ONTOLOGY and the
VICIOUS-CIRCLE
PRINCIPLE

ONTOLOGY and the VICIOUS-CIRCLE PRINCIPLE

Charles S. Chihara

CORNELL UNIVERSITY PRESS

ITHACA AND LONDON

First published 1973 by Cornell University Press.
Published in the United Kingdom by Cornell University Press Ltd., 2-4 Brook Street, London WiY iAA.

International Standard Book Number 0-8014-0727-3
Library of Congress Catalog Card Number 72-4569

Composed by St. Catherine Press, Ltd.
Printed in the United States of America by Vail-Ballou Press, Inc.

Librarians: Library of Congress cataloging information appears on the last page of the book.

To H. B.

Preface

This is a book about Platonism in mathematics and about the vicious-circle principle. The emphasis throughout is on the philosophical aspects of these topics, but some treatment of mathematical and logical points of a purely technical nature was unavoidable. I have attempted to keep the discussion relatively free of obscure logical notation and recondite technical details, so as to make the book accessible to the nonspecialist with some background in elementary logic and mathematics. In keeping with this aim, I have, for the most part, used the logical terminology and notation of Mates's well-known *Elementary Logic*. In certain places, I have found it convenient to use certain notational devices popularized by Quine, such as '---α---' and quasi quotes. I have generally followed Russell's practice of using the term 'class' as synonymous with 'set'. As in Mates, single quotation marks are used to indicate that what is being referred to is the expression appearing within the quotes. Double quotation marks are used as "scare quotes" and for quotation. The conventions adopted here may raise problems for some readers when I quote an author, such as Bertrand Russell, who uses double quotation marks to "mention" a word or symbol. Fortunately, such occasions are few in number and the careful reader should have no difficulty determining what the author intended.

Research for this book was begun in earnest in the 1964-1965 academic year at the University of Pittsburgh, where I was an Andrew Mellon Postdoctoral Fellow. I am pleased to acknowledge the generous assistance I received that year from the university and its philosophy department. Most of the basic ideas in this book are to be found, in somewhat inchoate form, in a paper I wrote then. Although that paper was never published, it was sent to various

vii

philosophers (notably Richard Cartwright and Hilary Putnam) with whom I discussed it and from whom I received helpful criticisms. Some of the ideas in that paper were further discussed and developed in courses I gave in Berkeley from 1965 to 1971, and I am grateful to many students for stimulating and, in some cases, significantly influencing my thoughts on these topics. Of these students, I should like to mention in particular Oswaldo Chateaubriand, Telis Menas, Len Sasso, Tom Schaffter, and John Steel. I am also grateful to the following students for assisting me in getting the manuscript ready for publication: Yutang Lin, Ian Carlstrom, Alfred Van Schoick, Bob Ray, Bill Hopkins, and Andre Orianne. Lin and Carlstrom were especially helpful in checking, simplifying, and developing parts of the exposition of the main ideas in the appendix. I should also like to express my gratitude to Dale Ogar and Nancy Shaw for typing the technical portions of the manuscript, to Ruth Anderson for supervising the typing of successive versions of the manuscript, and to the University of California for a Humanities Research Fellowship that enabled me to spend a good part of the 1967-1968 academic year working on this book. Thanks are also due to George Myro, Tony Martin, David Shwayder, and Hans Sluga for reading and commenting on portions of the manuscript. Another philosopher who should be mentioned is Charles Parsons, who read an early version of the book in its entirety in early 1969 and made a number of helpful criticisms. Hao Wang should be thanked for his willingness to discuss his ideas on predicativity via the mails. I should also like to thank Max Black for his editorial assistance and encouragement. I am especially happy to acknowledge the many ways in which my wife has assisted me in the writing of this book. It is to her that I owe the expression 'mythological Platonism' which, for good or ill, occurs with great frequency in Chapter II.

At various times, material from this book has found its way into papers I have delivered before academic groups. Early versions of Chapter I were read in Berkeley in the 1965-1966 academic year, once at the Logic Colloquium and once at the Philosophy Club Collo-quium. In 1971, much of Chapter II was read at the Logic Colloquium and later at the Philosophy Faculty Seminar of the University of Washington. Part of Chapter III was delivered

before the Hume Society of Stanford University in 1967. Another
paper on ontological commitment overlaps the material in Chapter III; this was read at the 1970 University of Georgia Conference
in Philosophy. Some of this material has appeared elsewhere,
and I am indebted to the following for permission to reprint:
Doubleday and Company, Inc., and David Pears, for "Russell's
Theory of Types," from *Bertrand Russell: A Collection of
Critical Essays*, edited by David Pears (New York, 1972); and
NOÛS, Vol. II, 1 (February 1968), for "Our Ontological Commitment to Universals," by permission of the Wayne State University Press.

CHARLES S. CHIHARA

Berkeley, California

Contents

Introduction

He [the nominalist] is going to have to accommodate his natural sciences unaided by mathematics; for mathematics, except for some trivial portions such as very elementary arithmetic, is irredeemably committed to quantification over abstract objects.

W. V. O. QUINE

When I first read these words in *Word and Object* several years ago, I wrote in the margin: "This philosophical doctrine should be soundly refuted." It was only much later, while I was working on an essay on the vicious-circle principle, that an idea came to me as to how one might construct such a refutation. Although I would not claim to have refuted Quine, this essay is the result of that idea.

It may appear strange to the reader that Quine is not discussed until after the chapters on Russell and Gödel. Something should be said in explanation of this fact. That Russell's ideas should be relevant to Quine's is hardly surprising in view of the fact that Quine has, for many years, been a student of Russell's logical works; the chapter on Russell is meant to serve as an introduction to the kinds of considerations that led Quine to espouse Platonism. In addition, I believe this chapter provides some needed historical background and perspective for the discussions that follow. The chapter on Gödel is intended to introduce and clarify Quine's Platonism in another way. It was once suggested to me that Gödel's argument for Platonism is essentially the same as Quine's. That there are similarities cannot be denied; but the differences require quite different responses from the nominalist. I believe that a comparison of the two arguments facilitates understanding Quine's position, the contrast putting it into sharper focus.

As one might assume from the title of this essay, I also concern myself with the vicious-circle principle. I should like to emphasize right from the start, however, that I make no attempt to provide a comprehensive discussion of it, encompassing all of the relevant mathematical, logical, or philosophical issues. Instead, I concentrate on the claim that the vicious-circle principle provides a solution to the various paradoxes that Russell's early logical writings made so famous. Specifically, I concern myself with the arguments given in support of the position that reason demands that we conform to the vicious-circle principle, that nonconformity is unreasonable, illogical, or scientifically unsound, and that the paradoxes are the result of failure to adhere to this principle.

It is primarily with this aim that I analyze the philosophical and logical writings of Russell and Poincaré. I begin the essay with a discussion of Russell's proposed solution to the paradoxes, even though Poincaré published the view that the paradoxes stem from viciously circular definitions before Russell did. This is because Russell's writings provide a much better introduction to the problems than Poincaré's do.

Poincaré's writings pose special difficulties for the expositor. Poincaré was not a systematic philosopher who carefully examined and reexamined his many philosophical pronouncements in order to present a general, overall account of the nature of mathematics. For the most part, the key ideas of his philosophy of mathematics were expounded in the course of discussing some specific philosophical issue or controversy, such as the logicist's thesis that mathematics is "reducible" to logic, and were not explained in depth or in detail. What emerges from Poincaré's philosophical writings is a collection of faint sketches, from which one does not seem able to obtain any sort of coherent philosophical view at all. After pointing out in Chapter IV some of the difficulties in interpreting Poincaré's philosophical claims, I argue in Chapter V that one can indeed make a great deal of sense of Poincaré's ideas if one interprets the sentences of mathematics and set theory in a particular anti-Platonic way. To this end, I show how one can interpret the sentences of Hao Wang's formal set theory Σ_ω in a way that "fits" Poincaré's intuitive ideas regarding mathematics and the paradoxes.

Hence, this essay is concerned both with the vicious-circle principle and with Platonism in set theory. One might expect that

Platonism would be relevant to a study of the vicious-circle principle from the fact that predicative set theories (roughly, set theories that conform to the vicious-circle principle) are generally contrasted with Platonic set theories. What has not been widely appreciated is the extent to which Russell and Poincaré based their respective justifications of the vicious-circle principle on a rejection of the Platonic doctrine that sets exist. It is my contention that not only does an examination of Platonism in set theory throw light on the vicious-circle principle and the reasons philosophers have given to justify adopting the principle, but conversely an analysis of the reasons philosophers have given for adopting the principle makes clearer some of the plausibility and attractiveness of Platonism in set theory.

The dispute between predicativists (those who advocate adhering to the vicious-circle principle) and Platonists involves two quite distinct issues: on the one hand, there is the question of whether mathematics ought to be completely reconstructed and developed in accordance with the principle; and on the other hand, there is the ontological question of whether or not sets exist. How these two questions are related will become evident in the following chapters.

ONTOLOGY and the
VICIOUS-CIRCLE
PRINCIPLE

CHAPTER I

Russell's Solution
to the Paradoxes

In the introduction to Russell and Whitehead's monumental work on the foundations of mathematics, *Principia Mathematica* (*PM*), we are told that the logical system presented "is specially framed to solve the paradoxes which, in recent years, have troubled students of symbolic logic and the theory of aggregates" (p. 1). What are these paradoxes? What is meant by a "solution" to them? And what is the solution proposed? Did Russell and Whitehead succeed in finding a solution? These are the principal questions I shall discuss in this chapter.

1. Russell's Attitude Toward the Paradoxes

> Hardly anything more unfortunate can befall a scientific writer than to have one of the foundations of his edifice shaken after the work is finished.
>
> This is the position I was placed in by a letter of Mr. Bertrand Russell (Frege, [31], p. 234).

Frege was understandably dismayed by Russell's letter, for Russell had clearly brought out an inconsistency in his *Grundgesetze*. That Frege's logical system is inconsistent is a fact pure and simple. That the mathematics of the period was also inconsistent is not so obvious. Russell, for example, regarded himself as having discovered a "paradox" rather than a contradiction in mathematics. And when a variety of other paradoxes were discovered—paradoxes that seemed to be quite similar in nature to Russell's but which did not involve the notion of set or class—Russell became convinced that "the trouble lay in logic rather than mathematics and that it was logic which would have to be reformed" ([107], p. 76).

1

Russell's paradox is so well known that it may be thought unnecessary or tedious to state it here. However, I think it worthwhile to compare the version Russell gave in his important 1908 paper with more recent versions. Russell begins by letting W be the set of all sets which are not members of themselves. He then infers that for any set x, $x \in W$ if and only if $x \notin x$, and hence that $W \in W$ if and only if $W \notin W$. Nowadays Russell's paradox is usually expressed by making use of a first-order language somewhat as follows: It is suggested that many (or most) mathematicians of this period accepted an (unrestricted) *axiom of abstraction*, which says that for every property (or condition), there is a set whose members are just those objects having the property (or satisfying the condition). This axiom is given thus

$$(\exists x)(y)(y \in x \leftrightarrow \phi y).$$

Taking ϕy to be the property of not being a member of itself, which we can express "$y \notin y$", we get

$$(\exists x)(y)(y \in x \leftrightarrow y \notin y),$$

and hence we can infer for some x

$$x \in x \leftrightarrow x \notin x.$$

It is generally thought that the conclusion to be drawn from this derivation is simply that the set theory accepted at this time was inconsistent. But it is clear that Russell did not view the paradox this way.

Consider the familiar story of three salesmen at a convention, who decide to stay the night at the same hotel. To save money, they agree to share a room. Since the room costs $30, each contributes $10. Later on, however, the desk clerk discovers that he should have charged the salesmen only $25 for the room and thus sends the bellhop up to their room with the $5 change. The bellhop, deciding that it is too difficult to split $5 three ways, returns only $3, pocketing the remaining $2. Now, since each salesman originally contributed $10 and subsequently received $1 back, we can conclude that each spent only $9 for the room. Thus the three salesmen spent $27 for the room, and the bellhop received $2; this makes $29. But they originally started with $30. So what happened to the other dollar?

Needless to say, there is no temptation here to attribute any sort of contradiction to mathematics. And in so far as one sees a puzzle, one naturally enough looks for some sort of solution. One need not look far, for it soon becomes apparent that the situation is described so as to mislead the reader into analyzing the financial situation improperly: it is suggested that from the original $30, $27 was spent and, in addition, $2 was given to the bellhop, whereas the $2 that went to the bellhop came out of the $27 spent. So there is no problem about what happened to the $30: $27 was spent ($25 for the room, $2 for the bellhop) and $3 was saved.

Russell evidently thought that the paradoxes troubling him were also to be solved by pointing to some sort of mistake or confusion. He tells us in his autobiography that he thought there must be "some trivial error in reasoning" responsible for the paradoxes ([108], vol. 1, p. 147). Russell's attitude toward the paradoxes can be likened to that of a person who is given one of the paradoxes of Euclidean geometry found floating around mathematics departments: the person does not seriously consider the possibility that geometry is contradictory or that, say, some angle really is identical to the sum of another angle plus itself; he is certain that there is some fallacy in the "proof." And just as we would say of some of these paradoxes that they rest upon an unjustified assumption that there exists a line with such and such properties or that one can construct a line with such and such properties, so Russell became convinced that the paradoxes he was concerned with rested upon equally unwarranted assumptions regarding the existence of certain sorts of large totalities. Russell was led to this position by Poincaré's suggestion that the paradoxes resulted from definitions that were viciously circular (Poincaré, [62], pp. 307-308). Following this suggestion, Russell formulated a principle that would distinguish and, so to speak, rule out the guilty totalities. This principle became known as the *vicious-circle principle*.

2. The Vicious-Circle Principle

Russell's own statements of the principle are vague and obscure.

(1) Whatever involves *all* of a collection must not be one of the collection.

(2) If, provided a certain collection had a total, it would have members only definable in terms of that total, then the said collection has no total ([102], p. 63; *PM*, pp. 31, 37).

Russell writes in a footnote: "When I say that a collection has no total, I mean that statements about all its members are nonsense" ([102], p. 63).

(3) Given any set of objects such that, if we suppose the set to have a total, it will contain members which presuppose this total, then such a set cannot have a total. By saying that a set has "no total," we mean, primarily, that no significant statement can be made about "all its members" (*PM*, p. 37).

(4) No totality can contain members defined in terms of itself ([102], p. 75).

(5) Whatever contains an apparent variable must not be a possible value of that variable ([102], p. 75; [100], p. 640).

If we examine the first three statements above, we see that (1) contains the term 'involves', whereas (2) uses 'only definable in terms of', and (3) contains neither of these expressions but instead the word 'presupposes'. This fact prompted Gödel to claim that Russell proposed three different vicious-circle principles.[1] But admitting that 'presuppose' does not ordinarily mean 'only definable in terms of' or 'involves', it is by no means obvious that we are dealing with three different principles; for surely there is more to getting at what was Russell's point than merely reading his explicit statements of the principle. We can examine his applications of the principle, and we can analyze the theory of types for further clarification of it.

Logicians commonly interpret the vicious-circle principle as a device for severely limiting the abstraction axiom so as to yield a consistent set theory.[2] On this interpretation the principle requires that "impredicative specifications" be eschewed; and although one

---

[1] Fraenkel and Bar-Hillel claim that Gödel *shows* that Russell gave us three different principles rather than three different formulations of a single principle ([29], p. 175). This is an overstatement: Gödel does not *show* any such thing, he only claims it. ([38], p. 218).

[2] See Quine, [84], p. 243; Fraenkel and Bar-Hillel, [29], p. 176; also Beth, [5], pp. 497-500.

does not find complete unanimity as to how 'impredicative specification' is to be defined, the general idea can be given as follows:
a specification of a set A by means of the schema

$$(x)(x \in A \leftrightarrow \phi x)$$

is impredicative if the set A, were it to exist, or any set presupposing
the existence of A, falls within the range of a bound variable in the
specification.[3] The principle so interpreted shall be called 'the set-
theoretical vicious-circle principle'. This version of the vicious-circle
principle restricts the abstraction axiom just to predicative specifications. No doubt this statement of the principle is not as clear as
one would like, but it will be of some use in the following discussion,
if only as an object of comparison.

Let us now see how the vicious-circle principle, as stated above,
can be used to obviate Cantor's paradox. This paradox begins with
the classical theorem that the cardinality of a set S is always less than
the cardinality of $P(S)$, the set of all subsets of S (or the "power set
of S"). Let U be the set of all sets. Since every element of $P(U)$ is
a set, we can conclude that $P(U) \subset U$. It follows that $P(U)$ is equinumerous with a subset of U. On the other hand, U is obviously
equinumerous with a subset of $P(U)$. Hence, by the Schröder-
Bernstein theorem, the cardinality of U is identical to the cardinality
of $P(U)$.

To see how impredicative specifications enter into this paradox,
we need only examine some typical proof of the theorem used in the

[3] The clause 'or any set presupposing the existence of A' is somewhat vague.
One wants to have the abstraction axiom limited to specifications in which
not only does A not occur within the range of a bound variable in the specification, but also, for example, no set containing A, no set containing a set
containing A, no set that can only be defined in terms of A, and so on. This
clause is not always included in explications of 'impredicative specification'
(cf. Fraenkel and Bar-Hillel, [29], p. 176). Quine uses the clause, 'or any set
whose specification might presuppose A' ([84], p. 242), but I find this clause
even more vague and misleading than the one above. In any case, some such
clause is clearly needed not only to bring the principle closer both to Russell's
statements of the principle and to his actual practice in constructing his set
theory, but also so that the principle is sufficiently strong to bar contradictions
(see Wang, [117], pp. 640-641).

paradox. Somewhere along the way, it is proved that there cannot be a one-one correspondence between S and $P(S)$, the power set of S; and the proof usually proceeds along the following lines.[4] Let us suppose that ϕ is such a one-one correspondence, that is to say, suppose that ϕ is a set of ordered pairs with the properties:

(i) $\langle x, y \rangle \in \phi$ only if x is a member of S and y is a member of $P(S)$;

(ii) for every element x of S, there is one and only one element y of $P(S)$ such that $\langle x, y \rangle \in \phi$;

(iii) for every element y of $P(S)$, there is one and only one element x of S such that $\langle x, y \rangle \in \phi$.

Then let α be the set specified as follows:

$$(x)(x \in \alpha \leftrightarrow x \in S \ \& \ (y)(\langle x, y \rangle \in \phi \rightarrow x \notin y)).$$

It follows that α is a member of $P(S)$. Hence, there is a unique element z of S such that $\langle z, \alpha \rangle \in \phi$. If $z \in \alpha$, then by the above specification of α, $z \notin \alpha$. But if $z \notin \alpha$, then $z \in \alpha$. Hence it cannot be that there is a one-one correspondence between S and its power set.

Clearly, the above proof does not conform to the set-theoretical vicious-circle principle, since the specification of α is impredicative. Now Russell intended *his* vicious-circle principle to rule out as illegitimate and meaningless quantification over the totality of all sets and all statements about the set of all sets. Consequently, Cantor's theorem could not be applied to the case in which S is the set of all sets for two reasons: (1) One could not give the above specification of α since it would be illegitimate to have the bound variable 'y' range over the totality of all sets; (2) one could not speak of the cardinality of all sets since one would not even be allowed to speak meaningfully of such a set.

As I said earlier, the specification of α in the above proof of Cantor's theorem is impredicative since the bound variable 'y'

<hr/>

[4] The proof that I present here is essentially the one given by Cantor. Russell tells us that he discovered his paradox while attempting to discover some flaw in Cantor's proof ([105], p. 136). This is not very surprising in view of the obvious similarity between Cantor's proof and Russell's paradox.

ranges over the totality of all sets (which would include α as a member if α existed). However, any specification of the form

$$(x)(x \in B \leftrightarrow \phi x)$$

would be impredicative if 'x' or any bound variable in ϕx ranged over the totality of all sets. Hence, in the usual set theories, all specifications of the above form would be impredicative. But the specification of α is not impredicative simply because the bound variables happen to range over the totality of all sets. Let us suppose that in our specification of α, 'x' and 'y' are restricted to relatively small totalities, viz. S and $P(S)$ respectively (clearly, we cannot restrict these variables to smaller ranges without specifying a different set from the one intended). Even then, the specification would be impredicative since α would be a member of the range of 'y'.

Russell attempted to make his principle plausible by first presenting the reader with a cluster of paradoxes and then arguing in each case that there is a tacit assumption of a totality in terms of which, by a kind of impredicative definition,[5] a member of the totality is singled out with the paradoxical property that this member cannot be a member of the totality ([102]). In each case, Russell analyzed the contradictions as arising from the mistaken belief that it makes sense to have bound variables ranging over these totalities. It would seem that the specific analyses were not used to provide a kind of inductive support for the general principle: rather the reader was supposed to *see* the validity of the principle from these examples. Since Russell did not analyze the paradoxes as simply arising from the mistaken assumption that there are objects answering to impredicative definitions—Russell went further in claiming that basically it was the assumption that it made sense to make statements about (to allow a bound variable to range over) some large totality that gave rise to impredicative definitions and paradoxes—it is a clear indication that, in the case of the set-theoretical paradoxes, Russell intended his principle to do more than rule out the use of impredicative specifications in connection with the abstraction axiom.

[5] I use the term 'impredicative definition' here, since some of the paradoxes do not involve the concept of set. Instead of an impredicatively specified set, there are impredicatively defined propositions, numbers, and so forth.

Let me clarify this point by looking specifically at some of the paradoxes that Russell discusses in his 1908 paper. "Epimenides the Cretan said that all Cretans were liars, and all other statements made by Cretans were certainly lies" ([102], p. 59). What is peculiar about Russell's statement of this paradox is that no contradiction follows from the above as it stands. One would have to add, for example, that no distinction is to be made between lying and asserting what is false and that a liar is someone who asserts only false propositions. In any case, Russell seems to have had in mind essentially the following version (cf. [100], p. 643). Epimenides asserts a unique proposition q at time t, where q is the proposition that there is a proposition asserted by Epimenides at t which is false. Since q is the unique proposition asserted by Epimenides at t, we can conclude that for every proposition p, if Epimenides asserts p at t, then $p = q$. From these premises, we are supposed to conclude that q is true if and only if q is false. The reasoning proceeds essentially as follows:

Let $\ulcorner Ap \urcorner$ stand for $\ulcorner$Epimenides affirms p at time $t_0\urcorner$, and let $\ulcorner Tp \urcorner$ stand for $\ulcorner p$ is true$\urcorner$. We then can assert, as true, both 'Aq' and '$(p)(Ap \to p = q)$', where q is the proposition (expressed by) '$(\exists p)(Ap \ \& \ -Tp)$'. It follows that if Tq, then $(\exists p)(Ap \ \& \ -Tp)$. Hence we conclude that $-Tq$. On the other hand, if $-Tq$, then $(p)(Ap \to Tp)$, and hence Tq. So Tq if, and only if, $-Tq$.

Russell concludes from this paradox that we must reject the assumption that there is a totality of all propositions. But notice that another way of avoiding the contradiction would be to claim that the sentence 'Epimenides asserted the unique proposition q at t' either is false or does not express a genuine proposition (at least if the purported proposition is taken to imply that for every proposition p if Epimenides asserts p at t, then $p = q$). Or one might object that the sentence 'There is a proposition asserted by Epimenides at t which is false' does not express a genuine proposition.[6] Surprisingly, Russell does not even object that q is defined circularly. Evidently, he felt that these sentences must express genuine propositions if it makes sense to quantify over all propositions.

---

[6] This position is suggested by some remarks of Wittgenstein ([123], § 691).

Consider Russell's treatment of Richard's paradox. We assume that there is a class C of all decimals definable by means of a finite number of English words. Then, by essentially following the celebrated diagonal procedure Cantor used to prove that the set of real numbers is nondenumerable, one constructs a definition (consisting of a finite number of English words) of a decimal N, which could not belong to C. (Details will be supplied later, in Chapter IV, §1). The definition of N is impredicative, but again Russell does not simply declare the definition to be illegitimate—he says the definition is illegitimate because it is illegitimate to quantify over C.

Russell gives his own paradox a similar analysis. He is not content with rejecting the assumption that there is a class such as W; he claims that it is only by rejecting the assumption that there is a totality of all sets over which we can quantify that we can avoid the contradiction.

Finally, consider Russell's treatment of the Burali–Forti paradox. It seems possible to prove in the classical theory of ordinals that the set of all ordinal numbers has an ordinal number and that this ordinal number must be greater than any ordinal number. In this case, Russell claims that the notion of "all ordinal numbers" is not legitimate.

From these examples, one can see that Russell did not simply reject some impredicative specification or definition used in producing the paradox: he always rejected, in addition, the larger totalities in terms of which the relevant impredicative specifications or definitions were made. He always rejected as meaningless sentences involving quantification over these totalities. This gives us good reason for supposing that Russell intended his vicious-circle principle to do more than simply reject impredicative specifications —it was supposed to pare down the ranges of bound variables to some kind of manageable size. As we shall see, the underlying idea was that the legitimate ranges would have to be obtainable by a kind of process of construction (using predicative specifications) from some given totality of individuals.

It is not hard to see how rejecting impredicative specifications of sets led Russell to reject such large totalities as the totality of all sets as well. For as we have already seen, if any specification of the form

$$(x)(x \in \alpha \leftrightarrow \phi x)$$

is to be legitimate, the range of bound variables must be smaller than the universe of sets. But the actual arguments for rejecting these large totalities are not fully articulated ([102]). Russell seems to be claiming that if we do not reject as meaningless sentences containing quantification over, say, the class of all classes, there would be no rational grounds upon which we could avoid Russell's paradox. He seems to have believed that if the specification

$$(x)(x \in \alpha \leftrightarrow x \notin x)$$

were legitimate, the set α could not belong to the range of 'x'. Hence, 'x' could not range over the totality of all classes:

> That there is no such class results from the fact that, if we suppose that there is, the supposition gives rise (as in the above contradiction) to new classes lying outside the supposed total of all classes ([102], p. 62).

By the time *PM* was written, however, Russell was no longer content to rest his rejection of these large totalities on the paradoxes. In *PM*, he also analyzed the paradoxes in terms of his "positive" theory of propositional functions, and the meaninglessness of sentences containing quantification over such large totalities was supposed to follow from this theory.

3. The Need for a Positive Solution to the Paradoxes

Having agreed with Poincaré about the source of the paradoxes —the supposed source being, in each instance, a violation of the vicious-circle principle—one might think that this would have satisfied Russell's desire for a solution to the paradoxes. This was not so: for Russell, the vicious-circle principle was "purely negative in its scope"; he felt that an adequate solution to the paradoxes must provide a *positive* theory which would "exclude" totalities in accordance with the vicious-circle principle. "The exclusion must result naturally and inevitably from our positive doctrines, which must make it plain that "all propositions" and "all properties" are meaningless phrases" ([102], p. 63). Now why did Russell feel compelled to provide such a positive theory? Consider the following version of an elementary-school puzzle. For $n = 1$, we have $2n + 5 = 7n$. Subtracting 7 from both sides of the equation, we get $2n - 2 = 7n - 7$. Factoring, we have $2(n - 1) = 7(n - 1)$. Dividing both sides by $n - 1$, we have $2 = 7$. An elementary school boy, genuinely puzzled by the above, would gain some understanding of the puzzle by seeing that the absurdity results from dividing by 0. He might even formulate a principle: it is illegitimate to divide by 0. But as I interpret Russell, this would provide only a partial solution of the puzzle: to have a satisfactory solution, the boy must also discover why dividing by 0 is illegitimate and why it gets him into trouble. To gain the required insights, it may be necessary for the boy not only to make explicit the definitions of multiplication and division, but also to gain, in terms of these definitions, a clear understanding of the algebraic operations one is allowed to perform. One can see why Russell did not feel it was enough to point out that some step in the proof of each of the paradoxes violated his vicious-circle principle and why he felt it necessary to produce a positive account of logic and mathematics in terms of which one could see both why violating the vicious-circle principle leads to contradiction, and also how to avoid such vicious-circle paradoxes in the future.[7] Thus, Russell was faced with the major task of "analyzing" the basic concepts of logic and mathematics in such a way that, in the case of each of the paradoxes, some crucial definition, specification, or proposition could be shown to be meaningless, presupposing as it were an "illegitimate" range of a bound variable. Furthermore, one condition of adequacy of the analysis was that the restrictions placed on the ranges of bound

[7] Cf. Russell's early statement: "*Il importe de remarquer que le principe du cercle vicieux n'est pas lui-même la solution des paradoxes de cercle vicieux, mais seulement la conséquence qu'une théorie doit fournir pour apporter une solution. Autrement dit, il faut construire une théorie des expressions contenant des variables apparentes qui fournisse comme conséquence le principe du cercle vicieux. C'est pour cette raison que nous avons besoin d'une reconstruction des premiers principes logiques, et que nous ne pouvons pas nous contenter de ce simple fait que les paradoxes sont dus à des cercles vicieux*" ([100], pp. 640-641).

variables by the theory not be *ad hoc:* "the restrictions must result naturally and inevitably from our positive doctrines."

The positive theory that Russell developed about how and why we should restrict the ranges of variables is his "theory of types." So the theory of types is a theory about, among other things, what it makes sense to say. The expressions 'theory of types' and 'type theory' have also been used to refer to formal systems of logic and formal set theories in which the variables are restricted in such a way that the ranges of variables form a hierarchy similar to the hierarchy of types of *PM*.[8] I shall use both senses in this work. But I trust it will be clear from the context which sense is intended in any particular case.

In the schoolboy puzzle, the student could begin his task of gaining the necessary understanding of multiplication and division by picking up an appropriate book on the subject and looking up the relevant definitions. Russell's project had no analogous starting point. In so far as definitions existed of such terms as 'class' and 'proposition', they were thought by Russell to be inadequate. Russell was forced to provide his own analyses of these notions.

What is meant by 'analysis' is a very difficult question. There is no general agreement among philosophers about what an analysis is supposed to be, and it is especially difficult to say anything both accurate and precise about Russell's notion. In analyzing the notion of class, Russell wished to clarify and make precise what we mean (or at least what mathematicians mean) when we (they) make affirmations involving the term. This is only a rough explication, as can be seen from the fact that Russell was not always concerned with showing what we *do* mean: he was at times more intent upon showing us what we ought to mean (or what we can legitimately mean), and this latter aim sprang from his desire not only to clarify what we mean, but also to straighten out what we mean.[9]

---

[8] For examples of this use of the expressions, see Wilder, [121], p. 226, and Wang, [118], p. 406.

[9] Cf. Russell's comment about his theory of descriptions: "I was concerned to find a more accurate and analyzed thought to replace the somewhat confused thought which most people at most times have in their heads" ([107], p. 243). See also David Pears, [61], pp. 18-23.

A study of the paradoxes made it obvious to Russell that our ideas of class and proposition needed straightening out, so he did not feel compelled to explicate only what we do mean. Russell would not have abandoned his analysis of class simply because it gave a distorted account, at certain points, of what mathematicians say, and he was perfectly willing to allow, as a consequence of his analysis, that mathematicians sometimes speak nonsense when they talk about classes. But although Russell was willing to allow his analysis to "deviate" from mathematical practice, he evidently felt that any adequate analysis must at least satisfy a *criterion of conservation:* the analysis must be such that the great body of mathematical truths accumulated over the centuries can be salvaged. For Russell, then, there were two necessary conditions that his analysis had to satisfy to be satisfactory: (1) it had to satisfy the criterion of conservation, and in such a way that (2) the mathematics that was preserved would have a solid foundation, free of contradiction.[10]

4. The Role of the "No-Class" Theory in Russell's Solution

Considering the magnitude of Russell's undertaking, it is not surprising that the construction of the positive part of the solution was what he found most troublesome. In the *Principles* (Appendix B), Russell had already hit upon a device for avoiding some of the paradoxes. Roughly, the underlying idea was to restrict the range of the variables occurring in the open sentences in a way that would prevent the specification of such "classes" as the class of all classes that do not belong to themselves: variables would be restricted to entities of certain types, where individuals, classes of individuals, classes of classes of individuals, and so on, were held to be of different types. The system of set theory sketched there—a system that would now be roughly classified as a *simple type theory*—was not, however,

---

[10] Russell's reconstruction of mathematics has many points in common with his *reconstruction of empirical knowledge* (cf. [100], p. 649). As Pears writes concerning the latter, "he felt himself pulled in two opposite directions. On the one hand he wanted to save as much as possible. But on the other hand he wanted what was saved to be firmly based on sound foundations, and well and truly saved" ([61], p. 23).

free of difficulties.[11] And as a result, Russell felt that he had not yet found "the true solution" to the paradoxes. Without discussing the more technical aspects of this early version of type theory, it is easy to give some reasons for Russell's dissatisfaction: in the first place, the restrictions placed upon the ranges of variables in open sentences were devised *ad hoc* and, indeed, seemed counterintuitive; secondly —and this is a reason Russell himself gives—the device of stratifying the "universe of discourse" into different types did not show him how to avoid "semantical" paradoxes of a quite similar nature, and this suggested to him that he had not yet arrived at a sufficiently deep insight into the mechanism of these paradoxes ([98], p. 527).

Russell tells us that he worked on this problem throughout 1903 and 1904 until, in the spring of 1905, he achieved what he considered a partial breakthrough: the Theory of Descriptions.[12] In his important paper "On Denoting," Russell provides a method for translating sentences containing denoting phrases of the form 'the such-and-such', that is, what he later called 'definite descriptions', into sentences not containing such denoting phrases.[13] In *PM*, expressions of the form '$(\imath x)\ \phi x$', which supposedly correspond to the definite descriptions of English, are defined contextually as follows. A sentence containing '$(\imath x)\ \phi x$', which I shall represent '---$(\imath x)\ \phi x$---',[14] is simply an abbreviation for

$$(\exists y)[(x)(\phi x \leftrightarrow x = y)\ \&\ ---y---]$$

and no meaning is given to '$(\imath x)\ \phi x$' standing alone.

[11] See Wang, [119], §2.

[12] [107], p. 79. That the discovery of the Theory of Descriptions led to Russell's solution to the paradoxes is related by Russell in several other places. In his autobiography, he says that the Theory of Descriptions "was the first step toward solving the difficulties which had baffled me for so long." In a letter to Lucy Martin Donnelly of June 13, 1905, Russell wrote: "[it] throws a flood of light on the foundations of mathematics" ([108], vol. 1, pp. 152, 177).

[13] I do not discuss the details of Russell's Theory of Descriptions, since the reader can find several thorough accounts elsewhere and such a discussion is not needed to understand Russell's solution to the paradoxes. Those not familiar with the intricacies of this aspect of Russell's philosophical development can find a vigorous account given in Linsky, [52].

[14] I follow the notation in Quine, [80], here.

Russell's Theory of Descriptions is relevant to his quest for a solution to the paradoxes for more than one reason. Not only was the theory explicitly used in *PM* in the actual development of mathematics from the axioms, but also it paved the way for his no-class theory by serving as the model for his analysis of propositions involving class referring expressions.[15] As he puts it:

> What was of importance in this theory was the discovery that, in analyzing a significant sentence, one must not assume that each separate word or phrase has significance on its own account. . . . It soon appeared that class-symbols could be treated like descriptions, i.e., as non-significant parts of significant sentences. This made it possible to see, in a general way, how a solution to the contradictions might be possible ([106], p. 14).

How Russell analyzed class referring expressions can, perhaps, best be shown by stating the key definitions regarding classes in *PM*. In the following, the sentence represented as occurring to the left of the expression '$=_d$' is to be regarded as an abbreviation for the sentence represented as occurring to the right; the exclamation mark indicates that the variable immediately preceding it ranges over propositional functions called 'predicative functions'. (I shall discuss predicative functions shortly.)

$$*20.01 \text{ ---} \hat{x}\psi x\text{---} =_d (\exists\phi)[(x)(\phi! \ x \leftrightarrow \psi x) \ \& \ \text{---}\phi!\hat{x}\text{---}].$$
$$*20.02 \ x \in \phi! \ \hat{z} =_d \phi! \ x$$
$$*20.07 \ (\alpha) \ \text{---}\alpha\text{---} =_d (\phi) \ \text{---}\hat{x}\phi! \ x\text{---}.$$
$$*20.08 \ (\exists\alpha) \text{---}\alpha\text{---} =_d (\exists\phi) \text{---}\hat{x}\phi! \ x\text{---}.$$

In order to translate set-theoretical sentences into sentences about propositional functions, the above definitions should be supplemented by conventions that determine the order in which the class terms are to be eliminated. For as Gödel has pointed out, the order

---

[15] Cf. Russell's comments in [105], pp. 181-182: "We must seek a definition on the same lines as the definition of descriptions, i.e., a definition which will assign a meaning to propositions in whose verbal or symbolic expression words or symbols apparently representing classes occur, but which will assign a meaning that altogether eliminates all mention of classes from a right analysis of such propositions."

in which one eliminates these "incomplete symbols" is by no means insignificant ([38], p. 212). Such complications need not detain us here however. The following example will give the reader at least some idea of how one can use the definitions above to eliminate class symbols in *PM*. Starting with

$$(\exists\alpha)(y)(y \in \alpha \rightarrow -y \in \alpha)$$

one can use *20.08 to get

$$(\exists\phi)(y)(y \in \hat{x}\,\phi!\,x \rightarrow -y \in \hat{x}\,\phi!\,x)$$

and then use *20.01 to obtain

$$(\exists\phi)(y)(\exists\theta)(z)((\theta!\,z \leftrightarrow \phi!\,z)\ \&\ (y \in \theta!\,\hat{x} \leftrightarrow -y \in \theta!\,\hat{x}))$$

which in turn can be translated by *20.02 into

$$(\exists\phi)(y)(\exists\theta)(z)((\theta!\,x \leftrightarrow \phi!\,z)\ \&\ (\theta!\,y \leftrightarrow -\theta!\,y)).$$

Thus, in *PM*, sentences containing class referring expressions are treated simply as abbreviations for sentences containing expressions denoting propositional functions. It is because of this feature that the set theory of *PM* is frequently called a "no-class" theory.[16]

Before examining the relevance of the no-class theory to Russell's proposed solution to the paradoxes, it might be helpful to say something about propositional functions. Given that the *basic entities* of Russell's system of logic and set theory turn out to be not sets, but propositional functions, it is surprising that the precise nature of these propositional functions is left unclear. In *PM*, Russell admits that the "question as to the nature of a [propositional] function is by no means an easy one" (p. 39).[17] So rather than carrying on a detailed discussion of propositional functions at this point, let me merely state those salient features of propositional

[16] Russell himself used the term 'no-classes' to describe his theory. See [101], p. 45, and [100], p. 636.

[17] In this work I do not always give Whitehead his share of the credit for a remark appearing in *PM*. This is primarily for stylistic reasons, although I must confess to thinking that the main philosophical ideas in *PM* are due to Russell. Russell, himself, says "Broadly speaking, Whitehead left the philosophical problems to me" ([107], p. 74).

functions about which there can be little controversy. A propositional function has an argument range and a value range. For each
argument, the value of a propositional function is a proposition,
so propositional functions are similar to Fregean concepts. It
should be noted, however, that whereas Frege's concepts always
take *truth values*, propositional functions take truth values only
indirectly, through their propositional values, so to speak.

In Frege's system, concepts are stratified into different levels:
there are first-level concepts, second-level concepts, third-level concepts, and it would seem that one could go on to higher and higher
level concepts. The variables of the system are restricted so that
no variable that ranges over objects can also range over concepts;
furthermore, no variable that ranges over concepts of one level can
also range over concepts of another level. (One might say that
Frege's system is a simple type theory for concepts.) However,
Frege could see no reason for sorting the *objects* of the system into
different ranges: object variables ranged over all the objects. Since
the extensions of concepts were all lumped together as objects,
Frege's sorting of entities into different ranges for variables did not
save his system from Russell's paradox.[18]

Like Frege before him, Russell too evidently felt that logic could
not prevent variables from ranging over all the objects in the universe: restricting variables to only part of the totality of objects
must have seemed artificial and unmotivated to Russell.[19] This is
where the "no-class" theory came in: it allowed Russell to drop the
assumption that classes are objects or things, and thus gave him
hope that his type-theoretical solution to the paradoxes might still be
saved from the charge of arbitrariness. By making propositional
functions the *basic entities* of his system, he felt he could justify
the type-restrictions on the ranges of variables along the lines that
Frege took—except, of course, the justifications would have to

[18] Cf. Carnap [11], pp. 138f.

[19] Cf. Russell's early statement: "*Si donc le principe du cercle vicieux doit
être vérifié, il faut que les classes ne soient pas parmi les valeurs possible d'une
variable entièrement illimitée, ce qui est une autre manière de dire qu'il faut qu'il
n'y ait pas de classes*" ([100], p. 646).

proceed in terms of the nature of propositional functions instead of concepts.

Although I have not yet discussed the actual justifications Russell gives for his type-restrictions, enough has been said to indicate the essential role the "no-class" theory plays in this justification. So we now have a partial reconstruction of the reasoning that led Russell to adopt his "no-class" theory. Let us recall at this point that Russell was for various reasons dissatisfied with the *type theory* sketched in the *Principles*. The main reason for his dissatisfaction was that the simple type theory did not obviate certain "semantical" paradoxes which were thought to be essentially of the same sort as the set-theoretical ones. Russell came to believe that the "no-class" theory provided him with the means of dealing with this difficulty also, the basic idea being that, by means of the "no-class" theory, all the paradoxes could be reduced to paradoxes about propositions and propositional functions, so that the type theory would obviate them all.[20] Clearly then, the "no-class" theory was central to Russell's solution to the paradoxes.[21] It is a curious fact that mathematical logicians seeking to explicate Russell's vicious-circle principle and his predicative conception of set tend to ignore the "no-class" theory completely.

[20] Cf. [109], p. 38.

[21] My explanation of Russell's frequent statements to the effect that the discovery of the theory of descriptions enabled him to find his way to his solution of the paradoxes differs markedly from Quine's. In "Russell's Ontological Development," Quine makes the following suggestion: "If we try to be casual about the difference between use and mention as Russell was fifty and sixty years ago, we can see how he might feel that whereas a theory of types of real classes would be ontological, his theory of types of propositional functions had a notational cast. In so far, his withdrawal of classes would be felt as part of his solution of the paradoxes," ([87], p. 308). Needless to say, I believe one can give a much more charitable interpretation: the theory of descriptions led Russell to his "no-class" theory, which in turn was thought to be the key discovery in the quest for a solution of the paradoxes, since it seemed to provide him with the crucial step in finding a justification for his type restrictions, and thus for his vicious-circle principle, and it allowed him to treat all the paradoxes, including the set-theoretical ones, in terms of propositions and propositional functions.

5. *The System of Orders*

Before discussing Russell's justification for his type-restrictions, it may be helpful to say something about the system of orders to be found in *PM*. In a *simple* type theory, the "universe" is generally sorted into mutually exclusive totalities over which variables are allowed to range, each variable being restricted to one and only one of these totalities.[22] These ranges, which I shall call 'TYPES' (using upper case letters to distinguish these ranges from the *types* of *PM*), can be given as follows:

TYPE 0: individuals (or objects as distinguished from classes);
TYPE 1: classes of individuals;
TYPE 2: classes of classes of individuals;
   ⋮

Now the classification of ranges of variables in *PM* is more complicated than this. What are classified are not individuals and classes but individuals and propositional functions; and propositional functions contain more complexity than classes. In *PM*, propositional functions are sorted into *orders*, and indeed into *types* within orders, each type being a totality over which a variable is allowed to range. The open sentence '$x \in \alpha$' is not considered to be significant unless the variables 'x' and 'α' range over the appropriate types. Now each propositional function belongs to one and only one type and *a fortiori* to one and only one order. The order of a propositional function depends upon the structure of the formula of *PM* (which contains a circumflex variable) used to denote it. To avoid clumsy and lengthy locutions, when a formula of *PM* used to denote a propositional function contains a variable or quantifier, I shall say simply that the propositional function contains the variable or quantifier. Complications arise in the theory because the system comprises not only monadic propositional functions (functions with only one argument variable) but *n*-adic propositional functions as well. Since relations can be handled in set theory by means of ordered pairs, it may be thought that the *n*-adic propositional functions are unnecessary and that these complications are avoidable. Unfortuna-

---

[22] The system Russell envisaged did not have all these features: not all variables were restricted to one and only one of these ranges ([98]).

tely, if we followed the usual procedure of defining functions to be sets of ordered pairs and taking ordered pairs to be sets (say, unordered pairs of unordered pairs), Russell's type-restrictions would preclude there being any function that has arguments of one type of entity and values of a different type. However, the system becomes unwieldy and messy if *n*-adic propositional functions are included, so I shall simplify the following discussion by restricting it to monadic propositional functions.

In *PM*, it is assumed that there is a totality of objects called 'Individuals', these individuals being of order 0. Variables that range over these individuals are also said to be of order 0. Each variable ranges over one and only one type; and in general, variables of order *n* are variables that range over entities of order *n*. Now the order of a propositional function is the least integer greater than the order of all of its bound variables (quantified or circumflex). Thus, the theory of order effectively eliminates *impredicative propositional functions* (that is, any propositional function $\phi \hat{x}$ that contains a bound variable ranging over a totality containing either $\phi \hat{x}$ or some propositional function containing reference to $\phi \hat{x}$).

The reader can get an idea of how the orders and types are distinguished in *PM* by the following considerations. Propositional functions of order 1 clearly can take only individuals as arguments. However, in order 2, we can distinguish two kinds of propositional functions: those that take individuals as arguments and those that take propositional functions of order 1 as arguments. Corresponding to these two kinds of propositional functions, we have two *types* in order 2. In order 3, we can distinguish four *types* of propositional functions: those that take individuals as arguments, those that take propositional functions of order 1 as arguments, and two kinds of propositional functions of order 3 that take propositional functions of order 2 as arguments, the two kinds corresponding to the two *types* of propositional functions of order 2 distinguished above. In order 4, it is easy to distinguish eight *types*, and continuing in this way, there will be 2^{n-1} different *types* of propositional functions of order *n*.[23]

[23] There seems to be some confusion about Russell's ramified type theory. Many believe that Russell divided his ranges into TYPES, and then subdivided

In *PM*, only finite orders are allowed. Given the restrictions placed upon the ranges of variables, it is easy to see why Russell did not accept transfinite orders: one cannot have a variable ranging over all the finite orders (or even finitely many orders) without violating the type-restrictions. Of course, one could have a propositional function of order ω if there were formulas in *PM* containing infinitely many variables, but this is explicitly excluded ([109], p. 53).

A propositional function is called *predicative* when it is of the next order above that of its arguments. Hence a propositional function of order 1 is a predicative propositional function of individuals. An exclamation mark placed immediately after a variable indicates that the variable ranges over predicative propositional functions. There is a distinct possibility of confusion as a result of the terminology adopted here, for 'predicative' in the above sense does not mean 'not impredicative' as one might easily suppose. All of the propositional functions of *PM* are predicative in one sense (that is, are not impredicative), although only certain ones are predicative in the other. Usually the context makes clear which sense is being employed.

The system of types described above can be made more perspicuous by the following notation.[24] Individuals will be of type T_0. Propositional functions of order 1 will be of type T_1. Propositional functions of order 2 taking individuals as arguments will be of type $T_{2.0}$. Propositional functions of order 2 taking propositional functions of type T_1 as arguments will be of type $T_{2.1}$. In this way we can build the hierarchy of types as follows:

$$\vdots$$
$$T_{4.0} \quad T_{4.1} \quad T_{4.2.0} \quad T_{4.2.1} \quad T_{4.3.0} \quad T_{4.3.1} \quad T_{4.3.2.0} \quad T_{4.3.2.1}$$
$$T_{3.0} \quad T_{3.1} \quad T_{3.2.0} \quad T_{3.2.1}$$
$$T_{2.0} \quad T_{2.1}$$
$$T_1$$
$$T_0$$

each TYPE into orders in accordance with the vicious-circle principle. One finds such an interpretation, for example, in Kleene, [46], p. 44.

[24] This was suggested to me by Len Sasso, although it closely resembles Wang's notation for the system R, described in Wang, [118], Chap. XXIV, Section 10.

In terms of this schema, a propositional function is predicative if its type is either T_1 or $T_{k,k-1}.\sigma$ (for some natural number k, with σ a sequence of the required sort).

The above exposition of the system is based primarily on section five of the introduction to the first edition of *PM*. The account given in *12 differs significantly from the above. In *12, we are told that predicative functions are matrices, that is, propositional functions containing no bound variables. By this definition, not all first-order propositional functions would be predicative! In contradistinction to this, we are told in the introduction that predicative functions of individuals are those that take individuals as arguments and that contain no bound variables that range over propositional functions. We are also told in *12 that the exclamation point after a variable that ranges over propositional functions indicates that the variable ranges over predicative functions (p. 164). But in the introduction, we are told that '$\phi! \hat{x}$' will denote *any* first-order propositional function (p. 51). Actually, the account given in the introduction comes closer to Russell's view that all first-order propositional functions are predicative and that, in general, a function of one variable is predicative if it is of order one greater than the order of its arguments ([102], p. 78).[25]

I do not wish to claim that the 2^{n-1} different types distinguished by the above procedure exhausts the totality of types of propositional function of order n. In *PM* (*9.131) there is a set of rules for sorting propositional functions into types, which complicates the structure considerably. By these rules, even if two propositional functions have the same argument variable and are of the same order, they would still be of different types if they had different types of bound variables or if the number of occurrences of quantifiers in one differed from the number in the other. Roughly, the rationale for this enormous proliferation of types seems to be this: it is thought, for some reason, that one cannot get propositional functions of the same

[25] In the introduction to *PM*, it is said that a function of "one variable" is predicative when it is of order one greater than that of its argument. I interpret the authors to be saying that a function with one *argument* variable is predicative. Such an interpretation seems to be required for consistency with other things said in this section of the introduction.

type from propositional functions of different types by merely changing argument variables into bound variables of quantification. It is thought that if two matrices f_1 and f_2 are of different types, and if g_j is obtained from f_j by such a change of variables ($j = 1, 2$), then g_1 and g_2 must be of different types also. But the logical justification for this principle is obscure. Notice that, by this criterion, there would be infinitely many types of monadic propositional functions of order j ($j = 1, 2, 3, \ldots$). The arguments given in the introduction do not seem to justify such a system of types. Indeed, the system described in the introduction seems to be quite different from the one described in *9. I shall assume in the following discussions, for the sake of brevity and perspicuity, that *PM* has the simpler structure sketched above.

Despite the various restrictions on the ranges of variables, the notation of *PM* does not indicate the type over which a variable ranges. Wishing to keep the notation as simple as possible, the authors argue that for their purposes such indications are not necessary:

> In practice, we never need to know the absolute types of our variables, but only their *relative* types. That is to say, if we prove any proposition on the assumption that one of our variables is an individual, and another is a function of order n, the proof will still hold if, in place of an individual, we take a function of order m, and in place of our function of order n we take a function of order $n + m$ with corresponding changes for any other variables that may be involved (p. 165).

Thus, the reader is left to specify whatever ranges he wishes for the variables so long as he conforms to the type-restriction of *PM*. Throughout *PM*, then, the formal development proceeds with sentences that are "systematically ambiguous" as to type.

6. The Justifications of the Type-Restrictions

Let us now examine the Russell-Whitehead justifications for the type-restrictions in *PM*. Basically, two sorts of arguments are used: one purports to show the need for sorting the universe into TYPES, along the lines of a simple type theory; the other argument aims at proving the need for the full-blown classification into orders and types. I shall begin with the former argument, which is based upon the "direct inspection" of a few examples. Let us scrutinize one of them. In a section entitled 'Why a Given Function Requires Arguments of a Certain Type', the authors of *PM* claim to show that if something that is not a propositional function can occur significantly as an argument of a propositional function, say $\psi\hat{x}$, then no propositional function can be an argument of $\psi\hat{x}$.

> Take, e.g., "x is a man", and consider "$\phi\hat{x}$ is a man". Here there is nothing to eliminate the ambiguity which constitutes $\phi\hat{x}$; there is thus nothing definite which is said to be a man" (p. 48).

Notice that this argument has some very unintuitive consequences. First of all, it is the reason there are no classes in *PM* containing both individuals and classes; for if there were such a class, then (given the "no-class" theory) there would have to be a propositional function true of both individuals and propositional functions— something that is precluded by this appeal to "direct inspection." Secondly, the argument seems to show that ($\hat{x}$ is a man) cannot be an argument of ($\hat{x}$ is a propositional function), for, using the above reasoning, we can examine '($\hat{x}$ is a man) is a propositional function' and conclude that there is nothing to eliminate the ambiguity that lurks behind ($\hat{x}$ is a man).[26] Hence, one would think that in all consistency, Russell and Whitehead should say that if '$\phi\hat{x}$' denotes a propositional function, then '$\phi\hat{x}$ is a propositional function' is meaningless. But they don't. For them '$\phi\hat{x}$ is a function' is not a statement containing an ambiguity; it is a true statement "about an ambiguity" (*PM*, p. 40). This last assertion is surely plausible— the argument from direct inspection, I believe, is not.

In evaluating this argument, I find I must return again to the question, What is a propositional function? According to *PM*:

> Let ϕx be a statement containing a variable x and such that it becomes a proposition when x is given any fixed determined meaning. Then ϕx is called a "propositional function" (p. 14).

Since a variable is defined to be a symbol of a certain sort (p. 4), the above definition suggests that propositional functions are

---

[26] I use parentheses in this section to indicate the scope of circumflex variables.

expressions or symbols, or more specifically, *open sentences* rather than what philosophers call 'attributes', which are supposed to be nonlinguistic in nature. The fact that Russell says explicitly that a propositional function "is an expression" provides some confirmation of this suggestion ([104], p. 230; [105], p. 155). Further evidence supporting this interpretation is to be found in another place where he says:

> A *propositional function of* x is any expression $\phi!x$ whose value, for every value of x, is a proposition; such is "x is a man" or "sin $x = 1$" ([101], p. 30).

This definition parallels the following definition found in *PM:*

> By a "propositional function" we mean something which contains a variable x, and expresses a *proposition* as soon as a value is assigned to x. ... Thus, e.g. "x is a man" or "sin $x = 1$" is a propositional function (p. 38).

Furthermore, Russell's own words on the subject provide us with an even stronger case:

> Whitehead and I thought of a propositional function as an expression containing an undetermined variable and becoming an ordinary sentence as soon as a value is assigned to the variable: "x is human," for example, becomes an ordinary sentence as soon as we substitute a proper name for "x" ([107], p. 124).

There is rather good evidence, however, that Russell also used the term 'propositional function' in a quite different sense. First of all, it should be noted that Russell sometimes used the term 'verb' to refer not only to a certain type of word, but also to *constituents of facts* "corresponding to verbs" ([104], p. 217). Thus, according to Russell, corresponding to the word 'loves' in the proposition 'John loves Mary', there is an element of the fact that John loves Mary (supposing the proposition to be true), which 'loves' *means* and which Russell also calls a 'verb'. Similarly, I believe, Russell used the term 'propositional function' to refer not only to open sentences, but also to something nonlinguistic which somehow corresponds to these open sentences. This is indicated by the fact that in *PM*, we find quantification over propositional functions in a way that, on the most natural reading, requires propositional functions to be not open sentences but qualities or attributes corresponding to open sentences.[27] For example, in *PM* (p. 56) and in Russell [105] (p. 189), the statement 'Napoleon has all the qualities that make a great general' is symbolized

$(\phi)[\phi!$ $\hat{x}$ is a quality required in a great general $\rightarrow \phi!$ (Napoleon)]

and '$\phi!$ (Napoleon)' is understood to mean 'Napoleon had the quality $\phi!\hat{x}$'. Furthermore, one use of the circumflex in *PM* suggests the attribute sense.

> When we wish to speak of the propositional function corresponding to "x is hurt," we shall write "$\hat{x}$ is hurt" ... though "x is hurt" and "y is hurt" *occurring in the same context* can be distinguished, "$\hat{x}$ is hurt" and "$\hat{y}$ is hurt" convey no distinction of meaning at all (p. 15).

Let us return to the "direct-inspection" argument, keeping in mind that there seem to be two distinct senses in which the term 'propositional function' is employed by Russell. If we interpret the authors of *PM* to be thinking here of propositional functions as being open sentences, then the sentence '$\phi\hat{x}$ is a man' is neither meaningless nor indefinite, given that '$\phi\hat{x}$' denotes some particular propositional function. Thus, if '$\phi\hat{x}$' stands for (denotes) 'x is a man', then '$\phi\hat{x}$ is a man' says that the open sentence 'x is a man' is a man, and hence what the sentence says is false, not meaningless or indeterminate.

It is possible that a use-mention confusion—an error into which Russell was inclined to slip—has occurred in this argument. Consider first of all the following passage, which occurs in the course of the statement of the argument:

> A function, in fact, is not a definite object, which could be or not be a man; it is a mere ambiguity awaiting determination, and in order that it may occur significantly it must receive the necessary determination which it obviously does not receive if it is merely substituted for something determinate in a proposition ([109], p. 48).

[27] Quine has made this point in several places. For more details, see [82], pp. 110, 122; and [72].

Now the sentence '$\phi\hat{x}$ is a man' can be obtained by substituting '$\phi\hat{x}$' for the occurrence of the name 'Socrates' in the proposition 'Socrates is a man'; but notice, what is substituted is not the propositional function, itself, but rather something that stands for (denotes) the function. It is possible that Russell and Whitehead reasoned as follows: In the sentence '$\phi\hat{x}$ is a man' let us suppose that '$\phi\hat{x}$' stands for the open sentence 'x is a man'. Then '$\phi\hat{x}$ is a man' means the same thing as 'x is a man is a man', which says nothing determinate: "it is a mere ambiguity awaiting determination."

If the authors of *PM* did reason in the above manner, then the argument can be seen to be an instance of the fallacy of equivocation. '$\phi\hat{x}$' must *stand for*, in the sense of denote, 'x is a man' for the conclusion of the argument to have the force Russell and Whitehead claim for it; but on the other hand, '$\phi\hat{x}$ is a man' means the same thing as 'x is a man is a man' only if '$\phi\hat{x}$' stands for, in the sense of *stands in place of* (as an abbreviation, say), 'x is a man'.

But could Russell and Whitehead have made such a logical slip? I shall merely contend that the above interpretation has some plausibility. Consider the following passage:

> "Implies" as used here expresses nothing else than the connection between p and q also expressed by the disjunction "not-p or q." The symbol employed for "p implies q," i.e. for "$\sim p \vee q$" is "$p \supset q$." This symbol may also be read "if p, then q" ([109], p. 7).

Now how are we to treat 'p' and 'q' in the above passage? They are called 'variable propositions'. But are they variables ranging over propositions or schematic letters (to use Quine's terminology) to be regarded as standing in place of sentences "expressing propositions?" Evidently the former, since quantification over propositions is allowed ([109], p. 129 and xxii). In that case, when 'p' takes as value the proposition expressed by '$2 + 2 = 4$' and 'q' takes as value the proposition expressed by '$2 + 3 = 5$', 'p implies q' takes as value the proposition expressed by 'The proposition expressed by '$2 + 2 = 4$' implies the proposition expressed by '$2 + 3 = 5$' '. But 'p implies q' may also be read, according to the above, as 'if p, then q' and hence we should be able to express the above proposition by

'If the proposition expressed by '$2 + 2 = 4$', then the proposition expressed by '$2 + 3 = 5$' ', which is nonsense. And we obviously get into the same type of trouble if we treat propositions as sentences. Thus, ' '$2 + 2 = 4$' implies '$2 + 3 = 5$' 'cannot mean 'If'$2 + 2 = 4$' then '$2 + 3 = 5$' '. So it looks as if Quine is right in claiming that the authors of *PM* were willing to treat 'p implies q' as 'if p, then q' because they did not distinguish clearly and keep distinct propositions from their names ([83], p. 97).

Thus, since it seems that Russell and Whitehead did commit use-mention errors in *PM*—and the above example is just one of many that I could cite in support of this claim[28]—it would not be surprising if the source of the "direct-inspection" argument were also a use-mention confusion.

On the other hand, we should explore the possibility that they did not make such a mistake. Suppose, for example, that they were thinking of propositional functions as being attributes rather than open sentences in that argument. In this case, propositional functions do not literally contain variables, although they are denoted by expressions containing bound variables. Hence, it surely cannot be determined by "direct inspection" that the sentence '($\hat{x}$ is a man) is a man' says nothing definite. For it is the attribute or, to use a term Russell sometimes used, the *quality* of being a man that is said to be a man. And in this case, too, I am inclined to say that the sentence is false, not meaningless. I fully realize, of course, that some philosophers have argued that it does not make sense to say of a *quality* that it is or is not a man. However, anyone wishing to maintain such a position regarding meaningfulness could hardly defend it by simply appealing to direct inspection.

This, perhaps, is a good reason for supposing that Russell and Whitehead meant by 'propositional function' neither open sentences nor attributes in the traditional philosophical sense. I shall return to this possibility shortly.

Now how is the "direct-inspection" argument relevant to the paradoxes? Consider the Russell paradox. The authors of *PM* argue that by examining examples such as the above, the reader

[28] For further examples, cf. Linsky, [52], pp. 7, 79.

will see that if '$\phi\hat{x}$' denotes some propositional function, then
'$\phi(\phi\hat{x})$' must be meaningless. It follows that, in the logical system
of *PM*, '$\alpha \in \alpha$' is meaningless also. This can be seen as follows.
In virtue of the no-class theory in *PM*, '$\alpha \in \alpha$' would have to be translated

$$(\exists\psi)[(x)(\psi! \, x \leftrightarrow \phi x) \,\&\, \psi! \, \hat{z} \in \psi! \, \hat{z}]$$

which is the same as

$$(\exists\psi)[(x)(\psi! \, x \leftrightarrow \phi x) \,\&\, \psi!(\psi! \, \hat{z})].$$

And if '$\alpha \in \alpha$' is meaningless, so is '$-\alpha \in \alpha$', so we cannot have any
class of all classes that do not belong to themselves.

I now turn to the argument used to support the distinctive stratification of propositional functions into orders and types that
characterizes the ramified theory of types in *PM*. The argument
proceeds from the principle that a propositional function always
presupposes (as part of its meaning) its values and never vice versa,
so I shall refer to this argument as "the presupposition argument"
(p. 39; cf. also p. 54). The main idea behind this principle is that a
propositional function is essentially *derivative;* it is only given
a totality of propositions ϕa, ϕb, ϕc, . . . that one can then have a
propositional function $\phi\hat{x}$ which, for a given argument, denotes one
of the above propositions; and then the values, that is, the propositions in its value range, are part of the meaning of the propositional
function. From the above principle, it is argued that no propositional
function could belong to its own argument range. Thus, if $\phi\hat{x}$
belonged to its own argument range, then one of its values would
have to be $\phi(\phi\hat{x})$, and this proposition would presuppose $\phi\hat{x}$,
which contradicts the above principle. For a similar reason, it is also
argued that no propositional function referring to or "presupposing"
$\phi\hat{x}$, such as $\hat{x}(\psi x \,\&\, -\phi x)$, could belong to the argument range of $\phi\hat{x}$.
It is easy to see how these considerations are extended to rule out
the possibility of impredicative propositional functions; for in *PM*,
one derives a propositional function containing quantification over
some range R from propositional functions containing an argument
variable ranging over R. Of course, this "constructive procedure"
might be questioned. It might be argued (say, by Fregeans) that this

procedure is, itself, in need of justification and is not required by reason. (I shall develop this idea in the next section).

In evaluating the above argument, I think it is safe to say that the conclusion is by no means compelling if one takes propositional functions to be open sentences. The principle used in the argument is surely not self-evident. Why could there not be a totality of sentences

> 'John' contains three words.
> 'John is tall' contains three words.
> 'x contains three words' contains three words.
> $\vdots$

from which one can extract the open sentence 'x contains three words' and which belongs to its own argument range? Is not the sentence

> 'x contains three words' contains three words

perfectly coherent and "well defined," so to speak?

On the other hand, if we take propositional function to mean "attribute" or "property," the argument is even less clear since the nature of attributes is less clear than the nature of open sentences. And it is still difficult to see much plausibility to the principle used in the argument. Why must an attribute be "derivative" in the above sense? Thus, we seem to be driven both by the "direct-inspection" argument and by the above argument to search for some third interpretation of the term 'propositional function'. One possibility that suggests itself is that a propositional function is essentially what one might call the *sense* or *meaning* of a predicate (or perhaps open sentence). Despite the vagueness and unclarity of the notion of sense, such an interpretation would help explain why propositional functions are supposed to be so intimately connected with the expressions of *PM* denoting them. Thus, if the propositional function denoted by $\phi\hat{x}$ is the meaning of the open sentence ϕx, then it would be easy to see how there could be a connection between the logical properties of $\phi\hat{x}$ (e.g. its order) and the nature of the quantifiers occurring in ϕx. But will the above two arguments become more plausible when we interpret 'propositional function' in this way? Hardly. I cannot see how this interpretation makes the arguments any more intelligible and convincing than the previous interpretations.

There are other possibilities one might try. Thus, if one concentrates on the presupposition argument, one might suppose that a propositional function is some sort of (extensional) mathematical function. It would then be very sensible to say that a propositional function presupposes its range of values and its argument range. For if a propositional function were a set of ordered pairs, practically everyone would agree that such a set could not be one of the elements of an ordered pair that belongs to it. It seems unreasonable to interpret Russell in this way, however, since the no-class theory was supposed to eliminate sets from the ontology of *PM* in favor of propositional functions.

Perhaps, then, we should take propositional functions to be *intensional* mathematical functions that determine sets of ordered pairs. But is it so obvious that such a function cannot take itself as an argument? I suppose one might argue that a mathematical function of this sort *correlates* objects in its argument range with objects in its value range, and hence cannot be one of the things correlated. But why not? The argument has some intuitive appeal, but it is by no means self-evident or logically compelling. Besides, this interpretation does not enable us to get a valid, or even convincing, argument out of the "direct-inspection" argument. There seems no way of determining by direct inspection that a propositional function (of the above sort) that takes individuals as arguments could not take as an argument another propositional function.

Frege gave a justification for his stratification of concepts into mutually exclusive totalities over which argument variables are allowed to range in his system. This gives rise to the hope that we can make sense of the above Russellian arguments by interpreting propositional functions to be, with only minor differences, Fregean concepts. This possibility will be explored in the next section.

7. A Comparison with Frege's Arguments

So as to keep this digression from growing too large, I shall attempt to restrict my discussion to a few central notions in Frege's philosophy of language and logic, avoiding wherever possible the many complex and subtle controversies surrounding Frege's views.[29]

I shall begin with a very brief sketch of some of Frege's key terms as they are applied in his analysis of sentences of a natural language. Consider the sentence

John is to the right of Mary.

According to Frege, the subject, 'John', is a proper name. Its reference is an object, namely, that person called 'John' who is being referred to. The grammatical predicate 'is to the right of Mary' is also said to have a reference. However, the reference of the predicate is not an object, but a *concept*.

I shall not attempt to explain why Frege felt it necessary to postulate references for predicates: this would require too lengthy a discussion to be appropriate here. However, I can give briefly one reason Frege had for postulating such things—a reason that Frege did not, so far as I know, actually give. I shall limit myself to a mere sketch here, since the main idea will be elaborated in a later chapter. One of Frege's reasons for developing his metaphysical doctrines was to supply an explanation and justification for his higher-order predicate logic; and his notion of quantification requires that there be entities over which the predicate variables are to range. Frege explained the truth conditions of sentences of his *Begriffsschrift* that contain predicate letters as bound variables of quantification not in terms of the substituends of the variables, but rather in terms of the possible values of the variables—now a standard way of explaining quantification. Thus, if one is to have a Fregean type of quantification with respect to predicate variables, there must be arguments within the range of these variables, and these arguments must be distinguished from the predicates that are the substituends of the variables: the arguments must be the references of these predicates.

Frege's distinction between concept and object needs further clarification. It might be thought, from the above example, that an object is the reference of only what grammarians call proper names.

---

[29] See Klemke, [47], for a good sampling of these controversies.

It should be pointed out that Frege's notion of proper name is broader than that of the grammarian. In the sentence

The smallest odd prime is divisible by three

the subject is not a grammatical proper name, but it is a proper name in Frege's sense of the term. Even the noun 'three', which occurs in the predicate, is said to be a proper name. Thus, the reference of 'the smallest odd prime' is held to be an object—an object that is also the reference of the other proper name that occurs in the sentence. The distinction between concepts and objects is thus made in terms of the distinction between predicates and proper names. The distinction between predicates and proper names is elucidated by means of various illustrations and metaphors. For example, the subject is said to be "complete" and not in need of a "complement," whereas the predicate does "require a complement" (Frege, [33], p. 569). Frege characterizes proper names as being "saturated" and predicates as being "unsaturated."[30] Corresponding to the different types of expressions, one finds in Frege's system different types of entities. For Frege, objects are saturated; concepts are unsaturated. The basic logical relation holding between objects and concepts is that of "falling under." The "falling under" relation is like the ∈-relation in set theory: the number six *belongs to* the set of numbers divisible by three, but the object six *falls under* the concept denoted by 'is divisible by three'. A concept, then, is what is denoted by an expression "containing a gap or empty place in need of completion," and is like a Russellian propositional function of one variable. Indeed, for Frege, a concept is just a special kind of a function: it is a function of one variable that always takes one of the two truth values for each argument. And analogous to the propositional functions of more than one variable that one finds in *PM*, there are *relations* in Frege's system. For the sake of simplicity, as in the case of my discussion of Russell's theory, I shall restrict my discussion of Frege's theory to objects and concepts.

So far, I have been talking about what Frege calls first-level

[30] For an interesting discussion of the metaphors 'incomplete' and 'unsaturated' see Marshall, [53], esp. pp. 265-266.

functions—those taking objects as arguments. To get second-level functions, we need to specify a function taking first-level functions as arguments. Thus, suppose we produce a gap in the sentence

$(\exists x)(x$ is divisible by three$)$

by dropping the predicate 'is divisible by three'. The result is an unsaturated expression, '$(\exists x)(x$ ————)', in need of completion by a predicate. What is denoted by such an expression is a second-level concept. We thus obtain Frege's own example of an expression, denoting a second-level concept: 'There is something which' ([33] p. 571). Now the first-level concept denoted by the expression 'is divisible by three' is not said to fall under the second-level concept denoted by 'There is something which'. Frege suggests that we say that the first-level concept *falls within* the second-level concept, so as not to confuse the relationship obtaining between concepts with the relation that an object has to a concept it *falls under*.

Although the above sketch of Frege's ontology is brief, I hope enough has been said to provide a framework for discussing Frege's justification for his hierarchy of types.

In the following discussion, I shall use the terms 'first-level expression' and 'second-level expression' to refer to the unsaturated expressions denoting first- and second-level concepts, respectively. Now Frege argues that only certain sorts of expressions are "fitting" for the argument place of unsaturated expressions ([34], p. 78). For example, it would be nonsense to say, "Is tall is divisible by three" or "Is divisible by three is divisible by three," whereas it makes perfectly good sense to say, "Two is divisible by three." (But Frege also argues that it makes sense to say, "The moon is divisible by Earth!") By means of such examples, Frege thought that the reader could be brought to see that only proper names fit the argument places of first-level expressions, only first-level expressions fit the argument places of second-level expressions, and so on. These logical properties of expressions mirror logical properties of the entities denoted by the expressions, according to Frege: "There are different logical places; some of them can be filled only by objects and not by concepts and others only by concepts and not by objects" ([33], p. 571). The conclusion that Frege draws is that only objects can be in the argument range of first-level concepts, only first-level concepts can be within the argument range of second-level concepts, and so on.

But why, one might ask, cannot a first-level concept be an argument to a first-level concept? After all, it would seem that we can refer to concepts by means of proper names. For example, the expression 'the concept denoted by 'is divisible by three'' seems to be a proper name in Frege's sense and it seems to denote a concept. Thus, it would seem that, if proper names fit the argument places of first-level expressions, then concepts can be within the argument range of concepts.

The Fregean answer to this objection is surprising: he maintains that we cannot refer to a concept by means of a proper name. He maintains this despite the fact that time and time again he himself uses such expressions as 'the concept *prime number*'. And did I not refer to a concept when I used the expression 'the concept denoted by 'is divisible by three''? Evidently not, if we accept Frege's position. For Frege, the expression 'the concept denoted by 'is divisible by three' ' is not an unsaturated expression but a proper name, and proper names denote not concepts but objects. For this reason, Frege postulated peculiar objects called 'concept correlates' for such expressions to denote.[31]

Frege's justification for the denial that we can refer to concepts by means of proper names is not very clear. Dummett argues that, given Frege's definitions of the terms 'object', 'concept', and 'relation', a definite description "cannot stand for anything incomplete like a relation": since a concept is explained to be that for which a predicate stands and an object is explained to be that for which a proper name stands, if we allowed that a definite description can

---

[31] It is not surprising that this strange doctrine of Frege's has produced much discussion. Geach reports that, according to Dummett, Frege took a less bizarre position in his posthumous papers ([37], p. 156). Supposedly, Frege's later position is identical with one proposed by Geach in several places ([35], [36], [37]). The general idea being that expressions like 'the concept denoted by 'is divisible by three' ' denote neither concepts nor objects. Geach argues that under logical analysis, such pseudo-proper names disappear from legitimate sentences containing them. (Shades of Russell's theory of descriptions!)

stand for a concept, the above explanation of the nature of concepts and objects would break down. ([26], p. 281). The reasoning, as it stands, is unconvincing. Why should the above explanation of the nature of concepts and objects fall to the ground? Evidently, Dummett thinks that if a concept could be an object, then given only the above explanation of concepts and objects there would be no difference between calling an entity a concept and calling it an object. But even if it were known by everyone that some concepts are objects (or even that all concepts are objects), to say that F is a concept would still convey something different from the statement that F is an object: the former would tell us that F is the referent of a predicate, whereas the latter would not. Obviously, more needs to be said to make Dummett's argument plausible. Thus, we need to ask: Why cannot something be both a concept and an object?

Frege evidently felt that such a possibility was precluded by the "fundamental difference of objects from concepts". In an attempt to convince others that concepts have logical properties that no object can have, Frege wrote that an object cannot "adhere" to another object without some sort of "liaison" [33], p. 570). Such a liaison, he tells us, cannot be an object, but must instead be a concept or relation. I do not have a very clear picture of what Frege has in mind here, but the following idea taken from an example of Russell's is suggestive ([99], pp. 49-50). Compare the list

John, the relation *is taller than*, Mary

with the sentence

John is taller than Mary.

According to Marshall, Frege tries to account for this difference by holding that the reference of 'the relation *is taller than*' is radically different from the reference of 'is taller than' ([53], p. 259). The latter supposedly denotes the link or "liaison" of the sort mentioned above.

Notice that the above Fregean doctrine raises a paradox: it implies that, in speaking of the reference of 'is taller than', one does not refer to the intended concept. Thus, one cannot state, by Frege's own doctrine, another thesis that he wished to maintain: one cannot say "The reference of 'is taller than' is a concept" and make a true statement. This has led to the charge that Frege's doctrine of concepts is "self-referentially inconsistent" (Resnik, [94], p. 339).

There is another way of explaining Frege's insistence that no concept is also an object. We can produce an argument from the Fregean criterion of the identity and difference of references—essentially Leibniz's Law—which says roughly that two expressions have the same reference if, and only if, they are interchangeable *salve veritate*.

Such an argument might proceed as follows: Suppose 'is divisible by three' and 'the concept denoted by 'is divisible by three'' refer to the same entity. Such an entity would have to be both a concept and an object. Leibniz's Law says that the result of replacing 'is divisible by three' in the sentence, 'Six is divisible by three', by 'the concept denoted by 'is divisible by three'' has the same truth value as 'Six is divisible by three'. But

Six the concept denoted by 'is divisible by three'

is not a (meaningful) sentence, and *a fortiori* is not a true sentence. Hence, the assumption that the two expressions refer to the same entity must be false. By a simple generalization, it is concluded that no concept can also be an object.[32]

Up to this point, I have been relying on what Frege says about concepts and objects where the distinction is explained in terms of the distinction between saturated and unsaturated parts of sentences (in papers such as [33]). If, however, one explains the distinction as Frege does in other papers, ("I count as *objects* everything that is not a function"), then there is no question as to whether an object can also be a concept, ([34], pp. 35-36). Still, the question remains: Can one refer to a concept by means of a proper name? In this case, it would be legitimate to ask: Must the reference of a proper name be an object? Thus, in either case, Frege would be faced with a problem. And in either case, Frege could give the sorts of arguments described above.

Despite the similarity Russell's direct-inspection argument bears to the above Fregean justification of his hierarchy of types, it is

---

[32] This argument is given by Marshall, [53], p. 266.

clear that there are significant differences, perhaps the most important of which is this: Russell did not accept Frege's view that we cannot refer to concepts by means of names or definite descriptions. Russell criticizes Frege on just this point ([99], app.). And in *PM*, we are given a device for constructing "names" of propositional functions:

> When we wish to speak of the propositional function corresponding to "x is hurt," we shall write "$\hat{x}$ is hurt" (p. 15).

In fact, it is just such a "name" that is used in the direct-inspection argument.

Since Frege's justification of his system of types is more cogent and plausible than Russell's, one might wonder why Russell did not simply accept a revised no-class version of Frege's semantics. I think one can see why Russell would not want to accept Frege's doctrine that one cannot refer to a concept by means of a definite description: as I mentioned above, it leads to a paradoxical (if not absurd) doctrine in which one analyzes the sentence '$1 = 1$' in such a way that '$= 1$' denotes a concept but cannot say of any concept that it is the denotation of '$= 1$'. This paradoxical position Russell certainly wished to avoid. In any case, Russell did reject the above Fregean doctrine, and as a consequence he could not give Frege's justification for his "simple type-structure."

But there is another reason Russell had for not accepting a no-class version of Frege's semantics; Frege allows impredicative concepts. According to Frege, the variable 'F' in the expression

$$Fx \text{ and } F \text{ (Socrates)}$$

ranges over all first-level concepts. But the concept denoted by

$$(\exists F)(Fx \text{ and } F \text{ (Socrates)})$$

(viz. the concept of *having a property that Socrates had*) is a first-level concept and thus falls within the range of the bound variable 'F' occurring in the expression used to denote it. Frege's method of determining a concept's level makes bound variables irrelevant to one's calculation of levels: argument variables are the crucial elements. Russell agreed with Frege that the propositional function denoted by 'Fx and F (Socrates)' could not belong to the range of the argument variable 'F'; but he also held that a propositional function obtained from it by quantifying over the range of 'F', such as $(\exists F)(F\hat{x}$ and F (Socrates)), could not belong to the range of 'F'.

It is difficult to say whether this difference in theory reflects a difference in meaning of the terms 'propositional function' and 'concept'. If we assume that the above terms are not significantly different in meaning, then it is hard to see how Russell could *prove* to Frege that his theory of orders is the logically correct one. The opposition between the two philosophers on this point would seem to be analogous to the opposition between Platonists and constructivists in set theory. However, it would seem that, *from a methodological point of view*, Russell's procedure is attractive. This will be argued in the following section.

8. *A Methodological Justification for a Hierarchy of Types*

Let us suppose that propositional functions are concepts or attributes that open sentences denote. In the following, I shall talk about "constructing" propositional functions in stages. Actually, this is just a metaphorical way of describing the process of defining (in stages) the open sentences that are supposed to denote the propositional functions. Now suppose that we wish to construct propositional functions that contain quantification over propositional functions (To simplify matters, I shall begin by restricting the discussion to propositional functions of individuals). Sound methodology requires that the ranges of the bound variables be made definite. Let us assume, as Russell did, that we can start with some definite totality of propositional functions that contain at most quantification over the "individuals." Undoubtedly, this assumption is infected with a significant amount of vagueness, but in any case, the assumption is no more doubtful than one with which Russell began. Then, since we have a definite totality of propositional functions, we can define new propositional functions by allowing quantification over this totality. These constructed propositional functions will give us a new range over which to quantify, so we can construct propositional functions of higher order. By defining propositional functions in stages in this way, we run much less chance of contradiction than if we presupposed, as did Frege, a totality of propositional functions, some of which are defined using quantification over the very totality to which the function belongs. If we follow the above Russellian procedure, we can be confident that each new propositional function will be well defined if the previously defined propositional functions are well defined. Thus, we can erect a "safe" hierarchy of types of propositional functions. It is easy to see how one can proceed in a similar fashion to construct a "safe" hierarchy of types of propositional functions that take both individuals and propositional functions as arguments. Of course, there is nothing in the above reasoning to rule out having variables that range over more than one type of propositional function: the hierarchy might be a sort of cumulative system. Furthermore, there seems to be no compelling reason for restricting oneself to only finite orders. In any case, such a hierarchy would bear a strong resemblance to the ramified hierarchy of *PM*.

Not surprisingly, there are passages in *PM* that suggest thoughts similar to the above. The following is a good example:

> Consider a function whose argument is an individual. This function presupposes the totality of individuals; but unless it contains functions as apparent variables, it does not presuppose any totality of functions. If, however, it does contain a function as apparent variable, then it cannot be defined until some totality of functions has been defined. It follows that we must first define the totality of those functions that have individuals as arguments and contain no functions as apparent variables (p. 54).

Such passages supply us with hints as to why Russell thought the paradoxes were due to some sort of vicious circle. Let me first state some of the more pertinent historical facts. In 1906, Russell published "On Some Difficulties in the Theory of Transfinite Numbers and Order Types," in which he suggested that, in view of the paradoxes, we must give up the belief that all conditions (properties, norms, or propositional functions) determine sets.[33] Using the term 'predicative' to characterize those conditions that do determine sets, Russell

---

[33] Roughly, this suggestion can be taken to be one advocating a restricted abstraction axiom.

posed the question: which conditions are predicative and which are not? Poincaré volunteered an answer to this question ([62]). He claimed that the paradoxes were due to viciously circular definitions and to the unwarranted assumption of the actual infinite.[34] He then suggested that the predicative conditions were those that do not contain a vicious circle. Evidently, it was from this suggestion that the term 'predicative' and 'impredicative' came to take on the sense described earlier in this chapter. Russell responded to these suggestions shortly thereafter. He said that although he disagreed with Poincaré on the question of the actual infinite, he agreed completely that the paradoxes were due to viciously circular definitions ([100]). It is also worth noting that in *PM* the reader is referred to Poincaré's article for support of the claim that the paradoxes result from some sort of vicious circle.

So one might conclude that Russell was satisfied with Poincaré's analysis of the paradoxes in terms of a vicious circle. However, Russell's "no-class" theory would seem to necessitate some differences in analysis. It would seem that, for Russell, the set-theoretical paradoxes do not result from defining some set in terms of itself as Poincaré suggested, but rather from defining some propositional function in terms of itself. Now, essentially, Russell analyzed each of the paradoxes as arising from the belief in some propositional function that is supposed to fall within the range of one of its own variables. So the basic question is: why did Russell think that such propositional functions have viciously circular definitions?

Suppose that a propositional function contains a quantifier ranging over a totality of propositional functions. It is natural to say of this propositional function that it has been defined in terms of the propositional functions of that totality. Thus, it is also natural to think that if $\phi\hat{x}$ contains a quantifier ranging over a totality to which $\phi\hat{x}$, itself, belongs, then $\phi\hat{x}$ has been defined in terms of itself, which is to say that the definition of $\phi\hat{x}$ is circular. One might then conclude that, since the paradoxes seem to result from such circular definitions, the definitions must be viciously circular.

Although the reasoning described in this section has some plausi-

[34] This will be discussed in some detail in Chapter IV.

bility, in the end Russell's claim to have solved the paradoxes simply does not ring true. There are many points at which one might question Russell's analysis of the paradoxes. Consider, for example, the set-theoretical paradoxes. Essentially, what Russell does is to translate such paradoxes into paradoxes about propositional functions, and then to argue, on the basis of his analysis of propositional functions, that in each case some step in the reasoning is illegitimate. But unless one is convinced that Russell's "no-class" analysis is indeed correct, why should one suppose that the illegitimate step in the paradox about propositional function is the "fallacious step" in the corresponding set-theoretical paradox? Well, why should one doubt that statements about sets get accurately translated into statements about propositional functions by the Russellian method? There are many reasons. For one, the set theory developed in *PM* has certain counterintuitive features, as for example the existence of infinitely many null sets. Besides, stratifying sets into types and restricting the variables to one type is not intuitively plausible. From the point of view of those who think that there really are sets that exist independently of human thoughts and practices, the vicious-circle principle is false. (Of course, if one thinks that there are such things as sets, as distinct from propositional functions, one would reject the "no-class" theory outright.) Thus, one might have legitimate doubts about the claim made by the authors of *PM* that the theory of types "leads both to the avoidance of contradictions, and to the detection of the precise fallacy which has given rise to them" (p. 1).

Another reason for being skeptical about Russell's proposed solution to the paradoxes is this: It is evident from the discussion in this and the preceding sections that Russell simply did not have a very clear notion of propositional function and that his use of the term was, at times at least, quite confused. If we drop the open-sentence interpretation, the nature of propositional functions is left extremely obscure. We have, at best, vague ideas of what they are, how many and what different kinds there are, how to distinguish one from another, and so on. (One wants to ask Russell: What makes you think there are such things?) The fact that there are such obscurities in the foundations of *PM* is no trivial matter, for it casts doubt on such fundamental statements of the system as the axiom of reducibility: One begins to wonder if the ranges of variables are well-defined totalities and hence if the question of whether there are nondenumerably many propositional functions in some range even has a definite answer.[35] This is one reason for thinking that Russell's solution to the paradoxes is defective: the attempted reconstruction of logic and mathematics, which is aimed at bringing out the logical fallacies that underlie the paradoxes, far from having set mathematics on a firm and unshakeable foundation, rests upon the dubious notion of the propositional function—a notion as much in need of analysis and reconstruction as the fundamental notions of mathematics with which he dealt.

Other reasons for questioning Russell's proposed solution to the paradoxes have already been suggested. Russell's positive theory of propositional functions was supposed to provide support for his vicious-circle principle. Indeed, the vicious-circle principle was supposed to be a consequence of his positive theory. In particular, the positive theory was supposed to justify both classifying propositional functions into the types of *PM* and also restricting the ranges of variables to one and only one type. After all, the system of types was supposed to be logically required and not merely an *ad hoc* expedient. Yet Russell was never able to provide an adequate justification for his system, nor could he justify his vicious-circle principle in terms of his positive theory. So, it is not surprising to find him appealing to the vicious-circle principle to justify features of his system of types (*PM*, p. 49). Not only are the direct-inspection and presupposition arguments unconvincing, but many of the distinctive features of his system receive no real justification at all. Why cannot a single variable range over the propositional functions of, say, $T_{4.0}$, $T_{3.0}$, $T_{2.0}$, and T_1? Not even the methodological considerations described in this section preclude such a possibility.

In saying that Russell did not solve the paradoxes, I do not wish to suggest that there is such a thing as a "solution" to the paradoxes or that there is some precise fallacy underlying each of the paradoxes. It seems quite possible that talk of "solutions" in the case of at least

---

[35] Cf. Putnam, [68], pp. 278-281.

some of the paradoxes is misleading and confused. One might take the position that the set-theoretical paradoxes merely expose the inconsistencies in our early systems of set theory. Given such a view, the problem facing us would not be that of finding a solution to some logically puzzling fallacies but rather that of reformulating our mathematical principles so as to avoid such inconsistencies. There seems to be no compelling reason for thinking there must be only *one way* of reconstructing mathematics.

There is no doubt that Russell's work comes off much better if it is looked upon not as an attempt to find *the* solution to the paradoxes, but rather as an attempt to find one reasonable way (not *the* right way) of molding our mathematical and logical principles into a consistent system. Indeed, if one were simply concerned with saving mathematics from the doubts produced by the paradoxes, there would be no pressing need to "solve" them: It would be sufficient to reconstruct mathematics in a "safe" system within which no vicious-circle paradoxes could be constructed. In this respect, Russell seems to have been to a great extent successful.

It is less plausible to maintain that *PM* obviates the need for a solution to the semantical paradoxes. Although it can be argued that the semantical paradoxes cannot be reformulated in the language of *PM* (and about this there is no certainty, as will be indicated in the following section), it is at least initially implausible to maintain that we can dispense with the expressive power of our natural languages and replace them with formal languages. (This topic will be examined in Chapter III, §4.) It also seems unreasonable to claim that our natural languages are "inconsistent" or that our informal reasoning is untrustworthy. In any case, I would argue that the semantical vicious-circle paradoxes no more show the inconsistency of English or the untrustworthiness of reasoning in English than the "pseudo-paradoxes" mentioned earlier do. So if there are such things as solutions to these paradoxes, Russell failed to uncover them.

9. *The Axiom of Reducibility*

Let us recall that Russell's reconstruction of mathematics was supposed to satisfy a criterion of conservation. Now in attempting to fulfill this requirement, Russell felt compelled to appeal to a special axiom of reducibility

$$(\exists\psi)(x)(\phi x \leftrightarrow \psi! \, x)$$

which says that given any propositional function $\phi\hat{x}$, regardless of its order, there is a predicative propositional function, $\psi!\hat{x}$, extensionally identical to $\phi\hat{x}$.

To facilitate explanation of the significance of this axiom, I revert to the schema (of §5), which depicts in a simplified form the hierarchy of types. Let us first look at just those propositional functions that take individuals as arguments, that is, look at the left-most column consisting of T_1, $T_{2.0}$, $T_{3.0}$, ... Now the axiom of reducibility says in effect that the construction of propositional functions of types $T_{2.0}$, $T_{3.0}$, $T_{4.0}$, ... does not result in any new extensions; so from the point of view of set theory, we might as well not bother with these propositional functions. Similarly, looking at propositional functions that take propositional functions of individuals as arguments, it is easy to see that we need not bother with $T_{3.1}$, $T_{4.1}$, $T_{5.1}$, ... since one is guaranteed by the axiom of extensionally identical propositional functions of type $T_{2.1}$. Consider now the columns starting with $T_{3.2.0}$ and $T_{3.2.1}$. By a parity of reasoning, it is clear that we can omit all the types in the columns directly above these two types without losing any sets. Recalling that $T_{2.0}$ did not add to the sets of T_1, it is not hard to see that the sets of $T_{2.0}$ are just the sets of T_1, and hence $T_{3.2.0}$ does not contribute any new sets over those obtained in $T_{3.1}$. Continuing in this way, one can see that the crucial types are: T_0, T_1, $T_{2.1}$, $T_{3.2.1}$, $T_{4.3.2.1}$, ... Thus, the effect of having this axiom is that one need not worry about the orders of propositional functions: adding this axiom to the other axioms of *PM* results in a set theory essentially equivalent to the usual simple type-theory.[36]

---

[36] This criticism has been made several times, e.g., recently by Quine ([84], p. 256). It seems to have been first made by Chwistek in 1921 (on this point, see Wang [118], p. 405). Philosophers like F. P. Ramsey and Rudolf Carnap, who advocate replacing the ramified type-theory with some sort of simple type-theory, generally do so on the grounds that, in this way, we can avoid many complications and also eliminate the need for the axiom of reducibility. It is also

Obviously, Russell called the axiom the axiom of reducibility because he regarded it as a device for reducing propositional functions to the lowest possible order. Russell wrote in his 1908 paper:

> This seems to be what common sense effects by the admission of *classes*. ... I believe the chief purpose which classes serve, and the chief reason which makes them linguistically convenient, is that they provide a method of reducing the order of a propositional function ([99], p. 81).

The reasoning by which common sense is supposedly able to reduce the order of a propositional function by assuming the existence of classes is to be found both in the 1908 paper and in *PM*. The *Principia* version, which I give below, is aimed at showing that by assuming "the existence of classes, the axiom of reducibility can be proved":

> For in that case, given any function $\phi\hat{z}$ of whatever order, there is a class α consisting of just those objects which satisfy $\phi\hat{z}$. ... Hence "$\phi\hat{z}$" is equivalent to "x belongs to α." But "x belongs to α" is a statement containing no apparent variable, and is therefore a predicative function of x. ... The assumption of the axiom of reducibility is therefore a smaller assumption than the assumption that there are classes (p. 58).

The first point to notice here is that the above "proof" rests upon considerably more than just the assumption that there are classes (that is, the assumption that classes of some sort exist), for the argument proceeds from the hypothesis that for *every* propositional function $\phi\hat{x}$, there exists a class containing just those objects of which $\phi\hat{x}$ is true. Secondly, it is clear that, in this argument, 'propositional

---

argued that the ramified type-theory is not necessary to eliminate the paradoxes. Generally, the paradoxes are separated into two sorts: the logical and the semantical. Then it is argued that the simple type-theory is sufficient to eliminate the logical paradoxes, whereas some linguistic device is devised to obviate the semantical paradoxes. See Carnap, [11], § 60*a*, and Ramsey [93], pp. 20f. Ramsey admits that his diagnosis of the paradoxes of the second kind was not original. Peano had suggested earlier, in response to the publication of Richard ([95]), that Richard's paradox does not belong to mathematics but to "linguistics" since N cannot be defined according to the rules of mathematics. (See Heijenoort, [41], p. 142).

as Russell did, it is easy to see that the above definition of identity could be used if, instead of the axiom of reducibility, Leibniz's principle were adopted. Since Leibniz's principle can be proved in *PM* by using the axiom of reducibility, Russell was prompted to say that the axiom of reducibility is a "generalized form" of Leibniz's principle ([105], p. 192).

Russell also wished to define 'natural number' in the way Frege did. As in the above case, the type restrictions of *PM* prevented a strict Fregean definition of the form 'A natural number is one which possesses all properties possessed by 0 and by the successors of all numbers possessing them', but the natural numbers, by means of the axiom of reducibility, could be defined in terms of all predicative propositional functions of the appropriate type.

The axiom of reducibility plays an essential role in the development of the real number system and classical analysis in *PM*. In particular, the axiom is needed in proving the theorem that every bounded class of real numbers has a least upper bound; it is also used in proving Cantor's theorems that the cardinality of a set is less than the cardinality of its power set and that the set of real numbers is uncountable. Thus, if we include this axiom among the axioms of *PM* (including the axiom of infinity), it would appear that one consequence of the axioms is that there must be uncountably many propositional functions of a certain type (since in *PM* propositional functions "go proxy" for sets and real numbers). However, if we take any natural language and construct open sentences from the sentences of this language, we get only countably many open sentences. Since we cannot get uncountably many open sentences from even a denumerable infinity of natural languages, if we regard propositional functions as being open sentences, the axiom of reducibility appears to be false (assuming that the other axioms of *PM* are true).

We should not be hasty in drawing such a conclusion, however, since we have a situation here similar to that of the Skolem paradox.[38] Assume for the present that propositional functions are open sentences. Then the theorem we interpret as saying that the set of

[38] Cf. Putnam [68], pp. 276-277.

real numbers is uncountable actually does not say that there is no one-one correspondence between the reals and the natural numbers —it says instead that there is no propositional function, no open sentence, of a certain sort that "correlates" the reals one-one with the naturals. Thus, including the axiom of reducibility among the axioms of *PM* does not, by the above reasoning, provide us with grounds for thinking propositional functions are not open sentences.

However, Russell obviously thought that the theorem of *PM* that, on the usual reading, says the reals are uncountable implies that it is impossible to arrange all the real numbers in what he calls a "progression" ([105], p. 84); and it is difficult to see why Russell should have thought this if he interpreted the theorem in the above manner. The essential point is: if propositional functions are open sentences, then many theorems of *PM* that are supposed to express theorems of classical mathematics do not have the consequences they are supposed to have.

Since Russell could hardly claim that the axiom of reducibility is self-evident, while attempting to justify the axiom in the above way, his pragmatic justification of the axiom marks an interesting shift from Frege's program of deriving arithmetic from self-evident logical laws.[39] Russell soon became dissatisfied with the axioms of his own system: he came to feel that the axiom of reducibility was at best a "dubious assumption," not at all appropriate as an axiom of logic ([105], p. 193). But the idea of justifying logical and mathematical laws in the way one justifies empirical laws was destined not to be disregarded so quickly. Some years later, Gödel became enthusiastic about this sort of justification and applauded Russell for taking this route ([38], p. 213). Gödel then went on to suggest that this type of justification might be used in the case of set-theoretical axioms ([39]). Quine, too, was sympathetic to this aspect of Russell's reconstruction of mathematics, as I shall emphasize in a later chapter.

As I said earlier, the axiom of reducibility has the effect of obliterating the separation of propositional functions into orders and of turning the set theory of *PM* into a *simple* type-theory. Since the

[39] The axiom of infinity has also been regarded by many critics of *PM* as a questionable logical law.

system of orders was constructed in accordance with the vicious-circle principle, one may suspect that the set theory of *PM* no longer conforms to the principle once the axiom of reducibility is added. This suspicion is strengthened by the following considerations. Supposing that, in a simple type theory, the real numbers have been defined to be lower Dedekind cuts of rational numbers,[40] and that '*r*' and '*x*' are variables ranging over the reals and the rationals respectively, then for any bounded set α, of real numbers, it is easy to prove that there is a set

$$\hat{x}(\exists r)(x \in r \ \& \ r \in \alpha)$$

which is the least upper bound of α. Now in a system such as *PM* without the axiom of reducibility, where the real numbers are effectively identified with certain predicative propositional functions, such a proof cannot be carried out, primarily because one cannot prove

$$(\exists \beta)(x)[x \in \beta \leftrightarrow (\exists r)(x \in r \ \& \ r \in \alpha)],$$

the difficulty arising from the fact that the propositional function $(\exists r)(\hat{x} \in r \ \& \ r \in \alpha)$, being of order higher than that of the real numbers, is not itself a predicative propositional function. This is not surprising since, given the usual interpretations of the vicious-circle principle, the principle "says" we are not allowed to infer the existence of a set answering to the above specification that falls within the range of '*r*'. Of course, the axiom of reducibility "says" that we are allowed to infer the existence of such a set, so it looks as if there is a conflict of principles.

In suggesting that Russell, in effect, abandoned one version of the vicious-circle principle when he accepted the axiom of reducibility, I do not wish to imply that the axiom of reducibility produces (or allows) *impredicative propositional functions*, that is to say, propositional functions that fall within the ranges of their own bound

---

[40] By 'lower Dedekind cut of rational numbers' I mean a set, *D*, of rational numbers satisfying the conditions: (*a*) not all rational numbers are elements of *D*; (*b*) if $r_1 \in D$ and $r_1 < r_2$, then $r_2 \in D$; (*c*) *D* contains no greatest element. To see how the real number system can be developed in terms of Dedekind cuts, see Landau, [51].

variables. There is no conflict of principles if one takes the vicious-circle principle to be a principle about only propositional functions, as is expressed above in (5) of section 2. However, the set theory of *PM*, when the axiom of reducibility is included, certainly does not conform to the set-theoretical version of the vicious-circle principle (described in section 2) that restricts the abstraction axiom to predicative specifications; and that is what I was arguing above. Indeed, consider the following abstraction axiom schema (which one would expect to be impredicative):

$$(\exists\beta)(x)(x \in \beta \leftrightarrow \psi x)$$

where $\psi\hat{x}$ can be of any order. That sentence translates into a sentence equivalent to

$$(\exists\phi)(x)(x \in \phi! \hat{y} \leftrightarrow \psi x)$$

which is an abbreviation for

$$(\exists\phi)(x)(\phi! x \leftrightarrow \psi x)$$

in *PM*. But the latter is simply the axiom of reducibility![41]

The acceptance of the axiom of reducibility introduces another difficulty which has suggested to some that Russell's appeal to the axiom was not consistent with his original insights or with the vicious-circle principle. As I noted earlier, one of the reasons for constructing the ramification of types was to avoid such semantical paradoxes as the Epimenides. Developing an argument of Chwistek's, Copi has argued that if we can express certain semantical concepts in *PM*, some of these semantical paradoxes can be reintroduced, and if we cannot express these semantical notions in *PM*, then we do not need the ramification of types to avoid them since they cannot even be formulated in *PM*.

Copi follows Ramsey in formulating the Grelling paradox along the following lines: We first assume that there is in *PM* some symbol 'D' that expresses the relation that obtains between symbols and what they denote. Assume '*w*' is a variable ranging over symbols.

---

[41] Perhaps this derivation lies behind Russell's claim that if the existence of classes is assumed, the axiom of reducibility can be proved.

(It is assumed that all denoting symbols are of the same type). We then define the symbol 'Het' as follows:

$$\text{Het}(w) \leftrightarrow (\exists \phi)(w D \phi! \hat{x} \ \& \ -\phi! \ w).$$

Now we must be given that

$$(\phi)(\text{'Het'} D \phi \hat{x} \leftrightarrow \phi \hat{x} = \text{Het}).$$

Then we can derive

$$\text{Het ('Het')} \leftrightarrow -\text{Het ('Het')}.$$

But the theory of orders prevents this contradiction from arising in *PM*, since Het must be of higher order than the bound variable 'ϕ' in its definiens.

Copi argues that the axiom of reducibility reintroduces the paradoxes in the following way:

> The reducibility axiom asserts that there is a predicative function formally equivalent [i.e., extensionally identical] to the function Het, call it 'Het$_r$' ([22], p. 192).

Hence, we get

$$(1) \ \text{Het('Het}_r\text{')} \leftrightarrow \text{Het}_r\text{('Het}_r\text{')}$$

and

$$(2) \ (\phi)(\text{'Het}_r\text{'} D \phi! \hat{x} \leftrightarrow \phi! \ \hat{x} = \text{Het}_r),$$

that is, 'Het$_r$' denotes a unique predicative function. Now assume

$$-\text{Het}_r\text{('Het}_r\text{')}.$$

Then by (1), we have

$$-\text{Het('Het}_r\text{')}$$

and hence, by the definition of 'Het',

$$(\phi)(\text{'Het}_r\text{'} D \phi! \hat{x} \rightarrow \phi! \ \text{('Het}_r\text{')}).$$

By (2), we get

$$(3) \ \text{Het}_r\text{('Het}_r\text{')},$$

and thus a contradiction. So we can conclude (3). However, by (1), we have

   Het('Het$_r$')

so from the definition of Het, we have

   $(\exists\phi)$('Het$_r$'Dϕ! $\hat{x}$ & $-\phi$!('Het$_r$')).

Using Existential Specification, we get

   'Het$_r$'Dϕ! $\hat{x}$ & $-\phi$!('Het$_r$')

and hence, by (2), and substitutivity of identity, we have

   $-$Het$_r$('Het$_r$').

The trouble with this argument is that it makes an assumption never justified in the discussion. Copi assumes (without so much as a word of hesitation) that if there is a predicative propositional function extensionally identical to Het, there is an expression in *PM* that denotes it ("call it 'Het$_r$' "). But what is the "it"? The axiom of reducibility does not assert the existence of a unique predicative propositional function extensionally identical to Het. So we cannot use a definite description in place of 'Het$_r$'. And we certainly cannot assume that there are names in *PM* for each propositional function, since on the standard interpretation of *PM*, there are uncountably many propositional functions and only countably many names.[42] Indeed, one might take Copi's argument as showing that there are propositional functions that are not denoted by expressions of *PM*.

This objection to Copi's argument is ironically similar to Ramsey's objection to Chwistek's attempt to resuscitate Richard's paradox in *PM* ([93], p. 28n). Ramsey argued that Chwistek had assumed, without justification, that some predicative propositional function of a certain sort must be definable in *PM*. Commenting on Ramsey's objection, Copi wrote:

> However, no mention is made in the Grelling paradox of effectiveness or finite definability or constructibility, so there is no objection to giving the reduced function Het$_r$ the name 'Het$_r$' and deriving the particular contradiction indicated previously ([22], p. 195).

[42] This objection to Copi's argument is mentioned in Church, [18], p. 155.

Notice that Copi speaks of *the* "reduced function Het_r", as if the axiom of reducibility asserts the existence of a unique predicative function extensionally identical to a given function.[43]

I do not wish to suggest, however, that there is nothing to the objections raised by Chwistek and Copi. The axiom of reducibility does cloud the Russellian solution to the paradoxes. I believe that when Poincaré and Russell argued that the paradoxes were produced by means of viciously circular definitions, they were on the right track—at least in the cases of the semantical paradoxes. Unfortunately, the original insight was lost in the attempt to carry out the ambitious program of reconstructing all of mathematics on a logical foundation; and the problems with the axiom of reducibility are symptoms of this loss.

There is one other point in Copi's paper that warrants comment. In the course of raising this objection to the ramified theory of types, Copi claimed that the system of orders was introduced "solely for the purposes of avoiding semantical paradoxes like those of Richard and Grelling" ([22], pp. 190-191). Although I would agree that avoiding the semantical paradoxes was *one* of Russell's purposes in devising the system of orders, it is obvious from this chapter that I would dispute Copi's claim. Copi seems to have ignored completely the plausibility of the vicious-circle principle and the constructivistic impulse in Russell's philosophy.

Now if, as seems quite possible, Russell was not true to one version of his vicious-circle principle, it is easy to see how he might have overlooked this inconsistency. As a result of the "no-class" theory, he seems to have restricted his attention to propositional functions. The version of the vicious-circle principle that applies to propositional functions says that no propositional function can belong to the range of one of its own variables. The axiom of reducibility does not violate this version of the vicious-circle principle, and this version may have seemed to him to be the crucial one. One might

[43] In [119], § 5, Wang also suggests that the Grelling paradox can be resuscitated in *PM* if one can express the denoting relation in *PM*. Wang does not state this "result" as confidently as Copi does (using such expressions as "we might wish to argue" and "it would seem"), and he gives no indication of how the difficulty I raised above to Copi's argument can be circumvented.

also conjecture that, having constructed the ramified system in accordance with the vicious-circle principle, Russell found that he could not carry out his project without resorting to the axiom of reducibility. Probably, adding the axiom did not appear very damaging to his position for many reasons: (1) it could be given some sort of intuitive justification; (2) the axiom seemed to him to be weaker than one attributing existence to classes; (3) no formal contradiction emerged from the addition of the axiom; and (4), if one were convinced of the truth of not only Russell's other principles but also the propositions of mathematics that could only be derived *via* the axiom of reducibility, one would hardly suspect a conflict of principles.

Of course, what has to be taken into account here is the fact that the set-theoretical version of the vicious-circle principle is an *informal* principle in accordance with which the system was constructed: it is not, itself, one of the axioms. For this reason, the addition of the axiom of reducibility does not conflict with this vicious-circle principle by producing a contradiction in the system; rather, it nullifies the influence of the principle.

Whether or not Russell succeeded in solving the paradoxes, there is no doubt that he furnished generations of philosophers and mathematical logicians with many important and fertile ideas for further investigation. In later chapters, I shall trace more closely the connection between the vicious-circle principle and some version of the "no-class" theory. If the justifications he gave were not convincing, at least part of the blame must attach to the obscurity and confusion that surround the notion of propositional function. Perhaps, by making this notion more precise, further progress could be made along Russellian lines. Russell's intuitions may have been sound in linking the vicious-circle principle to the "no-class" theory. These possibilities will be explored later on in this work.

In claiming that Russell's proposed solution to the paradoxes is defective, I am of course not suggesting that *PM* is a total failure. As I said before, we can regard *PM* not so much as an attempt to solve the paradoxes or to carry out Frege's program of deriving the theorems of arithmetic from self-evident logical laws, as an attempt to reconstruct classical mathematics within a consistent system. Besides, as the authors state in the introduction to *PM*, finding a solution to the paradoxes was only one of their aims. They also hoped to analyze mathematical ideas in terms of a relatively small number of primitive ideas and undemonstrated axioms. Besides this, they wished to show how mathematical propositions can be expressed in a precise and simple notation (*PM*, p. 1). It can be plausibly argued that these purposes were, to a large extent, achieved. As Kreisel puts it:

> One of the remarkable discoveries of the last century, clinched by the work of *Principia Mathematica*, is this: the bulk of the properties of mathematical objects which strike us as significant, can be expressed in this language. This is quite surprising because this language has a precise grammar and few primitives and casual inspection of common usage (even mathematics) suggests that the complexity of ordinary language is quite essential to its expressive power and flexibility. It is easy to forget this striking discovery when one finds that some significant distinctions cannot be expressed in predicate logic ([49], p. 215).

10. The "No-class" Theory and What There Is

From some of Russell's philosophical papers, the reader may get the impression that Russell thought he had proved that there are no classes; for he sometimes says that classes are "logical fictions," and, at one point, he baldly asserts: "There are no classes in the physical world" ([104], p. 268). But generally speaking his position in regard to the existence of classes was that of *agnosticism:* he simply didn't know whether classes exist or not.

It is a little misleading, however, to say that Russell did not assume that classes exist. After all, he did assert such things as: 0 is the class whose only member is the null-class. Obviously, Russell's agnosticism concerning the existence of classes should not be taken to imply that he thought we should refrain from all class-existence assertions. But the class-existence assertions Russell was willing to make were analyzed into assertions about individuals and propositional functions; and Russell did not think that these assertions forced him to admit into his ontology anything more than propositional functions and individuals. Hence, Russell did not assume that classes exist, in so far as classes are regarded as different from individuals and propositional functions, that is, in so far as classes are thought of in the usual, full-blown, way.[44]

Russell never claimed that his "no-class" theory proved that there are no classes, in so far as classes are thought of in the full-blown sense. The "no-class" theory was only supposed to allow him to adopt his position of agnosticism. He could then appeal to Occam's razor ("entities are not to be multiplied without necessity") as a reason for not postulating the existence of classes ([105], p. 184). But Occam's razor is no substitute for a proof of nonexistence. So naturally Russell was hesitant about asserting that classes do not exist.[45] He suggests in *PM* that one might be able to prove that classes (thought of in the usual way) cannot exist, by making use of "the ancient problem of the One and Many" (p. 72), but it is clear that, *at that time*, he did not think *he* had any such conclusive proof. Russell did disclose much later both that he did not think classes exist, and also why.

> A class of n terms has 2^n sub-classes. This proposition is still true when n is infinite. What Cantor proved was that, even in this case, 2^n is greater than n. Applying this, as I did, to all the things in the universe, one arrives at the conclusion

[44] Pears makes a similar point in [61], p. 20. Although I agree with much of his interpretation of Russell, it seems to me that Pears is slightly inaccurate when he suggests that when Russell says that classes and physical objects need not exist, he is really saying something about his analyses of these expressions. According to my view, Russell's "parsimonious analyses" provide the grounds for such claims as "classes need not exist."

[45] Pears suggests that Russell did not feel confident about denying the existence of classes because he had doubts about his "no-class" analysis, which sprang from doubts about the axiom of reducibility (Pears, [61], pp. 24-25). I do not think this can be a correct explanation for Russell's hesitation. For one thing, Russell clearly felt that the axiom of reducibility was a weaker assumption than that of the existence of classes. Secondly, Russell, far from expressing any serious doubts about the axiom of reducibility in the first edition of *PM* (despite the fact that he did express an unwillingness to deny the existence of sets), was quite confident that he had given an adequate analysis of set theory, and that he had detected the precise fallacy in the paradoxes (*PM*, p. 1). As I see it, Russell's reluctance to deny the existence of sets is straightforward and easy to understand: he simply lacked a proof of non-existence.

that there are more classes of things than there are things. It follows that classes are not "things." ... The conclusion to which I was led was that classes are merely a convenience in discourse ([107], pp. 80-81).

A similar attitude was expressed in 1918, when he wrote that the above argument provides a "perfectly precise arithmetical [sic] proof that there are *fewer* things in heaven and earth than are dreamt of in our philosophy" ([104], p. 260). Now why did Russell not present this argument in *PM* as definitely showing that classes do not exist? Perhaps at that time, he was not so confident of its cogency. After all, the argument requires the use of impredicative specifications and certainly seems to violate his vicious-circle principle. A better reason for not publishing the argument is that it is invalid. When Russell says, "it follows that classes are not 'things'," he concludes too much. This can be seen as follows: If we follow Russell's reasoning, we can infer from Cantor's theorem that if every class were a thing, there would be more things than there are things. Since an absurdity follows from the hypothesis that every class is a thing, we can conclude that not all classes are "things." But the conclusion only implies that some classes are not "things," not that no classes are "things." Of course, concluding that some classes are not "things" is the direction that axiomatic set theory took.

CHAPTER II

Gödel's Ontological Platonism

1. A Sketch of Gödel's Argument

Russell's "no-class" theory has certain obvious points in common with phenomenalism—the doctrine that statements about physical objects are, in some sense, reducible to (or translatable into) statements about sense-data. No doubt, the philosophical significance of the "no-class" theory is obscure in so far as the notion of propositional function is obscure; but if one were to rely upon Russell's definitions of the term 'propositional function' and thus construe propositional functions to be open sentences, it would seem that the "no-class" theory in *PM* was aimed at effecting a translation of statements about mathematical objects like numbers and sets into statements about concrete marks that human beings construct, that is, it would appear that Russell and Whitehead were attempting to remove from mathematics the apparent reference to nontemporal, nonspatial, abstract objects. Now Gödel believes that neither phenomenalism nor the sort of reductionism in set theory suggested by the "no-class" theory can succeed. According to Gödel, mathematics is built upon axioms concerning abstract objects that "exist independently of our definitions and constructions" and this Platonic content of mathematics cannot be "explained away" by the nominalist any more than the phenomenalist can "explain away" the references to physical objects ([38], p. 220). The failure of Russell's program is taken as "verification" of the view that the content of mathematics cannot be explained away nominalistically ([38], p. 224). Needless to say, Gödel does not regard Russell's reconstruction of mathematics as entirely successful—at least when viewed as a nominalistic reconstruction—the reason being that

Russell's program requires some such axiom as the axiom of reducibility, which can hardly be true unless one assumes the existence of abstract objects ([38], p. 231). The analogy between the "no-class" theory and phenomenalism, between statements about sets and numbers on the one hand and statements about physical objects on the other, is further developed by Gödel. He suggests that in the case of mathematics, there is something analogous to the perception of physical objects; indeed, he claims that there is something like a *perception of the objects of set theory* "as is seen from the fact that the axioms force themselves upon us as being true" ([39], p. 271). On this view, the analogue of perception for the mathematical case is mathematical intuition.

Gödel holds that the question of the actual *existence* of these objects of mathematical intuitions "is an exact replica of the question of the objective existence of the outer world" ([39], p. 272). Moreover, he claims that the assumption that these abstract objects exist "is quite as legitimate as the assumption of physical bodies and there is quite as much reason to believe in their existence" ([38], p. 220). Behind this remarkable claim is a further development of the analogy described above: from the belief that neither nominalistic reductions of set theory nor phenomenalistic reductions of physical theories can succeed, Gödel goes on to argue that abstract objects "are in the same sense necessary to obtain a satisfactory system of mathematics as physical objects are necessary for a satisfactory theory of our sense perceptions" ([38], p. 220). Apparently swayed by these considerations, Kreisel allows "that the realist assumption of external mathematical objects is not more *dubious* than that of physical objects" ([49], p. 186).

2. *Ontological and Mythological Platonism*

Before examining Gödel's line of reasoning in more detail, I should like to make an elementary distinction. In most philosophical discussions concerning the nature of mathematics, Platonism is contrasted with various "schools of thought" such as intuitionism, finitism, formalism, or constructivism. Roughly speaking, the contrast is generally made in terms (1) of the content of mathematical assertions and theories (What is mathematics about? Abstract objects? Mental constructs? Meaningless marks on paper?); and (2) of the intelligibility of certain mathematical theories and concepts (Is classical mathematics an intelligible theory? Does it make sense to speak of the set of all real numbers?); and (3) of the types of inferences that should be permitted in mathematics (Is the law of the excluded middle a legitimate principle in mathematics?).[1] By characterizing Platonism in these terms, however, a distinction of some philosophical importance tends to be obscured, if not overlooked entirely. The mathematician who feels no sympathy with intuitionistic qualms about the law of the excluded middle, who can see nothing wrong with such notions as the set of all real numbers or with impredicative specifications of sets, and who thinks that mathematicians theorize about abstract objects and not mental constructions or strings of symbols, would generally be characterized as a Platonist. I suppose the term 'Platonism' is used in so far as the abstract objects of mathematics are regarded as having certain features attributed to Plato's Forms; for instance sets are regarded as neither spatial nor temporal objects, it being thought absurd to say that the set of natural numbers is in such and such a location in space or that it came into or went out of existence at such and such a time.

But suppose a person who can thus be characterized as a Platonist wishes to take either no stand or a negative stand on the ontological question, "Do these abstract objects exist?" Surely we should distinguish this *Platonist* from the *ontological Platonists*, typified by Gödel, who believe actually that there are such objects as sets. Bernay's claim that "Platonism reigns today in mathematics" ([3], p. 276), is highly implausible if one supposes that by "Platonism" he meant ontological Platonism. Most working mathematicians continue to use so-called Platonic methods of reasoning and Platonic concepts despite the philosophical criticisms of intuitionists and the like, but this does not imply that they are ontological Platonists (most working mathematicians, I believe, would shy away from all ontological questions regarding the actual existence of sets), for one can hold that mathematicians construct their systems *as if*

[1] Cf. Bernays, [3].

they were describing existing objects, *as if* there are such things as sets and numbers, and that he reasons accordingly. Whether such abstract objects exist, he can say, is irrelevant to the question of whether the mathematical theories are intelligible. It is enough that such objects can be conceived. To distinguish Platonists of the latter sort from the ontological Platonists, I shall use the term 'mythological Platonist'.

By a mythological Platonist, I do not have in mind an irrational person who simply holds inconsistent beliefs or who is unwilling to accept the consequences of his own theories. A person studying a mathematical theory that asserts the existence of abstract entities need not commit himself to such entities: he could, for example, deny the existence of abstract entities and still remain consistent by remaining uncommitted to the truth of the mathematical theory he is studying. Indeed, as I shall argue later, he can even remain a mythological Platonist while allowing that the theory is *in some sense* true. But first, I should like to explore some of the more important differences between the ontological and the mythological Platonist.

Compare Gödel's attitude toward the paradoxes with that of a mythological Platonist. Gödel feels that the paradoxes point to a slight imperfection in our intellectual perception of sets. However, he sees no reason for scepticism in mathematics. Pressing the analogy between mathematics and the physical sciences, he writes: "The set-theoretical paradoxes are hardly any more troublesome for mathematics than deceptions of the senses are for physics" ([39], p. 271). A mythological Platonist, however, might take the position that the paradoxes only showed us that certain systems of set theory were inconsistent and that we must be careful to avoid certain pitfalls in constructing our new systems.

This distinction between ontological and mythological Platonism can be further illustrated by considering the significance for Platonism of Cohen's proof of the independence of the continuum hypothesis, the hypothesis that $\aleph_1 = 2^{\aleph_0}$. Cohen has shown that the continuum hypothesis is undecidable in the standard axiomatic set theories (Zermelo-Fraenkel, Gödel-Bernays);[2] and this has prompted some

[2] See P. Cohen, [21].

mathematicians to claim that the question of the truth or falsity of the continuum hypothesis is meaningless and that we should have different kinds of set theories just as we have different kinds of geometries. A mythological Platonist might agree with those who hold that the continuum hypothesis is neither true nor false. He might maintain that it has no truth value, since he is not committed to the view that there really are such abstract entities as sets. His position would then be analogous to a standard position regarding works of fiction—one in which the sentence 'Hamlet's nose was $4\frac{1}{2}$ inches long' is regarded as neither true nor false. To adopt such a position, even regarding fictional characters, is not completely uncontroversial, as can be seen from a glance at the recent philosophical literature (cf. J. Woods, [124]). But it does appear to be a reasonable option. Gödel's reaction to Cohen's proof is, of course, quite different. He is certain that no set of axioms we now have completely describes or characterizes the realm of sets, so the mere fact that the continuum hypothesis is independent of some widely accepted set of axioms is no reason for thinking either that there is no longer any question of its truth or falsity or that we can never discover whether it is true or false. After all, we know from Gödel's celebrated incompleteness theorem that even in the case of arithmetic every consistent axiomatic system that is "reasonably strong" has undecidable propositions. Gödel argues that, since it is unreasonable to label as meaningless the question of the truth or falsity of such undecidable arithmetical propositions, it is also unreasonable to do the analogous thing for the case of the continuum hypothesis ([39], p. 272). Gödel goes on to tell us that his stand is not based solely on his belief in the objective existence of sets. He suggests that all the data are not in: new mathematical intuitions may enable us to decide this question some day ([39], p. 270-2).

Recent discussions of Cohen's work on the independence of axioms concerning the powers of cardinals suggests that many mathematical logicians envisage a proliferation of set theories. Commenting on these independence theorems, Mostowski writes:

> Probably we shall have in the future essentially different intuitive notions of sets just as we have different notions of space, and will base our discussion of sets on axioms which correspond

to the kind of sets which we want to study . . . everything in the recent work on foundations of set theory points toward the situation which I just described ([57], p. 94).

Obviously, such a situation would pose no difficulties for a mythological Platonist. He could even allow that different set theories may prove useful to scientists for different purposes, just as different geometries have been useful in different scientific theories. For Gödel, on the other hand, the proliferation of set theories poses the thorny problem of determining which of the many set theories is the one that most truly describes the real world of sets.

It may be suggested that Gödel might evade this problem by allowing set theory to bifurcate into two theories, both of which treat entities that resemble the "sets" of our earlier theories, but in one of which, the continuum hypothesis holds, whereas in the other, the hypothesis does not hold. Unfortunately, this maneuver is hardly satisfactory. Gödel has argued that we have good reasons for thinking there are sets. But could he go on to argue that we have equally good reasons for postulating the existence of two new kinds of entities? Surely his argument would support the belief in, at best, one of the new kinds of "sets." So Gödel would have the problem of either deciding which of the two new theories is the true one—which differs little from the original problem—or of justifying belief in the existence of both sorts of new entities— which is none too easy to do.

Now Gödel believes that we, in some sense, perceive or "see" sets. So a deep problem for Gödel is, how can we humans perceive these abstract entities given that *they do not belong to the physical world* (as Gödel himself admits)? This difficulty in Gödel's Platonism is analogous to the mind-body problem inherent in Descartes' dualism —a problem which, despite the protestations by Cartesians that, after all, mind *must* interact with body, diminishes the plausibility of the philosophical theory that analyzes the human being as consisting of two radically different substances. Obviously, a mythological Platonist is not faced with Gödel's difficulty. Indeed, he could take the position that sets are purely figments of the imagination. He could then explain why many have felt that set theory is a "free creation of the imagination," and he could see some point to the traditional philosophical view that mathematics is an *a priori* (non-observational) science.

But if a mythological Platonist were to take the above position, how could he explain the fact that we are all inclined to classify many set theoretical statements as true—even those that assert the existence of sets? Suppose, for example, that he were to find the following sentence on a true-false examination on Fraenkel's set theory:

> There exists a set containing all the real numbers.

He would naturally be marked wrong for answering: "False, there are no such things as sets." But consider an analogous situation. On a true-false English literature examination, we would all put down 'true' for the following:

> Hamlet kills his father's brother.
> People no bigger than an ordinary man's hand inhabit Lilliput.

Notice that in the literature examination, we could understand the sentences to be saying: In Shakespeare's play, Hamlet kills his father's brother. In Swift's *Gulliver's Travels*, people no bigger than an ordinary man's hand inhabit Lilliput. The mythological Platonist can regard the set theory case in a similar manner. The question for him is not, "Does there really exist a set that contains all the real numbers?" but rather, "In Fraenkel's imaginary world of sets, does there exist a set that contains all the real numbers?" Of course, the explanation offered here is very rough. Further clarification is called for. So let us consider more fully the claim that in certain situations we would classify the sentence 'People no bigger than an ordinary man's hand inhabit Lilliput' as true. We know that if the sentence were uttered in the course of describing the contents of Swift's novel, it would be natural to say that what the speaker said is true. However, few anthropologists would take seriously an utterance of the sentence during a discussion of strange races of men. I should think some sort of distinction should be made between saying some statement is true on the grounds that this is what is said or implied in a work of fiction and saying that something is the case regardless of what is said in stories. So let us use the terms 'true to a story' and 'objectively true' to mark roughly the distinction we want. The above sentence would then be *true to a story* (viz., Swift's novel) but not *objectively true*. By making this distinction, we could allow the inference of 'There are tiny men no bigger than an ordinary man's hand' from the above sentence, so long as what is concluded is only that the sentence is true to the story.

I do not wish to suggest that the notion of a sentence being true to a story is a precise one. I would be the first to admit that the rules for the use of the term are somewhat vague. Thus, it seems reasonable to classify as true the sentence 'Hamlet did not have artificial arms' (otherwise how could he have fenced so well?). But what about the sentence 'Hamlet's indecision was due to an Oedipus-complex'? *Could* that be true? Or consider: 'Either Hamlet's nose was $4\frac{1}{2}$ inches long or it was not'. *Must* that sentence be true to the story? I am not certain. I would have qualms about taking the affirmative position.[3] Despite this vagueness, I think the distinction between *true to a story* and *objectively true* should be made.

To clarify these points and to bring out more vividly the distinction between ontological and mythological Platonism, I should like the reader to enter with me into a world called Myopia. The inhabitants of this world, the Myopians, have a strange practice: they tell their children a long story about a god called Myo, and the children seem to develop the capacity for continuing this story far beyond what is told to them. It would appear that the story is extendable without limit. Not only this, but almost all of these children agree on how it should be continued. Now and then a child may deviate slightly from the others, but these deviations are usually slight and, if noticed, are "corrected." Very infrequently, a child cannot continue. But if, after repeating the story for the child many times, encouraging him to go on, and continuing the story to new lengths, the child is still unable to tell the story beyond a certain point, he is

---

[3] Cf. J. Woods [124], p. 62. Woods gives a strange argument to support his contention that the law of excluded middle applies to fictional entities. He maintains that Hamlet's nose was either 4 1/2 inches long or it wasn't—it is just impossible to discover whether or not it was. But I find neither the argument nor the position very satisfactory.

considered in some respects mentally deficient. Now, the telling of this story is far more than a simple pastime. By tradition, the social and moral practices of the Myopians are based on the words and actions related in the story. A certain act might be condemned on the grounds that Myo explicitly refrained from such acts, or it might be justified on the grounds that Myo himself performed such acts. One open question for the Myopians, which has generated much controversy, is whether or not the use of artificial contraceptives is morally admissible. Since the story of Myo—at least as far as anyone can tell—does not explicitly decide this question, the liberals argue that the individual is free to choose whether or not he shall use such means. And their doctrine has become known as "the axiom of choice." Logicians and mathematicians of Myopia have investigated the question of the decidability of the axiom from the story, and they have concluded that neither it nor its negation can be inferred from the deeds of Myo occuring in that part of the story that anyone has ever investigated. This independence result has been taken as another reason for adopting the axiom. There are, however, ontological theists who argue that the question is by no means settled. These philosophers believe that the story relates actual events in the life of an actual immortal god. They argue that the ability of the people to continue the story is due to some sort of "direct intuition" of the universe that Myo inhabits. They also argue that only on their hypothesis can one explain the general agreement among the people about how the story is to be continued. To these ontological theists, it would be absurd to suppose that one might literally see Myo or discover traces of Myo in the land of Myopia, for they believe that Myo does not exist in the three-dimensional space of the Myopians.[4] Concerning the axiom of choice, these philosophers argue, using the law of the excluded middle, that Myo must have either used artificial contraceptives or not have used them while he was married to Lyo. The fact that the story does not decide this question only shows, on their view, that the Myopians' "perception" of the world of Myo is defective; it does not show that the question

---

[4] Cf. the belief of Catholics regarding Heaven and Hell. It is believed that Heaven and Hell really exist despite the fact that neither these "places" nor the souls that inhabit them exist in "physical space."

of the truth or falsity of the axiom of choice is a meaningless one. Besides, they add, the fact that the story is indefinitely extendable shows that all the data are not in: new intuitions may enable them to decide the question in the future. The mythological theists agree that the ever lengthening story may someday decide the question, but they do not allow that the story relates actual events. For these philosophers, the story is fictional—a kind of myth. Thus, when they allow that the sentence 'Myo used contraceptives' may be found to be true or false at some later date, they do not wish to suggest that the sentence may be found to be *objectively* true or false. It is just that all the data are not yet in, in the sense that the story, which is still being extended, may someday decide the question of whether or not the sentence is true to the story. Although they do not pretend to explain the fact that there is general agreement in the continuations of the story, some philosophers at M.I.T. (the Myopic Institute of Technology) suggest that the unlimited extendability of the story is explainable by postulating certain innate principles in the Myopians. Noting that the Myopians, as organisms, are basically alike and that they all receive essentially the same training in telling the story, they analyze the situation in terms of a mechanism which is given a certain input and which produces a certain output: An inference is then made about the nature of the mechanism. The philosophers suggest that the Myopian organism must have certain rules or principles "built into it," and they see no reason for appealing to perceptions or intuitions of another world.

Perhaps the above example can throw some light on the following puzzling passage in which Gödel argues that Cohen's independence result does not dispose of the question of the truth or falsity of the continuum hypothesis:

> The question of the objective existence of the objects of mathematical intuition (which, incidentally, is an exact replica of the question of the objective existence of the outer world) is not decisive for the problem under discussion here. The mere psychological fact of the existence of an intuition which is sufficiently clear to produce the axioms of set theory and an open series of extensions of them suffices to give meaning to the question of the truth or falsity of propositions like Cantor's continuum hypothesis ([39], p. 272).

This quotation seems to express the view that even if there were no objects of mathematical intuition, we might still come to see that the continuum hypothesis is true or false. But is there not a problem here? Suppose no sets exist, and suppose we know this. How, then, should we construe the claim that the continuum hypothesis is true? Reverting to the Myopians example, if it were known that no such person as Myo ever existed, what would it mean to say the sentence 'Myo used contraceptives' is true? We would probably understand the person to be making a claim about what is stated in, or inferable from, the story of Myo (that is, about what is true to the story of Myo). Of course, in the set theory case, there is no story to furnish the framework for such an analysis, but we do have a concept of set. We should look for an analogue of the notion of being true to a story.

The rough distinction between true to a story and objectively true can be extended. If we can speak of a sentence being true to Dante's *Divine Comedy*, why not go on to speak of a sentence being true to Dante's conception of Heaven (or to the concept of Heaven expressed in the *Divine Comedy*)? We could then say that the sentence 'There are angels in Heaven' is true to this conception. Notice that a mythological Platonist might make a similar distinction for statements about sets. He could then argue that when he says "There are no such things as sets," he is not contradicting the statement 'There are infinitely many sets containing the null set', he could say that the former is objectively true whereas the latter is only true to a concept of the universe of sets. The statement 'There are many null sets' would then be true to the Russellian concept of set expressed in *PM*, but false to Zermelo's concept of set.[5]

The distinction between *objectively true* and *true to a concept* that I am trying to make can perhaps be clarified in terms of the following example. Let us suppose that a group of people meet regularly to discuss their conception of Heaven. And suppose that after many years of discussion, they finally arrive at a common idea of Heaven. One of the discussants, a logician, decides to axiomatize

[5] This is a little misleading since one cannot assert that there are many null sets in *PM*. But one can see, in the meta-theory so to speak, that there are many null sets, many universal sets, many number ones, etc.

some of the more salient features of Heaven. He puts into the axioms of his first-order theory such sentences as:

$(\exists x)(x$ is an angel and x inhabits Heaven)

$(x)(x$ inhabits Heaven $\rightarrow - x$ has position in physical space).

Now it is said of these axioms that they are, in some sense, true—even self-evident. If it is objected that it is unreasonable to claim that one can know *a priori* that angels exist, the members reply that when they claim that the axioms are true, they mean only that the axioms truly characterize or express their conception of Heaven: they are not claiming that the axioms truly characterize reality.

The idea that a statement might be objectively false and yet true to someone's conception of an imaginary world may not seem so strange if we translate the question "Is $\ulcorner P \urcorner$ true to your conception of Heaven?" into "Do you imagine Heaven to be such that P?" When so translated, the question of whether a particular statement is true to one's conception of some universe may have a definite and easily obtainable answer. Such questions *are* asked, and most people can answer them without great difficulty. Obviously, we are not in so favorable a position to answer questions about objective truth.

Some students of set theory claim that they cannot conceive of the axioms of Zermelo-Fraenkel set theory being false. It would be strange if they were claiming that these axioms could not possibly be objectively false; for surely it is conceivable that no sets at all exist. Even Gödel would allow that. Probably, what is being claimed is that the axioms could not conceivably be false to a certain conception of the universe of sets. In these respects, then, the world of set theory would resemble Heaven.

I should like to use this rough distinction between *objectively true* and *true to a concept* to clarify a suggestion I made earlier: I said that a mythological Platonist is not committed to holding that the continuum hypothesis is either true or false. What I had in mind was this: he need not maintain that the continuum hypothesis is either true or false to his (or the relevant) conception of the universe of sets. It is easy to see that this sort of "rejection" of the law of excluded middle as it applies to fictional or imaginary entities does not imply a rejection of the classical laws of logic. Suppose that you are asked to imagine in some detail a man and woman fencing. And suppose you are asked such questions as: Is the man taller than the woman? Does the man have a beard? Is the woman slender? Is she black? Suppose you are then asked: Has the woman had her appendix removed? Or does she still have her appendix? Must those questions have "Yes" or "No" answers? Essentially what is being asked is this: Did you imagine the woman to have an appendix? Now the classical law of excluded middle might be cited in support of the claim that either you imagined the woman to have an appendix or you did not imagine the woman to have an appendix. But 'You did not imagine the woman to have an appendix' does not imply 'You imagined the woman not to have an appendix'. So, it is hard to see how logic can show us that either you imagined the woman to have an appendix or you imagined the woman not to have an appendix.[6] Similarly, I do not see why a mythological Platonist could not allow, without giving up classical logic, the possibility that the Zermelo-Fraenkel conception of sets is neither of a universe in which $\aleph_1 = 2^{\aleph_0}$ nor of a universe in which $\aleph_1 \neq 2^{\aleph_0}$.

It might be thought that the version of mythological Platonism sketched in this section simply postpones the appeal to abstract entities. For has not the mythological Platonist committed himself to acknowledging the existence of at least *concepts* when he speaks of sentences being "true to a concept" (or true to someone's conception of something)? And are not concepts abstract entities? The objector may feel that it is only by postulating the existence of abstract entities (concepts) that he can see how a sentence can be "true to a concept." But what underlies this objection? Why does the objector feel that the mythological Platonist has committed himself to the existence of concepts? Perhaps "semantical considerations" of the following sort underlie the objection: the objector may feel that the expression 'is true to concept C' must be analyzed in such a way that 'is true to' denotes a relation that obtains between sentences on the one hand and concepts on the other.

My response to this sort of objection is similar to Quine's and will become clearer in the following chapters (cf. Quine [81], § 45). But

---

[6] A similar point is made by Wittgenstein in [122], IV, § 17.

a brief reply may be in order here. The expression 'is true to C' need not be analyzed in such a way that a sentence s is true to John's concept of Heaven if and only if

$(\exists x)(x = $ John's concept of Heaven & s is true to x).

The mythological Platonist can regard the expression 'is true to' as an operator, which, when applied to a concept expression such as 'John's concept of Heaven', yields a predicate of sentences. From this point of view, there is no need to suppose that some abstract entity is being presupposed by the use of the expression 'is true to John's concept of Heaven': the expression is simply analyzed to be a complex predicate. In this way, the mythological Platonist could argue that he is not committed to quantification over concepts.

But does not this response restrict the mythological Platonist's use of such "concept expressions" as 'John's concept of Heaven' to contexts in which sentences are said to be true to some concept? Suppose, for example, that he wishes to deny that there is anything real that corresponds to, or "falls under," to use Frege's terminology, John's concept of Heaven. Would such a denial commit him to acknowledging the existence of concepts? Not necessarily; for the operator analysis described above can be extended to cover the new use. The mythological Platonist can regard 'corresponds to' and 'falls under' as operators, which yield predicates when applied to concept expressions.

But the operator analysis does not seem to be applicable to sentences like:

(1) John's concept of God is identical to Aquinas'.
(2) John's concept of God is that of God as a necessary being.

Must the mythological Platonist refrain from making such assertions? By making use of the operators defined above, he can provide rough paraphrases of such sentences. Much of the "sense" of (1) can be captured by asserting: "Any sentence true to John's concept of God is true to Aquinas', and conversely; and if anything falls under John's concept of God, it would have to fall under Aquinas', and conversely." Asserting (2) is not so different from asserting: "The sentence 'God is a necessary being' is true to John's concept of God; and if anything falls under John's concept of God, it would have to be a necessary being." Of course these analyses are only meant to be rough suggestions as to how the mythological Platonist could respond to the objection under consideration. Obviously, the details of the position would have to be worked out.

It should be emphasized, however, that I am not putting forward mythological Platonism as a completely satisfactory philosophical theory of set theory. This position was developed primarily for two reasons: first, to clarify (by way of contrast) Gödel's ontological Platonism, and secondly, to bring out weaknesses in Gödel's argument for his position.

Thus far, I have indicated how the mythological Platonist might explain his use of expressions involving such particular "concept expressions" as 'John's concept of Heaven'. It is more difficult to explain locutions involving "indefinite reference" to concepts. In particular, how can the mythological Platonist use such locutions as 'true to a concept', in which no particular concept expression is involved? He cannot allow, as the ontological Platonist can, that

(3) s is true to a concept

is to be analyzed as "saying"

(4) $(\exists x)(x$ is a concept & s is true to $x)$

at least, if the quantifier in (4) is to be understood in the usual way. However, he can give the following analysis of (3): There is a concept expression ϕ such that the sentence consisting of s followed by 'is true to' followed by ϕ is true. (The essential idea here is to make use of "substitutional quantification;" in regard to this see Quine [88], p. 231). Of course, the mythological Platonist would have to specify some range of concept expressions for the existential quantifier used in the analysis, but it is not difficult to see how he might do this.

It might then be objected that the mythological Platonist commits himself to at least the existence of expressions if he says of some sentence s that it is true to a concept. I shall defer responding to objections of this sort until the last chapter.

It is possible that an ontological Platonist may wish to develop a slightly different version of the objection described above. He may feel that the postulation of the existence of concepts is needed for purposes other than the theoretical explanation of the "semantics" of such expressions as 'is true to C' or 'falls under C'. The objector might argue that the existence of concepts is needed to explain, for example, how John can *know* that some sentence is true to his concept of Heaven. But to make this argument persuasive to the mythological Platonist, it would have to be shown that the only genuinely acceptable theories we now have that enable us to explain how John can know such things all require the postulation of the existence of concepts. If the Platonist could produce even one scientifically respectable theory that did provide us with the required adequate explanation, then such an objection would be very persuasive indeed; but this no Platonist has done. I admit that there is much about our talk of concepts, ideas, and images that I cannot adequately explain and that I do not fully understand. But I see in this no good reason for clutching at Platonic straws. Indeed, I doubt that the postulation of such nonphysical, nonspatial entities as concepts can be of any use in explaining what John can know. What genuine explanatory power does a theory gain by postulating the existence of abstract entities? The answer to this question is by no means clear from the theories Platonists have put forward so far; for their metaphysical theories have been notoriously lacking in the kind of verifiable consequences expected of adequate scientific theories. My doubts regarding the explanatory power of abstract entities will be more fully articulated in the next section.

3. A More Detailed Examination of the Argument

Returning now to Gödel's argument for ontological Platonism, I should like to point out that Gödel's reasoning can be separated into two parts, the first being concerned with the possibility of giving a nominalistic reduction of any "satisfactory system of mathematics." Now it is not perfectly clear what Gödel means by (or takes to be) a "satisfactory system of mathematics," but it is clear that Gödel thinks the predicative set theory of *PM* (minus the axiom of reducibility) would not qualify as such a system. It would seem that Gödel would expect a truly satisfactory system of mathematics to permit the derivation of the standard classical analysis and set theory. In any case, even if we all agree with Gödel that no such nominalistic reduction of mathematics is possible, this by itself does not commit us to ontological Platonism, since we can still espouse some form of mythological Platonism. It is the second part of Gödel's argument that attempts to force ontological Platonism upon us. Basically, Gödel reasons that, since we cannot give a nominalistic reduction of any satisfactory system of mathematics, mathematics demands the existence of abstract objects just as physical theories demand the existence of physical objects. Of course, acceptance of the claim that some physical theory implies the existence of physical objects does not, of itself, commit one to some form of realism, for it is still open to the phenomenalist, for example, to hold that this physical theory is not a true one. The point is: one is not tempted to say that we ought to believe in the existence of ghosts just because some theory of ghosts demands (or implies) the existence of ghosts; for unless we are also given some good evidence for the theory, itself, we have as yet not been given any good reason for believing in ghosts. Hence, underlying Gödel's argument is the belief that we have good reason for maintaining that a satisfactory system of mathematics is (objectively) true. What supports this belief? Gödel holds that, corresponding to the sense experiences that support our empirical theories, there are mathematical experiences that support our mathematical theories, so it is ultimately our mathematical experiences that demand the existence of abstract entities ([38], p. 220). Mathematical theories are supposed to be based upon genuine experiences upon which we should place as much confidence as we place upon our sense experiences.

But what makes Gödel think there are such mathematical experiences? The following quotation provides us with an answer:

> But, despite their [the sets'] remoteness from sense experience, we do have something like a perception also of the objects of set theory, as is seen from the fact that the axioms force themselves upon us as being true. I don't see any reason why we should have less confidence in this kind of perception, i.e., in mathematical intuition, than in sense perception, which induces us to build up physical theories and to expect that future sense perceptions will agree with them (Gödel [39], p. 271).

But even if we grant that there are such "mathematical experiences," must we assume that the mathematical theories we construct in response to these experiences are true? Must we assume that the axioms of set theory are true in order to explain our mathematical intuitions? I can find no convincing reasons for thinking we must.

Recapitulating my criticism of Gödel's argument, I have granted, for the sake of argument, that the *content* of any "satisfactory system of mathematics" can no more be "explained away" nominalistically than the content of our physical theories can be explained away phenomenalistically. But since Gödel claims that physical objects must be postulated to explain our sense experiences,[7] much more is needed to justify Gödel's claim that "there is quite as much reason to believe in" the existence of sets as in physical objects: we also need to show that we have to assume that our "satisfactory system of mathematics" is *true* in order to explain our "mathematical experiences." This, for some reason, Gödel does not do [38].

It is *not* obvious that we get the best explanation of our mathematical experiences by postulating the existence of abstract entities. Indeed, it is by no means obvious to me that we can give a reasonable explanation of these phenomena even if we do postulate the existence of sets. Gödel focuses on the experience of an axiom forcing itself upon us as being true. I suppose that what is impressive about this sort of experience is the fact that there is so much agreement in intuitions. This agreement lends some plausibility to the Platonist's claim that there is some objective reality being perceived. Thus, Gödel explains our mathematical experiences by postulating a nonphysical universe of abstract objects which we, in some unexplained way, perceive. However, I doubt that many empirical scientists would find such an explanation at all convincing.

Let us consider more carefully this phenomenon that Gödel describes as that of some axiom forcing itself upon us as being true. I do not see why we should regard this as an instance of intuiting or in some sense "perceiving" the objects of set theory. Could not my hypothetical logician, axiomatizing his group's concept of Heaven,

---

[7] "Physical bodies are necessary for a satisfactory theory of our sense experiences" (Gödel [38], p. 220).

claim that the axioms force themselves upon him as being true? Of course, the relevant sense of "true" does not yield the conclusion that he can "perceive" Heaven and its inhabitants.

Perhaps my qualms about Gödel's doctrine of mathematical intuition can best be illustrated by a more "real" example drawn from recent philosophical discussions of the ontological argument for the existence of God. Many philosophers have conceived of the possibility of a perfect being whom they call 'God'. In analyzing this concept, they have been led to attribute to this being such properties as omniscience. Now imagine a systematic philosopher attempting to axiomatize this conception of God. He might ponder the possibility that God could be destroyed somehow, and conclude that this would be an impossibility in the case of a perfect being. He might ask himself whether a perfect being could be constructed, generated, or created by some other thing, and decide that this, too, is impossible. Then it might strike him as absolutely obvious that God cannot depend for his existence on anything, and he might express this "insight" by saying that *God is a necessary being*. So if the sentence, '*God is a necessary being*', were to be treated as an axiom of this philosopher's system, we might say that this axiom forced itself upon him as being true. But, making use of the distinction made in the previous section, I should think that it would be less misleading to say that it forced itself upon him as being *true to this concept of God*. For my imaginary axiomatizer need not think that there is anything that corresponds to his concept: he could be an out-and-out atheist, and still find himself forced to conclude that the concept he is analyzing is that of God as a necessary being. Of course, if something does correspond to this philosopher's concept of God, that is, if something "falls under the concept," then this thing would have to have the property of being a necessary being in the above sense; but, so far as I can see, nothing above *proves* that there is any such being. And the mere fact that, by going through some such process of analysis this philosopher should be able to arrive at axioms about which there is, among Christian philosophers, general agreement, would not imply that we humans are able to "perceive" God or that we have "theological intuitions." So far as I can see, the phenomenon that Gödel describes as that of axioms of set theory forcing themselves upon us as being true is really more like the above case of an axiom's forcing itself upon us as being true to a concept, than a case of perceiving objects "external to us" as Gödel suggests.

It is perhaps worth noting the sort of discussion that frequently precedes someone's getting another to see that 'God is a necessary being' is "true." The preliminary discussion seems to be necessary sometimes to get across the relevant concept of God. There seems to be an analogous situation in the set theory case. The agreement in mathematical intuitions I have been talking about is by no means universal, as can be seen from the controversy that took place at the turn of the century over the acceptability of the axiom of choice.[8] Nowadays, a teacher might talk about the intuitive universe his set theory is supposed to describe, in order to get his students to see that the axiom of choice or the power set axiom is "true." But this too suggests that the axioms are being accepted as true to a concept.[9]

Should we postulate the existence of sets to explain this agreement in intuitions, or this phenomenon of seeing that some axiom is true? Descartes once argued that, in order to explain the fact that he had an idea of a perfect being, it was necessary to postulate the existence of such a being. I should think it would be better to look for less fanciful explanations of such facts of one's intellectual history. (Should we not consider Descartes' Catholic education in searching for an explanation?) So also, if we wish to explain the existence of "mathematical intuitions" and the large agreement in intuitions we find among contemporary set-theorists, I think we should look for some sort of natural explanation before we turn to postulating nonphysical universes and extra-sensory perceptions. As a start in this direction, it is worth mentioning that the set-theorists who agree that certain axioms of set theory force themselves upon us as being

---

[8] See Black [6], p. 184. Cf. Zermelo's reply to his critics in [125].

[9] I am not claiming that *all* mathematical truths are of this sort. I would not say, for example, that arithmetical truths are only true to a concept. I focus on the axioms of the "standard" set theories since Gödel seems to allow that *PM* (minus the axiom of reducibility) does "explain away" the Platonic content of a significant portion of mathematics. In any case, I shall argue, in a later chapter, that such predicative set theories can be "reduced" to a nominalistically acceptable system.

true receive substantially the same sort of mathematical training. Furthermore, mathematicians, regarded as biological organisms, are basically quite similar.

On the topic of sets and concepts, Gödel once wrote:

> It seems to me that the assumption of such objects is quite as legitimate as the assumption of physical bodies and there is quite as much reason to believe in their existence. They are in the same sense necessary to obtain a satisfactory system of mathematics as physical bodies are necessary for a satisfactory theory of our sense perceptions ([38], p. 220).

When Gödel spoke of a "satisfactory system of our sense perceptions," he did not have in mind a theory that tells us about the actual production of sense perceptions in the way in which some psychological or physiological theory might someday tell us how normal human beings come to have any sense perceptions at all or how particular stimulations of specific nerves produce sense perceptions. Gödel is not committed to holding that we have a satisfactory theory of sense perceptions in that sense. What he had in mind coincides in certain important respects with Quine's views on the matter. Supposedly, we construct our scientific theories to square with, explain, and predict our observations and experiences. Now Gödel classifies our experiences into two categories: sense experiences and mathematical experiences. He then suggests that the theories of sense perceptions we now accept, such as present-day physics, chemistry, biology, and the like, are the most satisfactory of the alternatives that have been proposed; and these theories presuppose or require the existence of physical objects. Similarly, Gödel argues, any satisfactory theory of our "mathematical experiences," that is, any satisfactory system of mathematics, will presuppose the existence of sets and concepts.

What I have been arguing in this chapter is that we have not been given any good grounds for supposing that the classical systems of mathematics Gödel would regard as satisfactory (systems, that is, that are substantially stronger than predicative systems) must be true in order to square our mathematical perceptions with our theories. I have, in effect, questioned Gödel's idea that we should separate off mathematical perceptions from the totality of our experiences and explain them in a radically different way by postulating the existence of new sorts of entities. In the present situation, it is just as promising to seek an understanding and a theoretical explanation of our mathematical perceptions within the framework of our ordinary empirical sciences. We need not suppose that our mathematical theories describe some actual universe of abstract entities of which we have some extra-sensory perception. If this is so, considerations of theoretical and ontological economy should prompt us to resist the Gödelian view. Gödel's reasoning seems to lead to a massive population explosion of our ontology: if we use mathematical intuitions to postulate mathematical objects, it would seem that we could use "theological intuitions" to postulate theological objects like angels.

Thus, it is hard to see why one should accept Gödel's claim that we have just as much reason to believe in the existence of sets and concepts as we have for the case of physical objects, unless of course one believes that the considerations I have brought to bear on Gödel's case for abstract objects can also be applied against belief in physical objects. In that case, one might distinguish a phenomenalistic mythological realist from an ontological realist, in order to argue that we have no good grounds for thinking our empirical theories to be true, and in this way try to salvage at least one part of Gödel's argument for the existence of sets and concepts.

I do not claim here that no convincing argument of this sort can be given. And although I believe both that no such convincing argument has as yet been given and that this line of defense faces severe difficulties, it will serve my purposes to note that Gödel has not given any such argument.

4. Gödel's Fruitfulness Criterion

Besides mathematical intuition, there is, according to Gödel, another way in which mathematicians might reasonably be led to accept a new mathematical axiom: one might find that the acceptance of some new axiom would allow one to prove theorems which can be independently "verified" (proved) in the old system, but in a way that is simpler and easier than is possible without the axiom. Supposedly, the axioms of the classical real number system have been shown to be fruitful in this sense, since they were used to prove various number-theoretic theorems which were subsequently verified in a more cumbersome way by elementary means.

Now the question arises: Can this criterion of fruitfulness be used to shore up Gödel's argument for ontological Platonism? Let us first note that when Gödel introduced this criterion, he was not attempting to justify his belief in the existence of sets ([39]). He was primarily concerned with the question of how one might arrive at some new axioms of set theory, and he was not addressing himself to the question: How might one justify the acceptance of the usual axioms of set theory (taken as a whole)? When he said that "a probable decision" on the truth of some proposed axiom might be arrived at by studying its fruitfulness, he was not making a claim with which a mythological Platonist would necessarily disagree ([39], p. 265). A mythological Platonist might maintain that the fruitfulness of an axiom would give him a reason for developing his conception of the universe of sets in such a way that the axiom would be true to this conception. Thus, he might use fruitfulness as a guide in forming his conception of the universe of sets in roughly the way in which an author might use some recent theory of psychology in forming his conception of a character. A mythological Platonist might even hold that the fruitfulness of an axiom is a reason for thinking that the whole mathematical community will probably come to accept as standard some conception of the universe of sets to which the axiom is true.

Although Gödel himself did not attempt to justify his ontological Platonism by appealing to his criterion of fruitfulness, some of his comments suggest ways in which one might attempt to bolster his argument by appealing to this criterion. If, for example, one regards arithmetical propositions as having a role in mathematics similar to "observation statements" in the empirical sciences, one might argue that the axioms of set theory enable us to "predict" arithmetical propositions which can then be verified to be true by "finitary" means. The verified arithmetical proposition would then serve as confirmation of the axioms of set theory, the way observations may confirm some physical theory. In order to construct in this way a plausible argument for ontological Platonism, it is not enough to point to cases in which arithmetical propositions deduced from the axioms of set theory have been verified. The argument would not be plausible unless the predicted arithmetical propositions could not be adequately explained by equally plausible theories that do not presuppose the existence of abstract entities. Since the nominalistic response to such an argument would depend upon the precise mathematical predictions made and verified, I shall not develop this line of investigation further. It is possible that no philosopher will ever give such an argument. Gödel, himself, wrote:

> The simplest case of an application of the criterion under discussion arises when some set-theoretical axiom has number-theoretic consequences verifiable by computation up to any given integer. On the basis of what is known today, however, it is not possible to make the truth of any set-theoretical axiom reasonably probable in this manner ([39], p. 272).

So far, I have been discussing fruitfulness in mathematics. Gödel also suggested that one might someday use fruitfulness in physics as a criterion of truth of mathematical axioms. This suggestion points to a significant difference between mathematical theories and the theological "theories" discussed earlier: mathematics is an essential element in our scientific theorizing. Perhaps one can justify a belief in the existence of abstract entities by an appeal to the use of mathematics in the empirical sciences. Quine developed such an idea into a new argument for ontological Platonism. In his argument the emphasis shifts from the postulation of abstract entities so as to explain our mathematical experiences to the postulation of abstract entities so as to explain our sense experiences. The argument will be examined in some detail in the next chapter.

CHAPTER III

Quine's Ontological Platonism

1. A Sketch of Quine's Argument for Ontological Platonism

The considerations that move Quine toward Platonism are similar in many ways to those put forward by Gödel. Again, Russell's "no-class" theory provides us with a point of entry into the logic of the position. As I said before, the ontological significance of the "no-class" theory is obscured by the ambiguity of the term 'propositional function': if propositional functions are thought to be open sentences, *PM* may appear to accomplish an important reduction of set theory to nominalistically acceptable principles. Quine notes, however, that in *PM* predicate letters are used as bound variables of quantification. As a consequence, Quine argues, the propositional functions over which these bound variables are supposed to range must be regarded as attributes or qualities rather than open sentences:

> The effect of letting 'ϕ', 'ψ', etc., occur in quantifiers, now, is that these letters cease to be fragments merely of dummy matrices 'ϕx', 'ψx', etc., and come to share the genuinely referential power of 'x', 'y', etc. They must now be regarded as variables in their own right, referring to some sort of abstract entities, perhaps *attributes*, as their value ... ([72], p. 19).

Thus the sentence

$$(\exists \phi)(x)(\phi x)$$

should be read roughly as follows:

There is an attribute ϕ such that every individual has the attribute ϕ.

Since Quine believes that attributes are "no less universal,

84

abstract, intangible, than classes themselves" ([72], p. 22), he concludes that *Principia* does not provide a nominalistic basis for mathematics: "The universals posited by binding the predicate letters have never been explained away in terms of any mere convention of notation" ([82], p. 122).

Now Quine can see no way of reconstructing mathematics in a way that avoids quantifying (in effect) over universals or abstract objects of some sort. Applying his well-known criterion of ontological commitment to the case of mathematics, Quine concludes that classical mathematics "is up to its neck in commitments to an ontology of abstract entities" ([82], p. 13). He thus claims that the nominalist "is going to have to accommodate his natural sciences unaided by mathematics; for mathematics, except for some trivial portions such as very elementary arithmetic, is irredeemably committed to quantification over abstract objects" ([81], p. 269). Being himself unwilling to take such a drastic position regarding science, Quine chooses, reluctantly, to go the way of the Platonist, allowing into his ontology classes as well as physical objects ([82], ch. 7).

Despite the obvious similarities, Quine's reasoning in support of Platonism should be distinguished from Gödel's. For one thing, they differ in their attitudes towards the Russellian "no-class" theory. Gödel, for example, does not concern himself especially with the role of the quantifier, as does Quine, nor does he employ any criterion of ontological commitment. His reason for saying that the "no-class" theory does not succeed in effecting a nominalist reduction of mathematics is that to complete the program, the authors of *PM* were forced to include the axiom of reducibility (or some such powerful axiom) in their system; whereas Quine's reasoning is based upon considerations of the bound variables in *PM*. But more importantly, the postulation of abstract entities is thought by Gödel to be required by mathematics, itself, whereas Quine stresses the demands of the natural sciences. Thus, if it could be shown that the mathematics needed by the natural scientist could be reconstructed on a purely nominalistic basis, even though many high-powered mathematical systems developed these days by mathematicians could not be so reconstructed, Quine's argument would lose much of its force; whereas such a result would seem to be largely irrelevant to Gödel's argument. Both seem to agree, however, that the evidently Platonic content of mathematical theories cannot be explained or analyzed away in a purely nominalistic fashion.

2. Is Quine an Ontological Platonist?

The claim that Quine is an ontological Platonist may be criticized on the grounds that Quine once said that physical objects and classes are "convenient myths" ([82]). Thus, it may be thought that Quine favored some form of mythological Platonism. This objection (which has been raised more than once) is based upon a careless reading of Quine's writings and fails to take account of the qualifications Quine makes when he says that classes and attributes are myths. What Quine says is: "A platonistic ontology of this sort is, *from the point of view of a strictly physicalistic conceptual scheme,* as much a myth as that physicalistic conceptual scheme itself is for phenomenalism" (p. 18, italics mine). Later, he says: "*Viewed from within the phenomenalistic conceptual scheme,* the ontologies of physical objects and mathematical objects are myths. The quality of myth, however, is relative; relative in this case, to the epistemological point of view" (p. 19, italics mine). When these qualifications are not overlooked, it is easy to reconcile Quine's remarks about myths with his many statements about the existence of sets. When Quine made the above remarks, he was not especially concerned with what there is: his main aim was to introduce order and rational standards into ontological controversies. So he did not put forward his own ontological favorites (classes and objects). But one could see, he argued, that what is a myth to one person is a real existent to another. Unicorns are myths to us, but undoubtedly there were some ancient Greeks who took them to be as real as horses. Similarly, according to Quine, although most people do not regard tables and chairs as myths, they are myths *to a phenomenalist.*

Quine, of course, is neither a phenomenalist nor a nominalist. In [78] and [81] he is explicit on this point: he favors an ontology of physical objects and classes. I said earlier that a mythological Platonist either takes no stand or a negative stand on the ontological question of whether abstract entities exist. Since Quine takes a positive position on this question, he cannot be a mythological Platonist.

It has also been objected that labeling Quine a Platonist is "contentious."[1] Evidently many philosophers believe that Quine pretty clearly took the position of conceptualism in [82], p. 129.[2] What Quine says there is that, of the three positions, Platonism, conceptualism, and nominalism, conceptualism is the strongest . . . *from a tactical point of view.* I am not certain that Quine had adopted conceptualism at that time. His more recent writings certainly do not exhibit a conceptualist viewpoint (see especially [84]). In any case, even if Quine is a conceptualist in the sense of [82], this does not imply that he is not an ontological Platonist. Indeed, given Quine's view that conceptualistic set theories like the one outlined in [82] are ontologically committed to sets, it at least *seems* to follow from the acceptance of conceptualism that one ought to be an ontological Platonist.

3. Quine's Criterion of Ontological Commitment

Since Quine's criterion of ontological commitment seems to be a crucial element in his argument for Platonism, I shall examine this criterion in detail in this section. When it was the fashion to debunk traditional ontological questions as being pseudoproblems, based upon misconceptions of ordinary language, Quine took the radical position that these questions are "on a par with questions of natural science" ([82], p. 45). To make sense of ontological questions, Quine divided the question "What things or sorts of things exist?" into the two separate questions:

(1) What, according to a given theory, exists? (In Quinian terms: What are the *ontological commitments* of a given theory?)

(2) Which theories have we good reason to accept as true? Concerning the latter question, Quine did not maintain that there are simple tests or criteria for determining truth. However, he did claim that we can give rational grounds for accepting theories—even those that carry ontological commitment to such metaphysical entities as universals. Indeed, he claimed that we can give, in these cases, the same sorts of grounds that are used to support scientific hypotheses.

---

[1] Robert Burton raised this objection at the conference on ontological commitment held in 1970 at the University of Georgia. *Supra.* Preface.

[2] E.g., Fraenkel and Bar-Hillel [29], p. 337.

For, according to Quine, the considerations that guide a person in his choice of scientific theories are, where rational, "pragmatic" ([82], p. 46); and pragmatic considerations may prompt us to accept theories that require quantification over such universals as numbers and classes:

> Numbers and classes are favoured by the power and facility which they contribute to theoretical physics and other systematic discourse about nature. Propositions and attributes are disfavoured by some irregular behavior in connection with identity and substitution. Considerations for and against existence are more broadly systematic, in these philosophical examples, than in the case of rabbits or unicorns or prime numbers between 10 and 20; but I am persuaded that the difference is a matter of degree (Quine [88], pp. 97-8).

Here, Quine attempted to place question (2) within the arena of rational assessment. However, I shall concern myself in this section with various attempts to provide a rational, objective criterion for answering questions of the first sort.

Let me first present a very rough explication of the notion of ontological commitment, before beginning my critical examination of the criterion. Let us start with some examples of commitment. One can commit oneself to doing certain things by saying (in appropriate circumstances of course) "You can count on my help" or "I shall be available." Obviously, one can also commit oneself to accepting as true certain teachings, doctrines, and principles, by accepting a religion. Someone who accepts Catholicism thereby commits himself to accepting as true certain pronouncements made by the Pope. Analogously, Quine holds that saying certain things can commit one to affirming or accepting certain ontological assertions, and that accepting a theory can also commit one to accepting a whole ontology—hardly a surprising thesis. What is surprising in Quine's position, of course, is the claim that accepting present-day scientific theories commits one to universals or abstract entities.

Before getting involved in the details of our investigation, I should like to note that Quine's criterion is devised to apply to "discourse," i.e., to sentences, theories, and the like, in contradistinction to persons (Quine [82], p. 103). A person may or may not share the ontological commitments of his discourse. For example, someone who, in telling a fairy story, says "There exist in this land strange little men with wings," does not thereby commit himself to the existence of men with wings. On the other hand, a philosopher who puts forward a theory in which

$(\exists x)(x$ is a universal$)$

is affirmed, does commit himself to the existence of universals.

Given, then, that the criterion applies only derivatively to men, Quine holds that a person who asserts something that commits him to an unwanted ontology may be able to remove this commitment by restating his position in a more ontologically neutral form. As a very simple (and unreal) example of this, take the case of a person who, in constructing a theory of measurement and space, finds it necessary to assert something to the effect that there is a difference in length between α and β. Expressing his theory in a one-sorted, first-order language, he first asserts

(A) $(\exists x)(x =$ a difference in length between α and $\beta)$.

However, he finds that the acceptance of (A) engenders difficulties. The formation rules of the language require that sentences like

α is longer than β & $(\exists x)(x =$ a difference in length between α and β & $x = \alpha)$

be well-formed. The problem then arises: What are the truth conditions for such sentences? And does the totality of differences in length constitute a well-defined set? To avoid such problems, the person restates his assertion so that it reads

(B) α is longer than β ∨ β is longer than α.

Roughly speaking, by showing how to paraphrase his original assertion "There is a difference in length between α and β" into "α is either longer than or shorter than β," the person has shown how he can avoid being committed to the existence of differences in length.

Quine might be criticized as follows:[3] How can this method of paraphrase eliminate ontological commitments? For if (B) is an

---

[3] Cf., William Alston, [1], pp. 8-17.

adequate translation of (A), then they must say the same thing; in which case, (B) must have the same ontological commitments as (A). On the other hand, if (B) is not an adequate translation of (A), then the fact that (B) is not ontologically committed to differences in length is irrelevant to the question of whether (A) is. In either case, the above person would not have rid himself of any ontological commitments by this method of translation. This dilemma points to the conclusion that Quine is confused in thinking he can eliminate unwanted ontological commitments in this way.

I believe Quine could reply to this objection by making use of the distinction between the ontological commitments of a sentence and the ontological commitments of a person. He could argue that (A) is, whereas (B) is not, ontologically committed to differences in length, and hence (A) and (B) are not synonymous. Clearly, then (B) is not being put forward as eliminating the ontological commitments of (A). But the *person* in the example is able to rid himself of the ontological commitments of (A) by giving it up in favor of (B).[4]

I should now like to examine in more detail the question: of what is Quine's criterion supposed to enable us to determine the ontological commitments. On this question, Quine is not very clear. "Theories," "discourses," "forms of discourse," "doctrines," "remarks," and "sentences," are some of the answers he gives. What Quine means by 'form of discourse' is also not very clear. Since his earliest papers on this topic were concerned with the ontological commitments of languages ([69] and [70]), one might suppose that a form of discourse is some sort of language or language-form (that is, partially interpreted language). Thus, a typical first-order language that has been interpreted by specifying some of the predicates might be considered a "form of discourse." However, as I shall indicate later on, difficulties result from assuming that Quine intended his criterion to apply to "forms of discourse" in this sense. I shall avoid some of these problems by assuming in this essay that the criterion is to be applied to theories and sentences.

There are also some problems connected with Quine's use of the

---

[4] This way of answering the above objection is suggested by various things Quine says in [81], Chapter 7.

term 'theory'.[5] Quine says in *Word and Object* and related writings that a theory is a class of all those sentences "within some limited vocabulary appropriate to the desired subject matter" that a person believes to be true (or that some imaginary person might believe to be true); and he goes on to say that a theory need not be deductively closed ([90], p. 309). However, he writes: "A theory, it will be said, is a set of fully interpreted sentences. (More particularly, it is a deductively closed set . . .)" ([89], p. 51). Since the passages that follow this quotation strongly suggest that Quine accepts this characterization of theories, it would appear that, at least some of the time, a theory for Quine must be deductively closed. For purposes of simplicity and convenience, I shall regard theories as deductively closed. (All my main points would apply, with some small revisions, even if they were not).

On many occasions Quine has applied his criterion to single sentences. Since Quine sometimes suggests that his criterion was devised for determining the ontological commitments of *theories*, one might suppose that, for him, a single sentence is a kind of degenerate theory. Another reasonable hypothesis is that Quine's statements about the ontological commitments of some sentence is intended to be a statement about the commitments of some imagined theory asserting that sentence.

Quine has emphasized on several occasions that his criterion is meant only for those theories in quantificational form. Suppose then that we have some standard *uninterpreted* first-order quantificational language. How are we supposed to get the sort of fully interpreted theory that Quine talks about? The following quotation provides us with the answer:

> In specifying a theory we must indeed fully specify, in our own words, what sentences are to comprise the theory, and what things are to be taken as values of the variables, and what things are to be taken as satisfying the predicate letters ([89], p. 51).

[5] In an earlier paper [16], I noted some of the difficulties of interpretation, connected with Quine's criterion, that arose because Quine was so inexplicit about his use of the term 'theory'. Fortunately, since the publication of that paper, Quine has clarified his use of this term in at least two places.

Hence, to specify a theory in Quine's sense of the term, we need only select, from a first-order language, a set of assertions (not containing individual constants) and supply an interpretation of the relevant portion of the language by specifying what is to be the universe of discourse and which English predicates or "interpretive expressions" are to be assigned to the predicate letters of the theory (to use Quine's terminology in [80]).[6]

In the following, I shall refer to theories, interpreted as Quine requires, as "Quinian theories" or simply as "theories."

Let us now turn to a more detailed examination of Quine's notion of ontological commitment. To adequately evaluate Quine's claim that the acceptance of science commits one to universals, we need to find out not only what 'ontological commitment' means (which is not easy), but also how ontological commitment is related to Quine's criterion of ontological commitment: we need to know just what Quine's criterion is a criterion of. In his reply to Geach, Quine writes: "It is wrong to admit abstract entities and gloss over their admission. It was because I was persuaded of the wrongness of this latter course that I undertook to sharpen the standards whereby we judge whether or not a given discourse does carry commitment to entities of a given sort" ([74], pp. 158-9). He then states his criterion thus: "My standard suffices for doctrines expressed in quantificational language, and it is, I repeat, simply this: the entities presupposed by a doctrine are those which must, in order that the doctrine be true, be in the universe with respect to which the quantifiers are construed" ([74], p. 159). From these passages, we can gather that Quine wished to develop a method for detecting and making clear the "admission of entities into one's ontology;" and evidently, to admit an entity into one's ontology is to *presuppose* the existence of the entity. So Quine devised a criterion for determining what entities a doctrine presupposes. Quine's method for detecting a person's glossing over the admission of entities into his ontology comes to this: first paraphrase his views into quantificational form; then apply the

---

[6] Predicates, in Quine's sense of this term, are considered by him to be interpretive expressions ([80], p. 136). However, in this essay, the logical notation and terminology will be that of Mates unless otherwise indicated (hence, the use of the expression 'English predicate').

criterion to bring out the existential presuppositions of his doctrines.

From the above, it would seem that Quine's criterion is one for determining what entities a doctrine presupposes that there is. However, in [82], p. 102, Quine suggests that his criterion is meant to be used as a standard for bringing out not all the existential presuppositions of a theory, but only the *explicit* ones, and he indicates that the class of explicit presuppositions of a theory should be distinguished from the class of presuppositions of a theory. Our difficulties in seeing clearly what Quine is trying to do are compounded by a third version of what his criterion is supposed to be. Quine first states his criterion as follows: "The ontology to which an (interpreted) theory is committed comprises all and only the objects over which the bound variables of the theory have to be construed as ranging in order that the statements affirmed in the theory be true" ([73], p. 11). Later he says: "The ontology of a theory is a question of what the assertions say or imply that there is" (p. 14). It would be reasonable to infer from these passages that Quine devised his criterion to determine clearly what a sentence or theory says or implies that there is; and this inference is further supported by the fact that Quine says in another place that the "question of the ontological commitments of a theory, then, is the question what, according to that theory, there is" ([76], p. 127). Finally, Quine sometimes sugests that this criterion is meant to enable us to see what a theory simply "says there is."[7]

We have thus been given four answers to our question "What is the criterion of ontological commitment a criterion of?" It is a criterion for determining what a theory (a) *presupposes* that there is; (b) *explicitly* presupposes that there is; (c) *implies* that there is; (d) *says* that there is.

Now do these all come to the same thing? I should think not. For surely we would all want to distinguish what a theory says that there is from what a theory presupposes that there is: indeed, ordinarily what is said to exist differs from what is presupposed to exist. One may find comparison of (b) with (a) difficult, because one may

---

[7] Cf., Quine [82], pp. 15 and 103; also Quine [81], p. 243 fn.

find the notion of explicit presupposition a little puzzling; but I believe one can think up some cases of explicit presupposition. Thus, in the introductory sections of the statement of a theory, it might be said that the existence of natural numbers will be presupposed, and in this case, it would be natural enough to say that the existence of natural numbers is an explicit presupposition of the theory. On the other hand, it would not be natural to say that this theory *says* there are natural numbers. Furthermore, in so far as I have any intuitive grasp of the notion of explicit presupposition, it strikes me as implausible that for any theory T, what T explicitly presupposes exists should coincide with what T (implicitly) presupposes, says, or implies exists.

In view of the fact that (a), (b), (c), and (d) seem to be quite different, it may legitimately be wondered how any one criterion could be an adequate criterion for determining all four. My own sense of wonder is increased when I read:

> But it is to the familiar quantificational form of discourse that our criterion of ontological commitment primarily and fundamentally applies. To insist on the correctness of the criterion in this application is, indeed, merely to say that no distinction is being drawn between the 'there are' of 'there are universals', 'there are unicorns', 'there are hippopotami', and the 'there are' of '$(\exists x)$', 'there are entities x such that'. To contest the criterion, as applied to the familiar quantificational form of discourse, is simply to say either that the familiar quantificational notation is being re-used in some new sense (in which case we need not concern ourselves) or else that the familiar 'there are' of 'there are universals' *et al.* is being re-used in some new sense (in which case again we need not concern ourselves) (Quine [82], p. 105).

Quine must have been confused when he made this claim. In this section, I shall argue against the adequacy of Quine's criterion, and none of my arguments will involve questioning the thesis that the existential quantifier has the sense of the English phrase 'there are'.

Actually, stating an adequate criterion of ontological commitment is not as simple as Quine supposed. Consider, for example, the two statements of the criterion quoted above. They both have a curious consequence: one can conclude that

$$(\exists x)(x \text{ is a table})$$

is *not* ontologically committed to any table, for if we ask of any particular table *t* whether *t* would have to fall within the range of the bound variable of the above sentence in order that the sentence be true, the answer is clearly "No."[8] Obviously, the criterion needs restatement. But I shall discuss Quine's more recent statements of his criterion in detail later on.

Quine may not have been entirely satisfied with his own groping attempts to explicate the point of his criterion, for in a recent paper he says:

> To show that a theory assumes a given object, or objects of a given class, we have to show that the theory would be false if that object did not exist, or if that class were empty; hence, that the theory requires that object, or members of that class, in order to be true. How are such requirements revealed? ([88], p. 93).

Later on in the paper, Quine answers his question: the objects that a theory "requires" are "those objects that have to be values of variables for the theory to be true" (p. 96). Thus, Quine states his well-known criterion of ontological commitment.[9] Notice that in the above quotation, Quine talks about what a theory *requires*. It would now seem that what he is trying to develop is a criterion for determining what objects, or sorts of objects, a theory *requires* in order that it be true. Now why should we need a criterion for this purpose? Each Quinian theory is supplied with an interpretation that tells us what the universe of discourse of the theory is. Then, if the interpretation tells us that the variables range over, say natural numbers, can we not say that the theory requires natural numbers in order that its assertions be true, and hence is ontologically committed to natural numbers? A misunderstanding regarding Quine's use of the term 'ontological commitment' needs to be cleared up:

> The trouble comes of . . . identifying the ontology of a theory with the class of all things to which the theory is ontically committed. . . . The ontology is the range of the variables.

[8] This is pointed out by Scheffler and Chomsky, [19], p. 74.

[9] The expression 'ontological commitment' is to be found in Quine's early papers on this topic. In [81], Quine began to use the term 'ontic commitment'. In this essay, I shall stick to the former term.

Each of the various reinterpretations of the range (while keeping the interpretations of predicates fixed) might be compatible with the theory. But the theory is ontically *committed* to an object only if that object is common to all those ranges. And the theory is ontically committed to 'objects of such and such kind', say dogs, just in case each of those ranges contains some dog or other (Quine [90], p. 315).[10]

It appears, from this quotation, that in determining the ontological commitments of a theory, we need not give any special weight to the particular universe of discourse specified by the interpretation —which explains why Quine applied his criterion to such sentences as '$(\exists x)(x$ is a dog)' without specifying any domain for the variable. From the point of view of a theory's ontological commitments, it makes no difference whether or not the theory comes with a specified universe of discourse.[11]

The quotation above was not meant to give us a criterion of ontological commitment; rather it was intended to explain the difference between the ontology and the ontological commitments of a theory. Still, the quotation warrants further examination. Suppose that we have a theory that asserts '$(\exists x)(x$ is a unicorn)', and suppose that the universe of discourse of this theory is specified to be the class of living animals. The ontology of this theory, it would seem, is the class of living animals. But does this ontology contain unicorns? Certainly, the class of living animals does not contain any unicorns. On the other hand, reasoning from the many examples Quine has given us, it is evident that such a theory is ontologically committed to unicorns. So are we to say that this theory is ontologically committed to a kind of entity even though there is nothing of this kind that belongs to the ontology of the theory? Another difficulty is that it would seem that all the possible ranges that can be assigned to the variables of the theory, that keep the interpretation of the predicates fixed, and that are compatible with the theory, must contain unicorns; and this suggests that the original range

[10] Notice that what Quine says the ontology of a theory is does not jibe with what he said earlier in [73], p. 14. If his readers have misunderstood him in this connection, he is largely to blame.

[11] Cf. my conjecture in [16], p. 65, as to what Quine means by 'theory'. That article was written before the above clarifying remarks of Quine's appeared.

assigned, namely, the class of living animals, must also contain unicorns. Take another example. Suppose a theory is interpreted to have as its domain the class of unicorns. The class of unicorns is the null set. So is the ontology of this theory the class of unicorns? Or does the theory have no ontology? Despite the many attempts Quine has made to clarify his ideas on ontology and ontological commitment, I for one would welcome further clarifications.

Perhaps we should return to Quine's statement of his criterion for more illumination. Recall that the criterion is supposed to enable us to determine what objects a theory requires in order that it be true. The question arose: Why do we need a criterion for this purpose? Why not say that the objects the theory requires are just those objects that (according to the theory) would have to exist in order that it be true? I suppose it would be said in reply that there are two expressions that are vague in the above suggestion: (1) 'would have to' and (2) 'exist'. *We still need a criterion to tell us what would have to exist (according to the theory) in order that the theory be true.* Now what is Quine's proposed criterion? The sorts of objects that would have to exist in order that the theory be true are just those that would have to be within the range of the bound variables of the theory in order that its assertions be true. But what progress have we made? We still have the vague notion "would have to" and instead of the term 'exist' we have the expression 'be within the range of the bound variables'. At first glance, it is hard to see why Quine should claim that he has given us a *criterion*. The difference between the *explicans* and the *explicandum* is so slight that one may wonder at the use of the term 'criterion' to mark the difference. Thus, one might say to Quine: If we need a criterion to determine what would have to exist in order that a theory be true, surely we also need a criterion to determine what would have to be values of the variables in order that the theory be true.

By way of contrast, let us examine a statement of a criterion of ontological commitment that more clearly deserves the title 'criterion'. In [17], p. 1014, Church states his own criterion as follows:

The assertion of $(\exists x)(M)$ carries ontological commitment to entities x such that M, where the letter 'x' may be replaced by any variable, the italicized letter '*x*' may be replaced by any name of the same variable, the letter 'M' may be replaced by any open sentence containing only the above variable, and the italicized letter '*M*' may be replaced by any name of this open sentence. (Of course, the usual notational conventions apply so that, for example, '$(\exists x)($'x is a horse'$)$' denotes '$(\exists x)(x$ is a horse$)$': for more on this see Mates [54], Chapter 2).

Here, we are given a clear and definite test for ontological commitment. We can determine definitely that the assertion '$(\exists x)(x$ is a horse$)$' carries ontological commitment to entities x such that x is a horse. By this criterion, we also know that '$(\exists x)(x$ is a ghost$)$' is ontologically committed to ghosts and not to unicorns. In general we need only look at the existential assertions of a first-order Quinian theory in order to determine its ontological commitments.

I should mention here that Chomsky and Scheffler state a criterion that is very similar to the above. In [19], p. 79, they present the following criterion:

A theory T makes a _____-assumption if and only if it yields a statement of the form '$(\exists x)(x$ is (a) _____$)$'.

However, I shall not concern myself with this version here since it is so similar to Church's criterion.[12]

To obtain some idea of how Quine applies his criterion, consider a second-order theory in which it is valid to infer

$$(\exists F)(\exists G)(\exists x)(Fx \ \& \ Gx)$$

from

$$(\exists x)(x \text{ is a dog} \ \& \ x \text{ is white}).$$

[12] At least, the Chomsky-Scheffler criterion is similar to Church's if one applies Church's criterion to theories as follows: A theory T carries ontological commitment to entities x such that M if, and only if, there is an assertion of T which carries ontological commitment to entities x such that M. On p. 1014, f.n. 4, Church says that a language carries the ontological commitments of every sentence that is analytic in the language. If a theory carries, in addition to the ontological commitments of its assertions, also the commitments of its language, we obviously get a "stronger" criterion than the one I have in mind. Church's criterion would then be similar to Cartwright's (see Cartwright [12]). Clearly it would not be acceptable to Quine.

According to Quine, the assertion of the latter sentence in a first-order theory does not involve commitment to such abstract entities as dogkind or whiteness, whereas the second-order theory does ontologically commit itself to these abstract entities by asserting the latter sentences. (See [82], p. 113 and pp. 120-2). The essential idea behind this application of the criterion is to be found in Quine's earliest articles on ontological commitment. For example, he asserts that "what entities there are, from the point of view of a given language, depends on what positions are accessible to variables in that language" ([70], p. 68). Quine applies this early version of his criterion to draw a distinction between nominalistic and realistic languages: "Words of the abstract or general sort, say 'appendicitis' or 'horse', can turn up in nominalistic as well as realistic languages; but the difference is that in realistic languages such words are substituents for variables . . . whereas in nominalistic languages this is not the case" ([69], p. 50). In these early articles, Quine concentrated primarily on the ontological commitments of *languages*, in contradistinction to theories, as can be seen from the above quotes. In expanding his criterion to cover theories, he had to go beyond mere accessibility to variables and take account of the *assertions* of theories. But he did not completely abandon his early views, as can be seen from the above example. Essentially, it was by applying his later criterion along the lines laid down by his earliest articles on the topic that he was led to charge the formal theory of *Principia Mathematica* with an ontological commitment to abstract entities. But who would have guessed from the formula 'what would have to be values of the variables' that we could apply the criterion in this way?

Now Quine has made two rather large claims for his criterion. The first is that ontological commitment belongs to "the theory of reference" rather than "the theory of meaning" ([82], pp. 130-1). The precise nature of this claim is not clear since the distinction between theory of reference and theory of meaning is only roughly made by Quine in terms of some examples: the notions of synonymy, significance, analyticity and entailment, he tells us, belong to the theory of meaning, whereas truth, denotation, extension, and naming belong to the theory of reference. In this paper, Quine goes on to say that if a concept were to be defined by using concepts from both areas, "we should probably reckon the hybrid concept to the theory of meaning—simply because the theory of meaning is in a worse state than the theory of reference" ([82], p. 130). One might conclude from this last statement that ontological commitment, as Quine "defines" it with his statement of his criterion, does not fall within the theory of reference, on the grounds that the phrase 'would have to', which appears in the statement, involves concepts taken from the theory of meaning. It should be noted that when Quine made the above claims, he did state a kind of criterion of ontological commitment that could be reasonably assigned to the theory of reference: "To say that a given existential quantification presupposes objects of a given kind is to say simply that the open sentence which follows the quantifier is true of some objects of that kind and none not of that kind" ([82], p. 131). However, it is easy to see that this criterion yields some very counterintuitive results. For example, a theory might assert '$(\exists x)(x$ is a ghost)' and still not be committed to ghosts.[13] It is not surprising that Quine has dropped this version of the criterion.

The claim that ontological commitment belongs to the theory of reference has been thoroughly criticized by Cartwright in [12]. Since Quine has never replied to the criticism and since he has not repeated his claim, one might infer that Quine has abandoned this early position. But to admit that ontological commitment belongs to that discredited area, the theory of meaning, is tantamount to admitting that ontological commitment is, itself, a muddled and unclear notion, in the same boat as the discredited notions of analyticity and meaning—something that Quine could hardly accept with an easy conscience.

The second large claim that Quine has made for his criterion is that ontological commitment "becomes objective and free of the old-time question-begging, once the theory is rendered in quantificational form" ([79], p. 3). To one contemplating Quine's vague statement of his criterion, it is by no means obvious that ontological commitment has become objective and free from question-begging.

---

[13] Essentially, this point was made by Cartwright in [12], p. 323.

Surprisingly, there is less doubt that Church's criterion satisfies the above two claims that Quine has made for his own criterion. Church's criterion does seem to fall within the theory of reference, since it makes no use of terms like 'necessity', 'meaning', and 'analyticity'. And the criterion is objective. I am not sure I would call it non-question-begging, but that may be because I am not sure I understand Quine's claim in this regard. Seeing how much better Church's criterion satisfies Quine's claims, it is reasonable to wonder why Quine, himself, did not adopt Church's version of the criterion. I suspect that the reason is: Church's criterion is, in certain respects, counterintuitive, being too stingy in handing out ontological commitments. For example, one cannot conclude that the assertion '$(\exists x)(x$ is a bachelor)' is committed to male human beings. And, strictly interpreted, Church's criterion does not allow us to say that '$(\exists x)(x$ is a set)' carries ontological commitment to an entity x such that x is an abstract entity. I should think that, to Quine, these consequences of adopting Church's criterion would be more than counterintuitive: they would make ontological commitment seem utterly trivial. Thus, we could claim that the usual Platonic set theories are not ontologically committed to abstract entities, on the grounds that the predicate 'abstract entity' does not occur in the vocabulary of the theory.

Unlike Church's criterion, Quine's allows us to go "outside" the target theory in determining ontological commitments. Quine tells us:

> There is certainly commitment to entities through discourse; for we are quite capable of saying in so many words that *there are* black swans, that *there is* a mountain more than 8800 meters high, and that *there are* prime numbers above a hundred. Saying these things, we also say by implication that there are physical objects and abstract entities; for all the black swans are physical objects and all the prime numbers above a hundred are abstract entities ([76], p. 128).

By Quine's criterion, the standard mathematical theories are ontologically committed to abstract entities even though they do not explicitly say there are such things. Quine tells us in various places that the standard set theories are committed to universals. Why?

Certainly, Quine did not think that by looking through a list of the theses of the theories, we should eventually find '$(\exists x)(x$ is a universal)'. However, Quine thinks we can assert

$$(x)((\exists y)(\exists z)(y \in x \ \& \ x \in z) \rightarrow x \text{ is a set})$$

and

$$(x)(x \text{ is a set} \rightarrow x \text{ is a universal}).$$

Evidently, we are allowed to use these universal affirmative sentences in determining ontological commitments.

The problem we now face is this: Which, or what kinds of, statements are we allowed to use in determining ontological commitments? The sentences that Quine uses in "going outside the theory" are all universal affirmative sentences. Are we restricted to such sentences? But before examining this "syntactical" aspect of the question, I should like to explore the problem from the "semantical" point of view. Can we use any *true* universal affirmative sentence? Quine's vague statements of his criterion do not help us much to answer this question. Let us explore this possibility by tracing some of the consequences of allowing all true universal affirmative sentences to be used. As I pointed out elsewhere, one unintuitive consequence of this interpretation is this: A theory affirming

$$(\exists x)(x \text{ is a chair} \ \& \ x \text{ was manufactured in 1966 by Lane Furniture Co.})$$

would be ontologically committed to walnut chairs if all chairs manufactured by the company in 1966 were, as a matter of fact, made of walnut ([16], pp. 33-4). Another unintuitive consequence is connected with the fact that '$(x)(x$ is a ghost $\rightarrow x$ is a unicorn)' is a true sentence. A theory affirming '$(\exists x)(x$ is a ghost)' would thus be ontologically committed to unicorns. Other problems result from interpreting the criterion in the above manner. Quine holds that set theory is ontologically committed to universals; and I am sure he would deny that it is committed to unicorns. To obtain these results, we must hold that '$(x)(x$ is a set $\rightarrow x$ is a unicorn)' is false. Since the last is true if '$-(\exists x)(x$ is a set)' is true, we must hold that nominalism is false. In this case, we seem to be begging the question in favor of Platonism. I think it is clear that Quine would not accept these consequences: some other line must be drawn between allowable and unallowable sentences.

Intuitively speaking, we wish to use only those universal affirmative sentences that are *necessarily true* or analytic: this is suggested by Quine's words "would have to be values of the variables" and also by the fact that the examples Quine gives us all seem to be sentences that would be classified by many philosophers as analytic or necessary truths. However, since Quine rejects the distinctions between analytic and synthetic statements and between necessary and contingent truths, this road does not appear to be open to him.

At this point, it is enlightening to compare Chateaubriand's criterion of ontological commitment with Quine's.[14] Chateaubriand suggests that we bypass the problem of distinguishing the class of necessary truths from the class of contingent truths by making use of the notion of theorems of a theory. For example, instead of talking about the necessary truths of arithmetic, we can talk about the theorems of arithmetic. By this maneuver, Chateaubriand has come up with an *ersatz* Quinian criterion of ontological commitment. He reasons that since such terms as 'implication' and 'validity' had been defined for formal languages in terms of, or relative to, a metatheory (which includes some set theory), he might be able to do something analogous for "ontological commitment." Why not define a criterion of ontological commitment relative to a theory?[15] At this point, I shall deviate somewhat from Chateaubriand's procedure and restrict my discussion of the criterion to first-order Quinian theories, the interpretations of which are given in English, supplemented by various notational devices. This restriction will enable me to formulate the criterion along the lines taken by Church

[14] Chateaubriand's criterion is set forth in detail in [13].

[15] Chateaubriand has observed that his criterion was anticipated, to some extent, by Beverly Robbins in [96]. In discussing Cartwright's revision of Quine's criterion, Robbins suggested that we formulate the criterion by making use of the idea of *being a theorem* instead of Cartwright's *following from semantical rules*. She added: "This purely syntactic version would make the assessment of the ontological commitments of a theory dependent on the capacities of proof in the semantic meta-theory" ([96], p. 536).

and to avoid some of the complications in Chateaubriand's formulation.[16] Then we can state Chateaubriand's criterion by means of a schema in which the letters 'S' and 'T' are to be replaced by names of theories, the letter 'x' is to be replaced by any variable, the italicized letter '*x*' is to be replaced by any name of the same variable, the letter 'F' is to be replaced by any open sentence containing only the above variable as a free variable, and the italicized letter '*F*' is to be replaced by any name of this open sentence. We shall say that S carries ontological commitment to an entity x such that F (relative to theory *T*) if and only if for some open sentence M, replacing the occurrences of the italicized letter '*M*' in (i) and (ii) below with occurrences of a name of M results in true sentences:

(i) $(\exists x)(M)$ is an assertion of S.
(ii) $(x)(M \to F)$ is an assertion of T.

Returning to the problem I raised earlier regarding Quine's criterion, Chateaubriand's suggestion comes to this: Those universal affirmative sentences we are allowed to use are simply those that are assertions of the relevant theory. Thus, a standard set theory will carry ontological commitment to universals—relative to a theory whose set of assertions contains

$$(x)((\exists y)(\exists z)(y \in x \ \& \ x \in z) \to x \text{ is a universal}).$$

The above suggestion of Chateaubriand's was first sketched in my paper [16]. Shortly after the publication of this paper, Quine delivered the John Dewey Lectures at Columbia university, in which he presented his new doctrine of *ontological relativity*: roughly, the doctrine that we can meaningfully ask about the reference of terms in some language only relative to some "background language," and we can ask about the ontology of a theory only relative to some "background theory with its own primitively adopted and ultimately inscrutable ontology" ([89], p. 51). He argued that it

---

[16] Obviously, about those theories to which this version of the criterion does not apply, the criterion says nothing. In particular, it does *not* say that higher order theories are not ontologically committed to universals, sets, concepts, and the like (relative to some other theory). Since I deviate from Chateaubriand's formulation, the defects of my formulation should not be attributed to him.

makes no sense to say what the objects of a theory are "absolutely speaking"; we can only ask "how one theory of objects is interpretable or reinterpretable in another" (p. 201). And he claimed that if, in specifying a Quinian theory, we say what the domain is and what the predicates are, we interpret the theory relative to our words and hence relative to our home language and the "over-all home theory" which lies behind this language (p. 202). Despite the fact that this doctrine suggests a similar thesis of the relativity of ontological commitment, Quine did not discuss his criterion. I should think it would be natural to try to develop some sort of Chateaubriand-type criterion of ontological commitment relative to this "over-all home theory" Quine talks about in his lectures. It is possible that Quine is moving in this direction. Recall that the universal affirmative sentences Quine used in determining ontological commitments were all sentences that would be classified as analytic by many philosophers. Quine rejects the analytic-synthetic distinction, but he does accept an "approximation": he says that a community-wide belief (or sentence accepted as true by the whole linguistic community) is his nearest approximation to an analytic sentence ([90], p. 310). The idea of community-wide beliefs, although vague, seems to provide us with a likely candidate for the class of assertions of the "over-all home theory" relative to which we can ask about the ontologies of theories we specify. But I only conjecture here, since Quine has not specifically said at any time, so far as I know, that he is dissatisfied with his own statements of his criterion.

Let us return to the "syntactical" question we raised earlier: Are we allowed to use only universal affirmative sentences in determining ontological commitments by Quine's criterion? Or can we use other forms of sentences? This question can be clarified in terms of Chateaubriand's criterion. According to this criterion, we may use only assertions of T of the form '$(x)(M \to F)$' in determining the ontological commitments of S relative to T. But does it not seem somewhat arbitrary to restrict the criterion in this way? Suppose, for example, that a sentence of the form '$(\exists x)(M) \to (\exists x)(F)$' occurs among the assertions of T. If S asserts '$(\exists x)(M)$', then it would be natural to say that S is ontologically committed to an entity x such that F relative to T. If we follow our intuitions on this point, we will get another version of Chateaubriand's criterion of ontological commitment relative to a theory.[17] In what follows, 'Chateaubriand's criterion' will refer to this second version unless otherwise indicated. But what of Quine's criterion? It is difficult to tell from Quine's statements of his criterion whether we are allowed to use sentences of the form '$(\exists x)(M) \rightarrow (\exists x)(F)$'. I have argued that one could reasonably interpret Quine in either way: on one reasonable interpretation, a theory asserting

(a) $(\exists x)(x$ is a winged horse)

would be ontologically committed to wings, whereas on the other interpretation, the theory need not be ([16]). Evidently, some philosophers have misunderstood my criticisms, for it has been objected that the unclarity I claimed to find in Quine's statements are due merely to the uncertainties that exist as to how we should paraphrase English predicates like 'is a winged horse'. But I am not asking if (a) can be paraphrased into

(b) $(\exists x)(x$ is a horse $\& (\exists y)(y$ is a wing $\& x$ has $y))$.

My question is about how to apply Quine's criterion, and it will not be answered by the statement that (a) can be paraphrased into (b). Fortunately, since the publication of my earlier paper, Quine has clarified his position. The problem is: How are we to understand the words 'such and such objects have to be values of the variables in order for the theory to be true'? Quine tells us that, for theories that include a complementary predicate for each predicate, the above words say the same thing as: "the predicates of the theory have to be true of such and such objects in order for the theory to be true" ([78], p. 95).

---

[17] Even though the above version is close to a criterion developed by Chateaubriand, it would be unfair to attribute its defects to him, for there are some significant differences. Actually, even the second criterion described above is artificially restrictive. Why restrict oneself to the single assertions of a theory in determining its ontological commitment   Why not take account of sets of assertions of T in determining the ontological commitments of T relative to T' ? By following this idea, Chateaubriand developed stronger criteria. However, it would take me to far afield to discuss such criteria. I discuss the second criterion here, since it is close to Quine's and since it facilitates clarifying some of my objections to Quine's views on ontological commitment.

To see how Quine's recent statement decides my "winged horse" question, notice that 'x is a winged horse' cannot be true of wings. If we allow that (a) can be true, it follows that 'x is a winged horse' need not be true of wings in order that (a) be true. It follows that (a) is not ontologically committed to wings. From this, we see that Quine has chosen a criterion that is closer to Chateaubriand's first criterion than to the second. It leads to some counterintuitive results; to see them more clearly, let us suppose that we construct a theory that asserts

(c) $(\exists x)(x$ is a full set of golf clubs).

And suppose that we explicate (in the meta-theory) the predicate 'is a full set of golf clubs' by asserting that a full set of golf clubs must contain nine irons and four woods. We can see that (c) is true only if there are golf clubs (indeed, irons and woods). But since the predicate 'is a full set of golf clubs' cannot be true of golf clubs, by Quine's criterion, (c) cannot be ontologically commited to them. What all this suggests is that Quine's criterion gives us, at best, sufficient conditions of ontological commitment rather than necessary and sufficient conditions as he claims.

John Searle has recently raised an objection to Quine's criterion that bears on this last point. Searle claims to show that "there is no subtance to" Quine's criterion ([111], p. 107). And he purports to construct a "*reductio ad absurdom* of the criterion" (p. 110). The argument proceeds as follows: Let 'K' be an abbreviation for a conjunction of statements which state all existing scientific knowledge. (We can take K to be the conjunction of all statements in some encyclopedia). We define the predicate 'P' as follows:

Px if and only if $x =$ this pen & K.

Proof: 1. This pen = this pen   (axiom)
       2. K (axiom)
       3. $\therefore$ This pen = this pen & K
       4. $\therefore$ P (this pen)
       5. $\therefore$ $(\exists x)Px$

Searle then writes:

> Thus, in the spirit of Q's ontological reduction we demonstrate that, in terms of Q's criterion of ontological commitment, the only commitment needed to assert the whole of established scientific truth is a commitment to the existence of this pen. But this is a *reductio ad absurdum* of the criterion (p. 110).

What are we to make of this argument? I must confess I still find it difficult to see the point of the above "proof" of '$(\exists x)Px$' from the axioms. At first, I thought Searle was arguing that one can deduce 5. from 1. and 2., that 5. is only ontologically committed to this pen, and that therefore 2. is only ontologically committed to this pen. But this reasoning is too absurd to be taken seriously. I have since learned from Searle that the proof was meant to show how '$(\exists x)Px$' is "based upon" the conjunction K. Although I am not sure I understand Searle on this point, it is clear to me now that the deduction is not essential to his argument. The main point of his *reductio* comes to this: Consider a theory, U, whose set of axioms contains only '$(\exists x)Px$'. By Quine's criterion, U is ontologically committed to this pen, but not to cats, dogs, people, etc., whose existence is clearly asserted, assumed, presupposed, or implied by the theory. Thus, we get a *reductio*.

There are many points that should be discussed in a full treatment of Searle's argument, but I wish here to make only one of them: The force of Searle's argument is greatly reduced if Quine admits (as I believe he should) that his criterion provides only sufficient conditions of ontological commitment and not necessary and sufficient conditions as it is supposed (and claimed).

When Searle's argument is turned against Chateaubriand's criterion, the situation is not so clear. If we get counterintuitive results from this criterion, it may be due to our choice of theories rather than to the criterion itself. This can be seen by making use of some ideas in Quine's John Dewey Lectures. To construct a Quinian theory, we must specify the predicates of the theory, that is, we must either say (in a meta-language) what the predicates are or assign predicates (interpretive expressions) from the meta-language to the predicate letters of the formal language of the theory. So a Quinian theory presupposes, as it were, what Quine calls a "background language" and a "background theory." It would be natural then to seek the ontological commitments of a Quinian theory relative to its background theory. For example, if we construct a theory V, that asserts

$(\exists x)(x$ is a bottle of acid)

the predicates 'is an acid', 'is acidic', 'is a proton donor', and 'yields hydrogen ions in water solution' need not even occur in the vocabulary of the theory; yet they are predicates of the background languages (in this case: English) and the background or "home" theory. And it is reasonable to suppose that chemistry would be part of this background theory. Hence, we might be able to say something definite about the ontological commitments of V relative to any reasonable first-order formulation of the background theory (making use of Chateaubriand's criterion). Or take the case of a theory that asserts '$(\exists x)(x$ is an infinite set of prime numbers)', but that has a vocabulary not containing the predicate 'is an odd number'. The background theory can be expected to include the usual theorems and laws of number theory. So we could argue, using Chateaubriand's criterion, that this theory is committed to odd numbers relative to any reasonable formulation of the background theory. Turning to Searle's theory, we can say that any reasonable formulation of its background theory will assert such things as

$(\exists x)Px \rightarrow (\exists x)(x$ is a cat)

so that we can expect this strange theory to be ontologically committed to cats, dogs, people, and so forth, after all—but relative to a reasonable formulation of its background theory. Of course, the notion of a background theory is, at this time, much too vague to allow us to be entirely satisfied with the above discussion, but it can be seen, at least in rough outline, how one might reply to the sort of objection Searle raised against Quine.

The above discussion makes it evident that Chateaubriand's criterion does not carry us very far toward getting the sort of "absolute" (nonrelative) criterion that Quine originally had in mind. Some may be inclined to claim that Chateaubriand's criterion is trivial and that the problems of ascertaining intuitively plausible ontological commitments have simply been shunted off to the task of formulating appropriate "background theories." Trivial or not, what I have called 'Chateaubriand's criterion' has difficulties of its own.

One difficulty with the criterion (and with other Church-type criteria) is that one ends up with some strange statements of ontological commitment. For example, it is easy to see that the criterion could tell us that:

(d) relative to W', W carries ontological commitment to an entity x such that $x = x$ and $(\exists y)(y$ is a golf club).

But what does (d) mean? It is not clear. One might understand it to mean that W is ontologically committed to something identical to itself and that there are golf clubs. Or one might read (d) as saying that W is ontologically committed to golf clubs. If we adopt the second reading, we shall run into another difficulty suggested to me by George Myro. Suppose that W asserts

$(\exists x)(x$ is a full set of golf clubs)

and that W' asserts

(e) $(\exists x)(x$ is a full set of golf clubs) $\rightarrow (\exists x)(x$ is a golf club)

but not

$(x)(x$ is a full set of golf clubs $\rightarrow x$ is a golf club).

Then we are inclined to think that, relative to W', W is ontologically committed to golf clubs according to the second criterion, but not so committed according to the first. However, (e) is equivalent to

$(x)(x$ is a full set of golf clubs $\rightarrow x = x$ & $(\exists y)(y$ is a golf club)).

So if we do adopt a policy of giving sentences like (d) the second type of reading, we shall have to say that the first and second Chateaubriand criteria come to essentially the same thing. We can eliminate some of these problems with strange commitments by tightening up the criteria so that the open sentence F must be quantifier-free.

But this way of dealing with the problem produces other counter-intuitive results.

A possible way of avoiding this problem is to view the unclear statements of ontological commitment that are generated by the criterion as "waste products" to be disregarded in toting up the commitments of some specific theory. Needless to say, this idea would have to be developed and made precise before it would be acceptable.

Another difficulty with this criterion was suggested to me by George Myro. Let us suppose that a theory T' asserts '$(\exists x)(x$ is a two-headed whale)'. Then, by Chateaubriand's criterion, if the vocabulary of T contains some predicate in the vocabulary of T', T would be ontologically committed to two-headed whales relative to T', regardless of what T asserts! To avoid such an unintuitive result, Chateaubriand once suggested that we formulate the criterion roughly as follows: T is ontologically committed to F's relative to T' if and only if either:

   a) T asserts $(\exists x)Fx$

or

   b) T asserts $(\exists x)Gx$, and T' asserts $(\exists x)Gx \rightarrow (\exists x)Fx$

but not

   $(\exists x)Fx$.

Such a criterion would certainly block the above sort of objection, but it generates some counterintuitive results of its own. For example, suppose T asserts

   $(\exists x)(x =$ the set of natural numbers$)$

but not

   $(\exists x)(x = 0)$.

Suppose also that T' is a theory comprising Peano arithmetic. Then it would be natural to expect T to be ontologically committed to the natural number 0 relative to T'. Unfortunately, it would not be so committed by the above criterion since T' asserts '$(\exists x)(x = 0)$'.

Perhaps these difficulties can be obviated without serious alterations of Chateaubriand's criterion; but I shall not pursue the matter here. It is apparent in any case that devising an adequate criterion of ontological commitment is no simple task.

4. *Extensionalism and the Problem of Abstract Entities in Mathematics*

I should now like to examine the claim that the nominalist will have to "accommodate his natural science unaided by mathematics." Why does Quine hold that a nominalist cannot use mathematics in his natural science? Evidently because he believes that the nominalist cannot assert the theorems of ordinary mathematics while remaining consistent with his nominalistic principles. He argues that "bound variables for classes or relations or numbers, if they occur in existential quantifiers or in universal quantifiers within subordinate clauses, must be renounced by the nominalist in all contexts in which he cannot explain them away by paraphrase" ([14], p. 128). To put the matter in slightly different terms, Quine holds that we would not find the usual mathematical theorems among the assertions of a consistent nominalist's scientific theories, because mathematics (except for some trivial parts of elementary arithmetic) is irredeemably committed to abstract entities. The basic problem for the nominalist, according to Quine, is "how to say what one wants to say of physical objects without invoking abstract objects as auxiliaries" ([81], p. 268).

When Quine talks about *how to say* certain things, as in the above quotation, he sometimes has in mind certain restrictions on the language to be used in saying the things. It seems likely that the problem he is posing to the nominalist is not just that of saying what is needed in science without presupposing that there are abstract entities, but of saying these things in a language having the austere grammatical structure that is Quine's "basic scheme for systems of the world"—an extensional language, that is, with Quine's "canonical grammar" of predication, quantification, and truth functions ([81], p. 228). There are two reasons for suspecting that Quine is placing such a strong restriction on what is an acceptable language of science. First of all, when Quine says that mathematics is committed to abstract entities, this suggests that he is using his criterion of ontological commitment; and, as we saw in the previous section, the applicability of the criterion requires that the target theory be given in a quantificational language with the standard interpretation of the quantifiers. Secondly, Quine poses the nominalist's problem within the context of a general discussion of the normative and methodological considerations relevant to determining what should be reckoned to be in the domain of scientific theories expressed in Quine's canonical notation ([81], p. 232). It is only after Quine has delimited the grammatical structure of science, that is, has settled the question of "what counts as a scientifically admissible construction," that he turns to the question of what should be in the ontology of science. I think it is reasonable to suppose that, for Quine, any acceptable scientific theory must be either in his canonical notation or at least paraphrasable into canonical notation.

Now why should the nominalist accept this view of science? Quine does support his position. He argues that we ought to state all our scientific theories in a language with such a structure because of the clarification and simplification of our "conceptual scheme" we thereby achieve ([81], § 33). Canonical notation eliminates many types of ambiguities found in sentences of ordinary languages. For example, the use of variables and parentheses enables us to eliminate ambiguities of cross-reference and grouping. Another theoretical gain from adopting Quine's canonical grammar is this: the set of sentences of the language will be specified by a small number of precise recursive rules, and as a result we can make use of proofs by induction on this set. More generally, we can apply the logical theory thoroughly developed by logicians. We thus have a probably sound and complete proof-procedure for the language.

To apply the standard first-order logical theory, however, the predicates of the language must be "well defined," so that, for example, if Fx is a monadic predicate and a is an object in the domain of the language, then Fx must either be true of a or false of a.[18] It may be recalled that Frege made a similar requirement of scientific

---

[18] It is clear Quine requires well-defined predicates of his canonical notation. See Quine [81], pp. 231-2.

languages. He argued that scientific rigor demands that all the concepts of a scientific language be sharply delimited: "If this were not satisfied it would be impossible to set forth logical laws about them" ([81], p. 33).

Of course, the above argument in support of restricting science to a Quinian extensional language would be unconvincing unless it were also shown that our present scientific theories can be reconstructed in such a language without serious loss. Quine does attempt to show in outline how this can be done ([13]). However, Quine does not do for the empirical sciences what Russell and Whitehead did for mathematics: in Quine's work, there is nothing comparable to the convincing detail that one finds in *PM*. He does not even give any examples of predicates that could clearly be used in his projected unified science. Predicates are troublesome for Quine because of the requirement of sharp delimitation. For example, natural predicates like 'bald', 'soluble', and 'living', would have to be either excluded or more sharply defined, since it is simply not the case that for each entity x, either x is bald or x is not bald, x is soluble in water or x is not soluble in water, etc. These difficulties are aggravated by the doctrine that the language of science is to have a "single unpartitioned universe of bound variables" containing both classes and physical objects. Perhaps, these difficulties can be overcome without much work, but I should like to see some of the details of this reconstruction carried out. On the whole, I find Quine's argument too sketchy to be convincing.

But there are other reasons for being skeptical about the thesis: it is not at all clear what precisely Quine is maintaining. A large part of Quine's sketch of his "regimentation" of the language of science consists in arguments that such notoriously nonextensional idioms as subjunctive conditionals and terms of propositional attitudes "have no place in an austere canonical notation for science" ([81], p. 225). For example, he argues that indirect quotation involves "evaluation, relative to special purposes, of an essentially dramatic act." Supposedly, we project ourselves into the speaker's state of mind and say "what, in our language, is natural and relevant for us in the state thus feigned" (p. 219). Unfortunately, says Quine, a strict criterion of faithfulness (or even a criterion of more or less faithfulness) to the dramatic act is beyond hope. Since the attributions of other propositional attitudes are no more in the spirit of objective science than indirect quotation, he argues, the use of these idioms should be eliminated from science. Quine qualifies his position by saying that he is not recommending that we eliminate idioms of propositional attitude from "daily use" or when we are merely using the terms to "dissolve verbal perplexities or facilitate logical deductions." As he says in another place, these idioms are not supposed to be eliminated from the market place or the laboratory (p. 228). His doctrine is only that we should limit ourselves to a canonical notation when "we are limning the true and ultimate structure of reality" (p. 221). "The doctrine is that all traits of reality worthy of the name can be set down in an idiom of this austere form if in any idiom, (p. 228). But these statements, themselves, do not come up to the high standards of clarity and precision Quine demands of science. What, after all, is the empirical "cash value" of saying that such and such is a trait of reality worthy of the name? And how *do* we decide when we are limning the true and ultimate structure of reality? And what does 'can' mean in the last of the quoted statements? Quine cannot be saying that it is *logically* possible for us to set down all traits of reality in his canonical notation, since he claims not to understand what is meant by 'logical possibility'. Perhaps he is only claiming that it is "theoretically possible" to do so. Very well, but can Quine explain the term "theoretically possible" in a way that will come up to his own high standards of scientific precision and clarity which he demands of the explanations and definitions of other philosophers? Of course, Quine might claim that he had in mind no special sense of 'possible' when he made the above claim. Well, if it is possible for Quine to actually reconstruct science in his canonical notation and if such a reconstruction would be as pragmatically desirable as he claims, why does he not actually carry out the reconstruction? Perhaps then we could see clearly what his claim comes to.

Another reason for questioning Quine's thesis of the extensionality of the language of science is this: Quine holds that the acceptability of a "conceptual scheme" is "as much a pragmatic matter as one's adoption of . . . a new system of bookkeeping" ([86], p. 125).

Hence, we should not decide whether or not to accept Quine's extensional language of science on the basis of merely considering the pragmatic advantages of accepting it: we should also consider the *disadvantages*. One powerful reason for not adopting a new system of bookkeeping would be the inordinate expense, time, and effort required to convert to the new system. Another would be the difficulty in teaching new bookkeepers the new system. By parity of reasoning, even if the reconstruction of our scientific theories to fit Quine's requirements could, in theory, be carried out, we should consider the enormous practical problems of actually completing the project and of teaching scientists the new system. Furthermore, Quine's logical grammar requires either giving up all sorts of useful psychological and sociological explanations (for example, those that make essential use of terms of propositional attitude) or separating off from these "contaminated" areas of scientific endeavor those theories that limn the true and ultimate structure of reality (whatever that means). Neither alternative is attractive from a pragmatic point of view. Clearly such disadvantages should be considered in evaluating Quine's thesis.

5. A Reconstruction of Quine's Argument

Several ways of rejecting Quine's argument for the existence of abstract entities are suggested by the preceding sections. One might argue that Quine's criterion of ontological commitment and, indeed, the whole notion of ontological commitment are so imprecise and vague that we cannot tell what it means to say "mathematics is ontologically committed to abstract entities." The strategy here would be analogous to the rejection of the claim that the statements of mathematics are synthetic *a priori* on the grounds that the analytic-synthetic distinction is muddled. A possible way of meeting this objection would be to reformulate the argument by using Chateaubriand's criterion, but this line of defense would seem to require further refinements. One might also reject Quine's argument on the grounds that it rests upon a vague and questionable thesis about the language of science.

But both these ways of saving nominalism are superficial, since it is easy to see how something very much like the argument can be stated without bringing in the notion of ontological commitment or the questionable thesis about the language of science. We may conveniently discuss this argument in terms of set theory since, as Quine puts it, all of mathematics can be "got down to" set theory. Actually, we need not adopt any position regarding the reduction of all mathematics to set theory. One need not even admit that functions, numbers, etc. can be regarded as sets. However, I shall treat the argument as if set theory were the essential element for the following reasons: (i) It simplifies the discussion; (ii) The problem facing the nominalist does not disappear even if the set-theoretical analyses of these entities are rejected; (iii) The discussion in terms of set theory will illustrate the central ideas; (iv) Since set theory is used by the scientist, it is clear that the nominalist must come to terms with the set theory used by scientists, regardless of the precise nature of the reduction of mathematics to set theory.

What is obviously crucial to Quine's argument is the claim that the nominalist must accommodate his natural sciences unaided by mathematics. Quine tried to convince us that we have good reasons for believing that there are abstract entities by arguing that, if we deny that there are such things, we must give up a great deal of science. But assuming that we accept the scientist's theories, must we also accept *as true* the mathematical theories needed to construct, express and apply these theories? Why cannot one take the position that the Platonic statements of mathematics are neither true nor false but meaningless? Quine suggests that (interpreted) mathematics—set theory, number theory, differential and integral calculus, and the like—should be regarded as an integral part of science "on a par with" physics, chemistry, economics, and so forth ([78], p. 231). He merely makes this strong claim without giving any supporting grounds. However, George Berry has responded to the extreme "formalistic" position in a way that has won Quine's approval.[19]

Berry argues that the extreme formalist is faced with a number of grave theoretical difficulties([4]). For example, how can he

---

[19] "I agree in general with Berry's admirable survey of the ontological options in set theory" (Quine [90], p. 346).

explain the usefulness of mathematics in the empirical sciences? He cannot argue, as can Quine, that predictions based upon mathematical laws are reliable because the laws are, themselves, true descriptions of what is the case. He has precluded himself from taking the position that the utility of mathematics is due to its truth (p. 255). There is also the difficulty of interpreting the statements the nominalist, himself, makes about mathematics: even if the mathematical statements, themselves, are meaningless, the nominalist can hardly treat his own statements about the system as meaningless. And since the usual syntax of set theory requires infinitely many sentences, the nominalist seems forced to assume infinitely many concrete objects. Besides these problems, such a nominalist must deal with the wide-spread intuition that many mathematical statements are both meaningful and true. Thus, it is argued, the most plausible and reasonable position to accept in this connection is this: Our scientific theories presuppose the truth of mathematics and we should be willing to accept the consequences of affirming the truth of a scientific theory.

Recall that Quine's aim in devising a criterion of ontological commitment was to develop a method for detecting something called 'the admission of entities into one's ontology'. Quine wished to use his criterion to make it clear when a philosopher admitted certain sorts of entities and then, glossing over this admission, denied that such entities exist. There were to be two steps in applying Quine's method: first, paraphrase the relevant sentence(s) into standard quantificational notation; and second, apply the criterion. But if the relevant sentences have already been expressed in a first-order language, as in the case of set theory, why not simply drop the criterion and rely on first-order implication (which is essentially what we do with Chateaubriand's criterion anyway)? If we proceed in this way, we can avoid many of the difficulties in the notion of ontological commitment thus far discussed. Thus, consider the case of a philosopher who is willing to affirm the axioms of a standard set theory formalized in a first-order language and who denies, just the same, that abstract entities exist. We can assume here that one of the theses of the set theory is

$$(\exists x)(\exists y)(\exists z)(x \in y \ \& \ y \in z).$$

Now suppose the philosopher accepts

$-(\exists x)(x$ is an abstract entity)

as a paraphrase of his assertion that there are no abstract entities. We can then ask the philosopher if he is willing to affirm

(5-1) $(x)((\exists y)(\exists z)(y \in x \ \& \ x \in z) \rightarrow x$ is a set)

and

(5-2) $(x)(x$ is a set $\rightarrow x$ is an abstract entity).

If (5-1) is rejected, we can inquire about the meaning of '$\in$'. If the philosopher rejects (5-2), this would signal a need for an investigation into what he thinks sets and abstract entities are. We should consider the possibility that the philosopher believes that a set is just a particular like a heap. Quine argues that such a belief rests upon an elementary confusion that should easily be cleared up ([82], p. 114). If, however, the philosopher were to accept (5-1) and (5-2), we could convict him of self-contradiction. Thus, it would seem, if we accept the truth of the mathematical theories used in the natural sciences, we cannot deny that there are abstract entities without involving ourselves in a contradiction.

To avoid this conclusion, a nominalist might reject the usual translations of mathematics into quantificational notation and deny that the standard formalized versions of set theory are true. But this strategy would be bizarre; it would seem only a desperate attempt to evade an unpleasant conclusion.

A less radical alternative would be to reject the paraphrase of the assertion that there are no abstract entities into

$-(\exists x)(x$ is an abstract entity)

where this quantified sentence is supposed to belong to the language in which the set theory has been formulated. It can be argued (and has been argued, as we shall see in the next chapter) that 'exists' has a special sense when it is used in mathematics; so one might maintain that the "sense" of the quantifiers used in set theory differs from that of the quantifier in the above sentence. To this move, however, Quine could reasonably request an explication of these two different senses (see [81], pp. 241-2). This line clearly leads to some deep philosophical questions.

Some philosophers may regard the whole issue as trivial, arguing that the question of whether or not abstract entities exist simply makes no sense. Now even if this position could be plausibly defended, not all the difficulties would disappear; for we should still be faced with the problem of trying to understand what is going on in set theory, where set-existence assertions are frequently made. One could hardly maintain that all set-existence assertions are meaningless, without being forced into the extremely counter-intuitive position regarding the nature of mathematics discussed earlier.

The Quinian argument I have reconstructed in this section does not rest upon philosophical assumptions regarding language of the kind implicit in the traditional arguments for the existence of universals that Quine has criticized: roughly speaking, it gets its real bite by taking the existential quantifier at face value and throwing the burden of explanation upon the anti-Platonist.

6. Ontological Reduction and the Löwenheim-Skolem Theorem

Evidently, within any of the standard set theories that have been axiomatized in a first-order language,[20] one can reconstruct the mathematics needed in the empirical sciences. The Löwenheim-Skolem Theorem shows that if the set of axioms of such a set theory has a model, it has a denumerable model. Hence, it might be argued that the nominalist can avoid Quine's Platonism by postulating denumerably many expressions and interpreting the set theory to be a theory about these nominalistic entities. The general idea is to meet the Quinian argument by actually effecting a nominalistic reduction of set theory on the pattern of the reduction of the real numbers to sets of rationals and of the natural numbers to sets of sets. In both of the above cases, the respective theories,—real number theory and arithmetic,—were preserved by the reductions. Let us suppose that a nominalist decides that he can effect a similar

[20] Throughout this essay, when I speak of "first-order languages" I have in mind languages with only countably many symbols.

reduction of the ontology of set theory to a denumerable ontology of expressions, while still preserving the truth of those sentences that are theorems of the set theory. We can imagine the nominalist arguing that the Löwenheim–Skolem Theorem, in effect, provides the required reduction. Let us assume that the set theory under consideration is formulated as an uninterpreted theory in a first-order language without identity (the identity sign being taken as a nonlogical constant). Now if the theory is satisfiable at all, it must be satisfiable by an interpretation with a domain consisting of denumerably many expressions.[21] Under this interpretation the theorems will all be true even though only expressions are within the range of the bound variables.

Before examining the notion of reduction that is central to this discussion, I should like to explore some of the difficulties facing the nominalist who attempts to avoid Platonism in this way. First of all, it might be said that, by the above reductive argument, the nominalist is forced to make dubious assumptions himself. The nominalist who postulates the existence of infinitely many expressions must be speaking of either types or tokens. Since types are abstract objects in the same category as sets, it would seem that he must have in mind tokens. But it is by no means obvious that infinitely many tokens exist.

In reply, the nominalist can admit that the Quinian argument compels him to make some assumptions that he otherwise would not make, but he can argue that his assumption of a denumerable infinity of tokens is weaker in both number and kind than the Platonist's assumption of the existence of uncountably many abstract objects: since practically everyone admits the existence of tokens, the nominalist is not forced to introduce a new category of entities but only infinitely many entities of a previously admitted type.

However, the difficulties facing the nominalist cannot be obviated so easily. The expressions that supposedly make up the domain of the reductive interpretation are not actually constructed by the

---

[21] This follows, for example, from the Henkin proof given in Mates [54], pp. 136-41.

nominalist. At best, he gives us a recursive rule for constructing as many of these tokens as we wish. To postulate the actual existence of all the expressions needed in the interpretation—a denumerable infinity of tokens—suggests that someone or something has completed an infinite sequence of distinct acts in a finite amount of time—surely an implausible hypothesis.[22] In fact, if the nominalist does postulate the existence of such a totality, we surely have good reason for thinking his postulation is false.

A second type of objection to the nominalist's reductive argument arises from a consideration of the various proofs of the Löwenheim–Skolem Theorem. Thus, in some proofs of the theorem, set theory, including the axiom of choice, is used. It might be argued that the nominalist presupposes the existence of sets in his very attempt to show that we do not have to presuppose the existence of sets. The nominalist might claim that in the case of the Henkin proof of the theorem, set theory is not used in any essential way; again, the difficulties cannot be dismissed so quickly. The Löwenheim–Skolem Theorem cannot even be stated without bringing in set theory. Thus, when the nominalist assets, 'If T has a model, T has a denumerable model', he must make sense of 'T has a model'. On the usual reading, the sentence says there exists a set (function or structure) of a certain sort. The nominalist might try to avoid this problem by replacing the Löwenheim–Skolem Theorem with the theorem: if T is consistent with respect to derivability, then one can interpret the sentences of T in such a way that all the bound variables and individual constants of the language refer to expressions and all the theorems of T come out true under this interpretation.[23] But the nominalist would still be faced with the problem of reinterpreting the definitions of 'true' and 'interpretation' so that the notion of set is not presupposed. And in addition, it would be incumbent upon the nominalist to show that where terms like 'set' and 'union' occur in the proof, one can treat such expressions as mere *façons de parler*.

A third objection to the nominalist's Löwenheim–Skolem reduction is outlined by Quine himself. In [85], Quine argues that the

[22] *Infra.* Chapter IV, § 3.3
[23] Mates, *op. cit.*

Löwenheim–Skolem Theorem does not provide a "true reduction" of the ontology of set theory to a denumerable universe. According to Quine, a genuine reduction of the ontology of a theory T to that of another theory T' must provide us with (a) a "proxy function," f, that maps the domain, D, of T into the domain, D', of T' and (b) an effective function, g, that maps the primitive predicates of T into the open sentences of T' in such a way that the following condition holds: any n-place primitive predicate, P, of T is true of $\langle \alpha_1 , \alpha_2 ,..., \alpha_n \rangle$ (where the α_i are elements of D) if, and only if, $g(P)$ is true of $\langle f(\alpha_1), f(\alpha_2), ..., f(\alpha_n) \rangle$ (pp. 204-6).[24]

Quine suggests that to justify the claim that some putative reduction is a genuine reduction, one must show that "the relevant structure" has been preserved, and this requires that the above mappings be supplied. Now the Löwenheim-Skolem Theorem does not, either explicitly or implicitly, supply us with any such proxy function: we cannot, from an examination of the demonstrations of this theorem, specify which expressions are "to go proxy" for the respective sets of our set theory. Hence, so Quine argues, the theorem does not provide us with a genuine reduction of the ontology of set theory to a nominalistically acceptable ontology.

Before considering a possible reply to Quine's objection to the Löwenheim–Skolem reduction, let us examine the proxy-function requirement in more detail. Several questions naturally arise in this connection. First of all, in order to reduce T to T', is it necessary to actually specify the proxy-function f? Or is it sufficient to prove that there exists such a function? Quine says a number of things that definitely point to the stronger requirement. He says, for example: "This third condition is that we be able to specify what I shall call a *proxy function*" ([85], p. 204); and "The standard of reduction of a theory θ to a theory θ' can now be put as follows: we specify a function" ([85], p. 205.); and "We have no ontological reduction in an interesting sense unless we can specify a proxy function" ([89], p. 60; see also p. 57). It is also noteworthy that all the cases of

---

[24] In stating his requirement in this way, Quine assumes that T contains only predicates, variables, quantifiers and truth functional connectives. He would apply his criterion to other types of theories by first "reducing" them to theories in the required form. See Quine [85], p. 205.

reduction that Quine cites as genuine—the reductions by Frege and von Neumann of natural numbers to sets, Carnap's reduction of impure numbers to pure numbers, and Dedekind's reduction of real numbers to sets of rational numbers—actually provide us with the required proxy functions. Of course, an analogous question arises in connection with the function g. In this case also, we evidently have to specify the effective function to have a true reduction.

It may be thought that, with the proxy-function requirement, no theory having a nondenumerable ontology can be reduced to one having a denumerable one. The following example will show that this is not the case. Let A be a deductive theory formalized in the first-order predicate calculus (without identity).[25] Its axioms are:

$$(x) - Gxx$$
$$(x)(\exists y)Gxy$$
$$(x)(y)(z)((Gxy \ \& \ Gyz) \to Gxz)$$
$$(x)(y)(Gxy \to -Gyx)$$

and it is interpreted as follows:

The domain: the set of real numbers
G: There is an integer n such that $①\leqslant n < ②$

Now this theory can be reduced to a theory B with a denumerable domain as follows: Let the domain be the set of integers, and let 'G' be interpreted as the English predicate '$① < ②$'. Now to satisfy Quine's proxy-function requirement, we simply map the real numbers onto the integers as follows: For every real number r in the interval $(n, m]$, where n and m are consecutive integers, $f(r) = m$. Clearly, for any real numbers r and s, there is an integer n such that $r \leqslant n < s$ if, and only if, $f(r) < f(s)$.

It is worth noting here that whether or not a given theory is reducible, by Quine's criterion of reduction, to another is independent of the nature of the assertions of the respective theories: we need only look at the domains and the sets assigned to the predicates of

---

[25] I use the expression, 'deductive theory formalized in the first-order predicate calculus', in the sense of Mates [54], Chapter II. The interpretation is also given in the standard way described in Mates [54], p. 73-4.

the theories. This, I believe, is a reason for viewing the proxy-function requirement with some suspicion.

Can the nominalist supply us with a proxy function in the case of the Löwenheim–Skolem reduction of the standard first-order axiomatized versions of set theory? No. To see why not, let us first assume that there are such functions f and g of the sort required by Quine. Let 'S' denote the domain of the set theory, and 'D' denote the denumerable domain of the nominalist's theory. Since S is nondenumerable and D is denumerable, there must be sets α and β such that $\alpha \neq \beta$ and $f(\alpha) = f(\beta)$. Now '$=$' is one of the primitive predicates of the set theory, so there must be an open sentence $g('=')$ that is true of $\langle f(\alpha), f(\beta) \rangle$ if, and only if, $\alpha = \beta$. It follows that $g('=')$ is not true of $\langle f(\alpha), f(\beta) \rangle$. But $\langle f(\alpha), f(\beta) \rangle = \langle f(\alpha), f(\alpha) \rangle$. Hence, $g('=')$ is true of $\langle f(\alpha), f(\beta) \rangle$. We can conclude that the proxy-function requirement cannot be satisfied for this case. Furthermore, as Tharpe notes, it is easy to see how this argument can be generalized to show that no theory with identity among its primitive predicates, or within which identity is definable, can be reduced (in accordance with Quine's criterion) to a theory with an ontology of smaller cardinality ([113], p. 155).

Now the nominalist might reply that he sees no reason for satisfying Quine's requirement of a proxy function. After all, what justification does Quine provide for his requirement? Essentially, what Quine does is examine a number of examples of reductions that he feels are clearly acceptable and then contrast these cases with the Löwenheim–Skolem reduction.[26] The trouble with this reasoning is

[26] It has been pointed out to me by John Steel that one of Quine's paradigms of reduction, namely Carnap's reduction of impure numbers to pure numbers, is analyzed in a questionable way. For unless the reduced theory is such an incomplete fragment of science as to be practically unusable, it is hard to see how the proxy-function requirement can be satisfied in the way proposed by Quine. One would expect any significant portion of science involving mixed numbers to include such statements as

Three feet = one yard
Two feet ≠ two degrees Centigrade.

However, the inclusion of such sentences in the theory to be reduced would preclude the proxy-function analysis advanced by Quine.

that the requirement of the proxy function is not well motivated: Quine's discussion makes it look as if he had simply introduced the new requirement to save the activity of making "ontological reductions" from trivialization. It is as if some board game had been ruined by the discovery of a simple procedure which enabled the beginning side to always win and the problem was to figure out a way of saving the game by changing the rules slightly. Insofar as we are concerned with the Quinian argument for Platonism, the crucial question is not whether the Löwenheim–Skolem Theorem effects a true ontological reduction (in Quine's sense of "ontological reduction") but whether the theorem enables the nominalist to have a mathematical system sufficient for the needs of the empirical scientist.

Quine does not discuss this problem in his papers on the Löwenheim–Skolem reduction. But one of his supporters has taken up the challenge. Harman asks: Why should we accept Quine's criterion of reduction? And he goes on:

> Quine argues that it distinguishes adequately those reductions we want to accept from those we do not want to accept as serious reductions. This may be true, but we would like to see how this criterion of reduction is connected with the sort of pragmatic considerations that lead us to prefer one theory to another ([40], p. 365).

Harman then puts forward an answer to this objection: "Quine's criterion of reduction explains what it is for the reducing objects to fulfill the purposes of the reduced objects" (p. 365).

Harman's defense of Quine's requirement, however, is far from satisfactory. Why is Harman so sure that all the original purposes of the reduced theory will be fulfilled by the reducing theory if the proxy-function requirement is satisfied? How, specifically, does the requirement explain what it is for the reducing objects to serve all the relevant purposes of the reduced objects? One expects further explanations from Harman; but he leaves the reader hanging. If we accept Harman's defense of Quine, then it looks as if the only part of a theory that is relevant to its original purposes is its structure. But have we been given any good ground for supposing that, for example, we can always tear a theory out from its web of logical connections with other theories and replace it with any other theory with which it is structurally isomorphic without losing any significant connections with sense experience? Suppose that we have a deductive theory formalized in the first-order predicate calculus, T, each predicate letter of which is given two quite different (intensional) interpretations so as to yield two Quinian theories T_1 and T_2. Suppose further that the interpretations yield isomorphic models of T.[27] Then, by Quine's criterion, we can say that T_1 is reducible to T_2. But recall that a Quinian theory always presupposes a background theory and a background language. Are the theoretical connections given by the background theory irrelevant to the "original purposes" of the theory? If so, it would be a surprising fact. Perhaps it would be best to consider a specific example. Let T be a deductive theory formalized in the first-order predicate calculus, the axioms of which are:

$$(\exists x)(\exists y)(\exists z)(x \neq y \ \& \ y \neq z \ \& \ z \neq x \ \& \ (w)(w = x \lor w = y \lor w = z))$$

$$(x) - Rx$$
$$(\exists x)(y)(Ty \ \& \ Oy \leftrightarrow y = x)$$

The theory Td will be obtained from T by interpreting the language as follows:

Domain: dogs that live in my neighborhood (this could obviously be made more precise if needed)

R: ① has retractable claws
T: ① has only three legs
O: ① is owned by Mr. Jones.

Theory Tc will differ from Td only in interpretation:

Domain: cats that live in my neighborhood

R: ① has non-retractable claws
T: ① has only three legs
O: ① is owned by Mr. Smith.

[27] For a definition of 'isomorphic model', see Mates [54], p. 177.

Now suppose that Td and Tc are both true theories. Then it is easy to see how the proxy-function requirement can be satisfied. So on the above supposition, we have:

Td is reducible to Tc.

But will Tc necessarily fulfill all the original purposes of Td? I doubt it. We can imagine that I accept, in addition to Td, a theory U that asserts such things as:

$(x)(y)(Dx \,\&\, Py \,\&\, xMy \rightarrow Ly)$
$(x)(Dx \,\&\, Hx \,\&\, Fx \rightarrow Gx)$

where the theory is interpreted as follows:

D: ① is a dog

P: ① is a paw print

M: ① makes ②

L: ① looks like such & such

H: ① is very hungry

F: ① is familiar with garbage cans

G: ① will probably look for food in garbage cans.

Now suppose that I wish to explain the overturned garbage cans in my back yard and the distinctive paw prints all around it. I can make use of both Td and U in my explanation. But can I give an equally plausible explanation if I replace Td with Tc? Not obviously.

I am not claiming that this example disproves Harman's claim. However, I do think it illustrates the need for a much fuller justification of the Quinian criterion of reduction than the one he gives. It also provides us with a reason for being suspicious of the view that satisfying the proxy-function requirement is a sufficient condition for a true reduction. But to explain more fully why I say this, I should like to discuss briefly the connection between reduction and dispensability. "A usual occasion for ontological talk is reduction, where it is shown how the universe of some theory can by a reinterpretation be dispensed with in favor of some other universe" (Quine [89], p. 55). From this quotation, it would seem that a reduction for Quine shows how an ontology *can be dispensed with*. But how does a reduction accomplish this? Quine begins his discussion of reduction by first discussing the reduction of one *notion* to another ([85]). But he soon shifts to discussing reductions of *systems of objects* to others, and he ends up discussing the reductions of *theories* to other theories. Now theories—at least Quinian theories —are supposed to have ontological commitments. Clearly, a reduction cannot eliminate the commitments of a theory; so when Quine says that a reduction shows how we can dispense with an ontology, it seems likely that he is speaking of the ontological commitments of persons rather than theories. Perhaps, then, he is saying something like the following: If T is reducible to T', then any person who accepts T (and who thereby accepts the commitments of T) can dispense with these commitments in favor of the commitments of T'. Unfortunately, a slight complication is introduced by the fact that Quinian theories come with their ontologies already specified (in a meta-language). To deal with this difficulty, I shall introduce the phrase "ontological presupposition" as follows: I shall say that T ontologically presupposes F's (or F's are among the ontological presuppositions of T) relative to meta-theory T' if either T is ontologically committed to F's relative to T' (using Chateaubriand's criterion) or the ontology of T is specified to be G's and $(\exists x)Gx \rightarrow (\exists x)Fx$ is an assertion of T'.[28] It would seem, then, that Quine is making the following claim: if T is reducible to T'', any person who accepts T can dispense with the ontological presuppositions of T in favor of the ontological presuppositions of T''.

But further revisions are needed if we are to avoid attributing an absurd claim to Quine. For suppose: (i) T is ontologically committed to F's; (ii) T'' does not ontologically presuppose F's; (iii) Mr. N accepts T.

It is clear that even if T is reducible to T'', that would not be a sufficient reason for saying that Mr. N can eliminate F's from his ontological presuppositions, for Mr. N may be committed to F's by some beliefs he has other than the belief in T. Perhaps we should take Quine to be claiming:

> (*) If T is reducible to T'', T ontologically presupposes F's, and T'' does not ontologically presuppose F's, then any

[28] This definition is not meant to be precise. For my purposes, even a rough notion will suffice.

person who accepts T and who accepts no sentence other than those in T that ontologically presupposes F's, can eliminate F's from his ontological presuppositions.

This version is still very crude and vague, but it should serve my purposes.

Let us now return to the Td and Tc example. Imagine that I accept Td. Now it seems conceivable that I might also accept no other sentence that ontologically presupposes *dogs that live in my neighborhood*. (Notice that the theory U does not presuppose *dogs that live in my neighborhood*.) In that case, by (*) and by the fact that Td is reducible to Tc, I can revise my list of ontological presuppositions by replacing *dogs that live in my neighborhood* with *cats that live in my neighborhood*! Surely we have arrived at an absurdity.

Now it might be objected that "ontological reduction," on Quine's view, only makes sense for precise theories not involving such empirical notions as that of dogs and cats. However, Tharp reports that Quine has indicated in a personal communication that he does intend his general theory of reduction to cover even such "muddy" cases as the reduction of the Eighteenth-Century theory of infinitesimals to the modern Weierstrassian version ([113] p. 163-164). It should be mentioned here that as Quine views the Eighteenth-Century theory, it attributes absurd properties to infinitesimals (cf. Quine [81], p. 248).

The example I have constructed above deals with theories with finite ontologies. Quine says: "Ontology is emphatically meaningless for a finite theory of named objects *considered in and of itself*" ([89], p. 62, italics mine). So it might appear that the difficulty I claim to find in Quine's proxy-function requirement is illusory. Actually, the main point Quine is making in the passage quoted is simply that ontological relativity holds trivially for the finite case: "What the objects of the finite theory are, makes sense only as a statement of the background theory in its own referential idiom." In any case, it is easy to alter the two theories in the above example so that they are infinite (even uncountable) theories: simply add to the domains of Td and Tc the real numbers and make suitable changes in the vocabularies. If it is objected that those portions of the domains do no work, add to the assertions of T some of the usual axioms of the real number system (with appropriate alterations).

Basically, the reason structural isomorphism of the sort that obtains between Td and Tc is not sufficient for reduction is this: There are all sorts of conceptual connections between Td and other theories we accept that are ignored in using Quine's criterion. To look at the situation in more Quinian terms, ontological reduction presupposes a background language and a background theory. Indeed even the interpretation we give in formulating Td and Tc presupposes a background language and theory. The term 'dog', for example, occurs in many statements we accept, other than those in Td. So it is easy to see that Td is conceptually related to many other theories we accept. These conceptual relations are ignored by Quine's criterion.

One might attempt to salvage Quine's criterion against this sort of objection by restricting the criterion to theories that are "complete" and not fragments of some more inclusive theory. But it would seem, from what Quine has written on other topics, that the criterion could then be applied only to the totality of someone's beliefs or to the whole of science.

But how could Quine have overlooked this basic point? Evidently by looking at only one sort of example, that is, reductions of theories of abstract entities. In discussing Frege's reduction of arithmetic to set theory, Quine mentions Russell's claim that more is needed for a reduction than a structure preserving model of arithmetic. Russell had maintained that we must also construct a method of translating "mixed contexts" in which arithmetical expressions occur with non-mathematical expressions. He held that we must provide for those sentences outside of arithmetic in which number terms and numerical relationships are involved—which is analogous, after all, to requiring that we provide for translating sentences outside of Td that involve (conceptually) dogs that live in my neighborhood. But Quine replies that this is no added requirement because we can say what it means for a class to have n members no matter how we construe the natural numbers so long as the numbers are ordered in a certain way. Essentially, Quine concludes that Russell has not found an added requirement for *this* case of reduction on the grounds that the requirement can always be met so long as the proxy-function requirement is met. He looks at other examples and draws the same conclusion. Thus, he fixed upon structure as the essential feature in a reduction, and ignored the problem of translating mixed contexts. He says "always, if the structure is there, the applications will fall into place" ([89], p. 44). It is unfortunate that in the earlier essay on reduction he did not consider any examples of reduction in which concrete physical objects were reduced, for in such cases, I do not think it is so obvious that preservation of structure guarantees translatability of mixed contexts.[29]

Is it possible, however, that Quine has given us sufficient conditions for ontological reduction so long as we are dealing only with purely mathematical theories or, perhaps also, theories dealing only with abstract entities? It is not so easy to come up with clearly acceptable counter-examples to such a thesis, and, in the case of mathematical theories, the thesis has some plausibility.

However, consider the following example. Under the intended interpretation, Wang's predicative set theory Σ_ω has an ontology of sets. It is easy to enumerate the entities in this ontology; so one can specify a proxy function, f, mapping the ontology of this set theory one-one onto the set of natural numbers. We can then define a binary relation R that holds between natural numbers as follows:

$$\alpha \in \beta \text{ iff } f(\alpha)Rf(\beta).$$

We can then specify a model of Σ_ω with the natural numbers as its domain and R as the extension of the $\in$ relation. Clearly this model is isomorphic to the intended model, so the proxy-function requirement is satisfied. But has the intended theory been ontologically reduced to this artificially constructed theory? If dispensability of ontology is a necessary consequence of reduction, then it would seem that the intuitive set theory has not been reduced to a theory about natural numbers. For the very definition of the reducing theory presupposes the ontology of the reduced theory. This example

---

[29] Cf. Nagel's discussion of reductions of scientific theories in [58]. There, he lays down a *condition of connectability* which effectively precludes the above sort of example from being a true reduction.

points to the need for restricting Quine's criterion to only cases in which one theory is reduced to another that is specified without reference to the reduced theory. Perhaps it could then be claimed with some plausibility that, with this restriction, Quine's criterion gives us sufficient conditions of ontological reduction, at least for the cases involving only mathematical theories.

The plausibility of the thesis, however, is deceptive. The difficulty in finding clear counter-examples to the claim may be due to the vagueness and unclarity of the notion of reduction. Indeed, as Chateaubriand points out, under one reasonable way of regarding reduction, the satisfaction of the proxy-function requirement shows not that the ontology of T has been reduced to T' but rather that T' is, in one important sense, ontologically committed to the ontology of T ([13], pp. 148f). The reasonableness of Chateaubriand's claim is brought out by a consideration of one of Quine's paradigms of ontological reduction: the reduction of natural numbers to sets. It is clear that the ontology of set theory is rich enough to include a totality of objects with all the structural properties of numbers. Commenting on this example, Chateaubriand writes:

> If in ignorance of the reducibility of number theory to set theory one had adopted both theories and posited numbers and sets as distinct entities, then once one realizes that number theory is reducible to set theory one sees that it is not necessary to posit numbers and sets as distinct entities. Quine wants to say that thereby one can repudiate numbers in favor of sets. But this is misleading . . . what we repudiate is our mistaken—or, at least, unnecessary—assumption that by adopting T and T' we had to posit numbers as distinct from sets. The ontology of numbers is not repudiated at all; it is merely shown to be part of the ontology of sets. ([13], pp. 148-9).

Chateaubriand contrasts the sort of proxy-function reduction that Quine talks about with the sort of reduction accomplished by Weierstrass in eliminating infinitesimals from the ontology of the infinitesimal calculus. In the latter case, the proxy-function requirement is not satisfied: nothing in the Weierstrassian theory goes proxy for the infinitesimals of the early theory. The beauty of the modern theory of limits is that we do not have to postulate infinitesimals or even entities that go proxy for them. In this sense, Weierstrass has shown us how to eliminate such entities from our ontology. It is clear that if we regard ontological reduction in the way suggested by Chateaubriand, it would be easy enough to find counter-examples to Quine's thesis of the sufficiency of the proxy-function requirement for the reduction of one purely mathematical theory to another. Quine would probably claim that the Weierstrassian theory did not effect a genuine ontological reduction; but it is not clear how he would justify this sort of claim other than by appealing to his proxy-function requirement—which, after all, is the very requirement under dispute. My intuitions of what is meant by 'ontological reduction' are certainly not sufficiently clear as to enable me to decide in Quine's favor.

The question now arises: Is satisfaction of the proxy-function requirement a necessary condition for a true reduction? As we saw earlier, Quine originally claimed that it was, and Harman supported him on this point. Quine, however, has had second thoughts about this claim. In the reprinted version of "Ontological Relativity," we find a note, hurriedly added in proof, in which Quine admits that there are ontological reductions that do not satisfy the proxy-function requirement. Actually, if dispensability is what one is after in a reduction, one wonders why satisfying the proxy function should be essential to a reduction.[30] Why not take the position suggested by Chateaubriand and allow that the Weierstrassian theory of limits does provide us with an ontological reduction of the early theory of infinitesimals? Or consider Russell's no-class theory, which is considered by many to have effected an ontological reduction: it does not satisfy Quine's criterion of reduction either. In *PM*, for each class α, there are many propositional functions with α as its extension; yet the no-class theory does not associate with each class a unique propositional function. And just how one would specify the required proxy function is not obvious. But even though the proxy-function requirement is not satisfied, it is generally agreed that the no-class theory does show how classes can be dispensed with in favor of propositional functions. Indeed, Quine, himself, says in several places that the no-class theory does effect a reduction

[30] Cf. Jubien [45], p. 538.

of the theory of classes to a theory of attributes ([82], p. 122; [84], p. 19, [78], p. 101). Thus, the question of whether one can specify a proxy function taking classes to propositional functions seems to be utterly beside the point: one simply does not need a proxy function to do set theory in *PM* and yet one does not commit oneself to sets in accepting *PM*.[31]

Let us review Quine's attempt to deal with the Pythagorean who claims that the Löwenheim–Skolem theorem enables us to reduce all theories to one with a denumerable ontology. We began with a vague intuitive notion of ontological reduction and some examples of what are purported to be reductions. Supposedly, the Pythagorean looked at these examples and claimed to find the essential property of reductions, namely, modeling. For the Pythagorean, a theory T is ontologically reducible to T' if one can construct a model of T using a subset of the domain of T' as the domain of the model. Of course, we are speaking here of interpreted theories— theories that come with their predicates and domains already specified—so we immediately see a peculiarity in the Pythagorean's claim. What does it mean to say such and such is a model of an interpreted theory? Evidently, M is a model of an interpreted theory T if, and only if, M is a model of T *uninterpreted* (that is, ignoring the particular interpretation of T that was given). In any case, Quine reconsidered the standard examples of reduction and came up with a new set of necessary and sufficient conditions for a reduction. Using his new criterion of reduction, Quine was able to reject the Pythagorean conclusion on the grounds that modeling is not a sufficient condition for a reduction. But Quine's critique seems questionable for various reasons. First of all, he has not given

[31] There is another aspect of Quine's theory of reduction that seems to me to be questionable. To prove that one can dispense with objects of a certain sort *via* Quine's proxy function, one is forced to adopt a meta-theory or "background theory" that takes the objects to be reduced as values of its variables. Quine dismisses this complication by saying that the reasoning involved in reduction is a form of *reductio ad absurdum:* We supposedly assume that the objects to be reduced are needed and then show that the objects are not needed. But one would like to see the reasoning spelled out in detail, so that the underlying assumptions could be scrutinized. For objections to Quine's reasoning on this point, see Tharp [113], pp. 157-8.

us any good reason for accepting his criterion of reduction. Secondly, an examination of some examples suggests that he has set forth neither necessary nor sufficient conditions for reduction.

In questioning Quine's views on reduction, I do not wish to suggest that I support the Pythagorean view. For if it is questionable that Quine has given sufficient conditions for ontological reduction, then how much more questionable is the view that modeling is sufficient. Besides, there is another, deeper, objection to Pythagoreanism (which also applies to the nominalistic reduction we have been discussing in this section). The objection arises from a consideration of the "applications" of mathematics to the physical sciences. To take a relatively simple example, consider the customary analysis of the motion of a free-falling projectile according to Newtonian mechanics. Roughly, the analysis proceeds by regarding position in space as (correlated with) ordered triples of real numbers and moments of time as (correlated with) real numbers. The projectile is regarded as a point occupying different positions in space at different moments of time. The set of positions (ordered triples) occupied by the projectile is the "path of the projectile." If $S = \{\langle x, y \rangle \mid y$ is the position of the projectile at moment $x\}$ is the "position function" of the projectile, then S', the derivative function of S, is the velocity function of the projectile, and S'', the derivative function of S', is the acceleration function of the projectile. Now from a knowledge of certain features of the empirical situation (boundary conditions) in addition to Newtonian mechanics and mathematics, one can construct an equation of motion of the projectile. For example, if one knows such things as the position and velocity of a bomb at the moment of release, the velocity of the wind, the force of gravity at the altitude of the release, and so on, one can calculate the path of the bomb and, in particular, the point of impact. Of course, in calculating the path of the projectile, one would make use of theorems of mathematics. The Platonist could explain and justify this use of mathematics by saying: the theorems are true statements that tell us what sets exist and how these sets are related to one another. The Pythagorean nominalist, however, cannot offer this Platonic justification for our procedures in the empirical sciences. He claims that there are no sets and that what we call axiomatic set theory is false if interpreted to be about sets. For the Pythagorean nominalist, it is only when the formalism is interpreted to be about some denumerable totality of physical objects, say, atoms, that it can be a true theory. But then, the question arises: Why should this theory of atoms shed any light on the empirical situation described above? In the above analysis, the open sentence 'y is the position of the projectile at moment x' is regarded as determining a set of ordered pairs. And set theory is supposed to tell us how this set is related to others such as S' and S". But if there are no sets and if formal set theory is false under the standard interpretation, what justifies us in applying mathematics as we do in the empirical sciences? I do not wish to claim here that the Pythagorean cannot answer these questions. I only wish to indicate the need for a much fuller explanation and development of the Pythagorean position. It is not enough to merely cite the Löwenheim–Skolem Theorem.

Thus, despite the weaknesses in Quine's approach to reduction, the nominalistic strategy sketched at the beginning of this section for circumventing Quine's Platonism involves a number of serious difficulties. Must we then succumb to the force of the Quinian argument? I think not. And my reasons will be given shortly. Since I borrow heavily from the ideas of Russell and Poincaré, I should now like to put into better focus the historical background of my position.

CHAPTER IV

Poincaré's Philosophy
of Mathematics

Henri Poincaré is generally credited with first espousing some form of the vicious-circle principle. Although Poincaré did not go on to construct a set theory that conforms to this principle, as did Russell, he did sketch the outlines of his philosophy of mathematics and science; and it is only in terms of these general philosophical views that one can adequately grasp his rejection of impredicative definitions and specifications in set theory. In the following, I shall argue that it is Poincaré's strong empirical tendencies that lie behind his anti-Platonic philosophy of mathematics. Poincaré's philosophical views regarding mathematics arise, I shall claim, out of an attempt to understand and explicate the nature of mathematics in terms of the activities of mathematicians and scientists, and without assuming the existence (in any ordinary sense of the word 'existence') of abstract objects.

Poincaré's philosophical writings present the expositor with serious problems. I have chosen to present only a rough sketch of Poincaré's philosophy in this chapter, indicating the salient doctrines and stressing the difficulties involved in reconstructing a coherent view of mathematics from the many paradoxical claims he made.[1] Although I shall attempt to bring out the rationale of his rejection of impredicative definitions in terms of his general philosophical views,

[1] For a more general exposition of Poincare's philosophical views regarding the nature of mathematics, see J. Mooij [55]. Mooij is concerned with tracing the historical connections between Poincaré's philosophy of mathematics and the writings of his contemporaries, Russell, Hilbert, Couturat, Zermelo, Brouwer, etc., and he does not seem to concern himself with the problem of making sense of Poincaré's paradoxical claims.

the larger task of making sense of his pronouncements on the nature of mathematics will be left for the next chapter.

1. Poincaré's Rejection of Impredicate Definitions

Poincaré admittedly got his ideas about impredicative definitions from Richard (see Poincaré [62], pp. 307-8, and [65], pp. 189-90). Richard stated his paradox essentially as follows:

Let E be the set of all decimals in the interval [0,1] that can be defined by a finite number of English words. We can arrange the finite sequences of English words in a sequence:

$$S_1, S_2, S_3, \ldots$$

where S_i precedes S_j if S_i contains fewer letters than S_j or, when equi-lettered, S_i precedes S_j in the lexicographical ordering of words. Let us eliminate from this sequence all those that are not definitions of decimals in [0,1]. We then get an ordering of the elements of E:

$$a_1, a_2, a_3, \ldots$$

where $a_j = .a_{i1}a_{i2}a_{i3} \ldots$ We now define a decimal $N = .n_1n_2n_3 \ldots$ as follows:

$$n_i = a_{ii} + 1 \quad \text{if } a_{ii} < 9$$
$$= 1 \qquad \text{if } a_{ii} = 9.$$

From the definition of N, it is obvious that N differs from a_i ($i = 1, 2, 3, \ldots$) and hence is not a member of E. On the other hand, since N can easily be defined in a finite number of English words, N must be a member of E ([95]).

As Richard analyzed this paradox, the definition of N would appear somewhere in the sequence $S_1, S_2, S_3, \ldots$ However it would not be meaningful "at the place it occupies," for it mentions the set E which has not yet been defined. Hence, it would be eliminated with the other elements of the sequence that are not definitions of decimals in [0,1].

Poincaré heartily agreed with Richard's diagnosis. He argued that E must be the set of all those decimals in the unit interval that can be defined in a finite number of English words "*without introducing the notion of the aggregate E itself:*" otherwise the definition of E

would be viciously circular. Now it is legitimate to define N in terms of E; but in that case N would not be a member of E.[2]

The Richard paradox, and indeed all the other related paradoxes, arise because, according to Poincaré, viciously circular definitions are used.

Unfortunately the above brief explanation did not remove the paradox. Poincaré's suggestion that the analysis of Richard's paradox could be carried over to the other paradoxes was especially controversial: many mathematicians could see nothing intrinsically wrong with impredicative specifications of sets. Poincaré argued that his critics were blind to the circularity of these impredicative definitions because of their belief in the actual infinite. Indeed, he went so far as to suggest that the paradoxes resulted from belief in the actual infinite. Russell replied to these claims regarding the paradoxes, saying that, although he agreed with Poincaré that the paradoxes were due to viciously circular definitions, he did not agree that the belief in the actual infinite was essential to the paradoxes ([101], p. 648). Russell suggested that the Epimenides paradox did not involve infinity. He also formulated other paradoxes which did not rely on the concept of infinity.

Eventually, Poincaré became convinced by Russell's argument. Poincaré discussed another paradox, not involving infinity and similar to the Berry paradox of the smallest natural number not nameable in fewer than eighteen syllables ([67]). Consider the English sentences, consisting of fewer than 100 English words, that uniquely pick out or specify some natural number. As examples, take:

>This is the least natural number.
>
>This natural number is the least natural number greater than the least natural number.

There are only finitely many such sentences, so there must be natural numbers that are not specified by these sentences. It then follows that there is a least number not so specified, say K. Consider, then, the sentence

---

[2] [65], pp. 189-190. A similar point is made in [62], pp. 307-8.

(S) This is the least natural number not uniquely specified by an English sentence of fewer than 100 words.

(S) must pick out the natural number K. But since (S) is, itself, an English sentence consisting of fewer than 100 words, K could not be a natural number not specified by an English sentence consisting of fewer than 100 words.

According to Poincaré this reasoning can legitimately take place only after we have succeeded in separating the natural numbers into two fixed classes; and this is held to be impossible:

> The classification can be conclusive only when we have reviewed all the sentences with fewer than one hundred words, when we have rejected those which have no meaning, and when we have definitively fixed the meaning of those which possess a meaning. But among these sentences, there are some which can have meaning only after the classification is fixed; they are those in which the classification itself is concerned. In summary, the classification of the numbers can be fixed only *after* the selection of the sentences is completed, and this selection can be completed only *after* the classification is determined, so that neither the classification nor the selection can ever be terminated ([67], p. 46).

As Poincaré understood the paradox, the sense of (S) is related to the class of *natural numbers not uniquely specified by an English sentence consisting of fewer than 100 words* in such a way that the denotation of (S) depends upon what is put into that class. If a "new" object is introduced into the class, (S) may change its denotation. It is this feature that Poincaré found crucial. He was thus led to distinguish predicative classifications from nonpredicative ones: predicative classifications are those that cannot be "disordered" by the introduction of new elements; nonpredicative classifications are those that are altered or disordered by the introduction of new elements ([67], p. 47). Thus, we can imagine ourselves classifying natural numbers into two categories,

D: those definable in fewer than 100 English words; and
N: those not so definable.

We proceed by first ordering in some way the English sentences of fewer than 100 words, and then going through the list picking out those that uniquely specify some natural number. Suppose we then come upon the sentence (S). In this case, according to Poincaré's analysis of the situation, we would be unable to determine which natural number should be assigned to this sentence until we had finished the job of sorting the natural numbers into the two categories D and N, for we need the fixed totality N to pick out its least element; on the other hand, we would be unable to finish the sorting so long as we had not yet determined which natural number should be assigned to those sentences whose "denotation" depends upon having a definite separation of natural numbers into categories D and N.

Notice that the above sense of nonpredicativity is distinct from Russell's. We thus have two senses of impredicativity to deal with.[3] However, I do not believe Poincaré's distinction between predicative and nonpredicative classifications is very clear. I suspect that it was hastily conceived in response to adverse criticism of his first diagnosis of the paradoxes. It is certainly not obvious why definitions classified as impredicative by Russellian standards should also be classified as nonpredicative in Poincaré's sense. Yet Poincaré also rejected these Russellian impredicative definitions as being viciously circular. This is indicated by the approval he gives to Russell's treatment of the paradoxes, by his examples of nonpredicative classifications, and also by the fact that he brands definitions of the following sort as viciously circular ([67], p. 70):

(1) We define X by postulating both that X is related in such and such a way to all the members of G and also that X is, itself, a member of G.

(2) We define Y by postulating that Y is related in such and such a way to X, that X is related in such and such a way to all the members of G, and finally that Y is, itself, a member of G.

[3] Recent work by mathematical logicians (notably Kreisel and Feferman) suggests there is an interesting connection between the two senses of impredicativity. See, in this connection, Feferman [27].

Before exploring Poincaré's reasons for treating such definitions as viciously circular, it would be well to look more carefully at Poincaré's distinction between predicative and nonpredicative classifications. In his statement of the distinction there is a curious phrase, which certainly bears investigation. What, we might ask, is meant by "introduce new elements"? Consider the example Poincaré gives of a predicative classification. We are to suppose that we have somehow defined only the natural numbers less than 100 and that, in some sense, the class of natural numbers increases as we define new ones. Now we can classify the natural numbers into two classes: those less than 10 and those greater than or equal to 10. This classification will not be disordered, he tells us, when we "introduce" 101, 102, 103, ..., and hence the classification is said to be predicative. Evidently, when we "introduce" new natural numbers we are supposed to add to the collection of natural numbers, so that somehow the class of natural numbers greater than 10 grows with each addition. But the classification is held to be predicative because those natural numbers *that have already been defined* do not shift from one category to the other with the addition of new natural numbers: the growth of the class of natural numbers greater than 10 does not necessitate any change in our classification of the natural numbers less than 10. As an example of a nonpredicative classification, we are asked to consider a classification of points in space into those that can be defined in a finite number of English words and those that cannot. Now some definitions will refer to all the points in space, and of these Poincaré writes:

> When we introduce new points in space, these sentences will change in meaning, they will no longer define the same point; or they will lose all meaning; or else they will acquire a meaning although they did not have any previously. And then points which were not definable will become capable of being defined; others which were definable will cease to be definable. They will have to change from one category into another. The classification will not be predicative ([67], pp. 47-48).

In response to this, one might ask: What precisely does 'introduce new points in space' mean? And why is a new point supposed to come into existence when it is introduced? What sort of thing is a point in space supposed to be that it can spring into existence just by being introduced or defined in some sense? Certainly, a Platonist would not accept such an analysis. Indeed it became evident to Poincaré that he could not convince a Platonist of the wrongness of impredicative classifications and specifications so long as the person remained a Platonist; this is one reason why he adopted the strategy of placing the dispute over the acceptability of impredicative definitions into the context of a general dispute about the nature of mathematics—a dispute between two schools of thought, one of which he called the 'Cantoreans' and the other—to which he, himself, belonged—the 'Pragmatists' (cf., [67], pp. 65-66).

Now from the pragmatist's point of view, the above definition of X in terms of G is viciously circular because it "is not possible to define X without knowing all the members of the genus G, and consequently without knowing X which is one of these members" ([67], p. 70). At first sight, this bit of reasoning seems lacking in logical coherence. Why should it be impossible to define X without *knowing* all the members of G? After all, to use Ramsey's example, one can define 'the tallest living person' as follows:

T is the tallest living person if, and only if,
a) T is taller than every other living person;
b) T is, itself, a living person.

There seems to be no good reason for supposing that this definition presupposes that we *know* all living persons. It is obvious that we must investigate further Poincaré's pragmatism if we are to gain any real understanding of his reasons for rejecting these impredicative definitions.

2. *Poincaré's Kantian and Operationalistic Tendencies*

Poincaré philosophized in a period in which the analytic-synthetic distinction and the *a priori–a posteriori* distinction were, for the most part, taken for granted. The Kantian question "Are there synthetic *a priori* propositions?" was considered live and important, challenging some of the best philosophers of the period. Poincaré, himself, took an active part in the controversies surrounding the logicists' claim that the true propositions of arithmetic are analytic, and not synthetic as Kant had thought. It is well known that Poincaré took the opposing position.

Poincaré never, to my knowledge, gave definitions of such terms as 'analytic' or 'synthetic', but it would seem that what he had in mind was similar to Frege's distinction. Roughly, the analytic sentences (or propositions) were held to be those that can be proved to be true using only logic and the definitions of the words or symbols used. Any true sentence (or proposition) that was not analytic was held to be synthetic. Poincaré also accepted the traditional *a priori–a posteriori* distinction: he distinguished truths (true statements, propositions, judgements, and so forth) known by means of experience and experiment from those known solely through deductive reason and intuition. Poincaré followed Kant in holding that there are some things we know through intuition, as for example that mathematical induction is a valid inference form and that certain axioms are true; he was thus Kantian to the extent that he believed in *a priori* knowledge of synthetic truths, and more specifically in thinking that arithmetical truths are synthetic *a priori* ([67], p. 43). But Poincaré did not agree with Kant's thesis that Euclidean geometry is synthetic *a priori*: as we shall see, Poincaré regarded the "statements" of geometry as being neither analytic nor synthetic.

To get a clearer idea of Poincaré's notion of *a posteriori* knowledge, it is worth noting Poincaré's view of experiment: "The experimenter puts to nature a question: Is it this or that? and he can not put it without imagining the two terms of the alternative. If it were impossible to imagine one of these terms, it would be futile and besides impossible to consult experience" ([63], p. 41). These words may bring to mind Hume's statement to the effect that the negation or contrary of any matter of fact is always conceivable. Of course many contemporary philosophers would disagree with this characterization of experiment; and I realize that many others would find the notion of *imaginability* too vague for fruitful discussion to be possible. It is clear that all of the above distinctions presupposed in Poincaré's writings would be questioned by some philosophers today. However, I do not wish to become involved in a discussion of the difficulties, raised by Quine and others, in making sense of, say, the analytic–synthetic distinction. It is enough for my purposes to sketch the framework within which Poincaré philosophized.

Determining whether a given sentence is analytic is not simply an exercise in logic, even if the sentence were known to be true, for where is one to find the relevant definitions of the terms in the sentence? In the controversial cases, as for example '5 + 7 = 12', there is generally widespread disagreement as to the correctness or adequacy of the various definitions proposed. Most of these controversial cases involve terms or words which we all seem to learn without being given any explicit, clearcut, definitions; so we are faced with problems very similar to those implicit in Russell's attempts to find a "true solution" of the paradoxes, discussed in Chapter I. Poincaré evidently believed that, in the case of many of these crucial terms, our usage reveals that we have *implicitly adopted* definitions of the terms; furthermore, he thought that by analysis we could discover what these definitions are. Thus, in attempting to explicate what is meant by 'happened at the same time' or 'simultaneity', Poincaré wrote: "To understand the definition implicitly supposed by the savants, let us watch them at work and look for the rules by which they investigate simultaneity. . . ."

When an astronomer tells me that some stellar phenomenon, which his telescope reveals to him at this moment, happened nevertheless fifty years ago, I seek his meaning, and to that end I shall ask him first how he knows it, that is, how he has measured the velocity of light" ([63], p. 30, 39). The above quotation also reveals an important feature of Poincaré's method of uncovering these "implicit definitions": time and again he asks, How do we know? How do we tell? What criteria do we use? Meaning, for Poincaré, is intimately connected with verification, ways of telling, and measurement. Thus, in discussing the notion of *force*, Poincaré wrote: "For a definition to be of any use it must tell us how to measure force" ([66], p. 98). And in analyzing the notion of point in space, he asked: "What do I mean when I say the object B is at the point which a moment before was occupied by the object A? Again, what criteria will enable me to recognize it?" ([66], p. 85).

Given this orientation, it is not surprising that Poincaré frequently gave "operationalistic" analyses of statements. As an example, consider the following quotation:

> When I shall say there is running in this circuit a current of so many amperes, that will mean: if I adapt to this circuit such a galvanometer I shall see the spot come to the division a; but that will mean equally: if I adapt to this circuit such an electrodynamometer, I shall see the spot go to the division b. And that will mean still many other things, because the current can manifest itself not only by mechanical effects, but by effects chemical, thermal, luminous, etc. ([63], p. 119).

The operationalistic tendencies are revealed even more strikingly by Poincaré's analysis of the notion of time. Poincaré held that physicists and astronomers apply a multitude of different rules for measuring time, depending on the particular case at hand, and thus make use of a variety of *definitions* of time ([63], p. 36). He thought that sometimes the physicist uses a definition in which all the beats of the pendulum are of equal duration, and that at other times the physicist supposed "by a new definition substituted for that based on the beats of the pendulum, that two complete rotations of the earth about its axis have the same duration" ([63], pp. 27, 28). According to Poincaré, "there is not one way of measuring time more true than another; that which is generally adopted is only more *convenient*" ([63], p. 30). Poincaré once expressed his philosophical position on time paradoxically by saying that the properties of time are "merely those of our clocks just as the properties of space are merely those of the measuring instruments" ([67], p. 18).

So despite Poincaré's strongly Kantian views regarding arithmetic and the existence of synthetic *a priori* intuitions, his philosophical outlook has many points in common with the "empiricism" of logical positivism and operationalism. Like the positivists and operationalists, Poincaré implicitly adopted a kind of *verification principle of meaning*. He considered the phrase 'absolute space' to be "completely devoid of meaning" ([65], p. 93). Why? Because he thought that we lacked any means of determining positions in absolute space, of verifying statements involving absolute position, and the like. "Not only can we not know the absolute position of an object in space, so that this phrase 'absolute position of an object' has no meaning ... but the phrases 'absolute size of an object' and "absolute distance between two points" have no meaning" ([67], p. 16). According to Poincaré, those who accept the notion of absolute space believe it is conceivable that everything in the universe might grow a thousand times larger in such a way "that the world would remain similar to itself"—an incomprehensible notion, in Poincaré's view of things, since the described event would be undetectable, our measuring standards, by hypothesis, having changed proportionately to everything else ([65], p. 94).

In attempting to understand Poincaré's philosophy of mathematics, it is especially important to take account of these empiricistic features of his overall philosophical view. (Perhaps this goes without saying, but compare the way logicians have been explicating Poincaré's concept of set.) As we shall see, a version of the verification principle is used in Poincaré's justification of his "no-infinity" theory and in his arguments against the Cantoreans or Platonists. And the operationalistic outlook certainly lies behind the following contention:

> Every mathematical theorem must be capable of verification. When I state this theorem, I assert that all the verifications of it which I shall attempt will succeed; and even if one of these proofs requires efforts which exceed the capability of a man, I assert that, if many generations, one hundred if need be, deem it appropriate to undertake this verification, it will still succeed. The theorem has no other meaning ([67], p. 62).

The above thesis is obscure in so far as the notion of verification is left obscure. This unclarity in the notion of verification generally presents a problem to one assessing the claims of verificationists, but the problem here is complicated by the fact that Poincaré, at times at least, regarded verification in mathematics to be something quite distinct from proof. There is a suggestion that what is proved by a proof is more general than the premises, requiring the use of mathematical induction for its proof, whereas what is verified by a verification is something particular like $2 + 2 = 4$ or $2 + (3 + 7) = (2 + 3) + 7$. From the examples he gives, I would suppose that the usual proofs given of the binomial theorem would be considered genuine proofs by Poincaré and not verifications, whereas a proof that a particular instance of the theorem holds, say,

$$(3 + 7)^4 = (3)^4 + 4(3)^3(7) + 6(3)^2(7)^2 + 4(3)(7)^3 + (7)^4$$

using only logic and the definitions of '1', '2', '3',... '+' and '×', would be considered a verification. It would seem that one *proves* general theorems and *verifies* particular instances of the theorem; one can verify a general theorem only in so far as one can verify a particular instance of the theorem (cf. [66], pp. 4, 10).

But this is all very rough and unclear. Another difficulty we run up against in trying to understand Poincaré's thesis about the content of mathematical theorems is the obscurity of what he means when he talks about the *success of attempted verifications*. The binomial theorem surely does not assert or even imply that every attempted verification will actually succeed: if Johnny Jones attempts to verify the above instance of the theorem and fails, we are not going to reject the theorem.

We can give a more sympathetic interpretation to Poincaré's thesis: we can take Poincaré to be asserting that every mathematical theorem makes a conditional statement of the following form:

> If one performs operation α, β, γ, ...
> then one will get results X, Y, Z, ...

Interpreted in this way, the thesis would be more in keeping with Poincaré's operationalistic inclinations. Then we can understand an "attempted verification" to be the actual performance of operations specified by the theorem, so that if one gets the results the theorem says one should get, the verification can be said to "succeed." A proof of the theorem, then, would prove that verifications must succeed. On this view, the binomial theorem says that for integers a, b, and $n(n > 0)$, if one takes the nth power of the sum of a and b, one will get the number one gets by taking the nth power of a, adding the product of $n!/(n-1)!$, the $(n-1)$ power of a, and the first power of b, then adding.... An "attempted verification" would then consist in actually (correctly) carrying out the specified operations for given a, b, and n. Even so interpreted, Poincaré's thesis will not be convincing to most philosophers—certainly not until it is shown in detail how mathematical theorems can be understood as asserting such conditional statements. I shall return to this point later on.

3. *Poincaré's Anti-Platonic Views on the Nature of Mathematics*

Poincaré's philosophy of mathematics can best be viewed as an expression of an anti-Platonist, empiricist attitude toward mathematics. Poincaré was convinced that the nature of mathematics could be understood without assuming the existence of what he would have considered occult objects. (In this, Poincaré was diametrically opposed to the views I have attributed to Gödel and Quine). Thus, like the later Wittgenstein, he continually attempted to explain mathematics in terms of the activities of the mathematician and scientist. He asked: What does the mathematician provide the physicist? He answered: a language. He asked: How can the mathematician gain knowledge without performing the sorts of experiments the physicist performs? How can "thought experiments" take the place, in mathematics, of experiments with instruments? He answered: Because the mathematician is not dealing with objects "external to him" as the Platonist thinks, but only with his own constructions. I wish now to examine some of the more important of Poincaré's anti-Platonic doctrines.

3.1 *The meaning of 'exist' in mathematics*. Poincaré's operationalistic tendencies also lie behind his contention that, in mathematics, the word "exists" does not mean what it does in physics or in ordinary everyday contexts: after all existence assertions are not verified or justified by mathematicians in the way they are by physicists. What, then, does the word 'exist' mean in mathematics? Poincaré adopted a position that, at one time, seems to have been popular. He claimed that the word "signifies exemption from contradiction"; he also said that it *means* "to be free from contradiction" ([65], p. 152, p. 180). Despite these apparently straightforward statements, Poincaré's actual position regarding "existence" is not straightforward. Surely he could not have thought that, in purely mathematical contexts, we ought to regard the word 'exist' as being *synonymous* with 'is free from contradiction'. Obviously, to say that a solution to such and such an equation *exists* is not to say that a solution to the equation is free from contradiction.

The following statements shed further light on what Poincaré is driving at. "The word 'existence' has not the same meaning when it refers to a mathematical entity as when it refers to a material object. A mathematical entity exists provided there is no contradiction implied in its definition, either in itself, or with the propositions previously admitted" ([66], p. 44). This quotation suggests that Poincaré was not attempting to give an account of what 'exist' means in all mathematical contexts. Notice that he speaks of the *definition* of the mathematical entity which is said to exist. The account seems hardly applicable to statements of the existence of solutions. Or consider the statement that for any set of natural numbers, there exists another set of which it is a member. Clearly, Poincaré's account does not apply to such statements since there is no specific definition to be examined for consistency.

A further problem raised by Poincaré's statements regarding mathematical existence is that they seem to contradict his position on impredicative definitions of sets: it would seem that he should allow the existence of all impredicatively defined sets so long as the definition is consistent. With these difficulties in mind, I shall turn to Poincaré's nominalism before attempting to explicate his position on mathematical existence.

3.2 *Mathematics as a language.* Another idea that Poincaré put forward in some of his writings is expressed by the dictum: Science speaks the language of mathematics. Like the dictum, 'exist' in mathematics means 'to be free from contradiction', the claim above has been advanced many times (it goes back at least as far as Galileo); but it has rarely, if ever, been investigated or analyzed in depth even though it is in need of clarification. On the face of it, it is absurd to suppose that mathematics is literally a language like English or German. As I mentioned above, Poincaré completely rejected the Platonist's picture of the mathematician as the investigator and discoverer of properties of supra-sensible abstract entities. In Poincaré's view, the mathematician only constructs "languages" and "systems of symbols," guided sometimes by practical needs and at other times by a kind of sense of aesthetics ([63], p. 77). Yet these languages and systems turn out to be extremely useful—indeed at times absolutely necessary—for progress in science.

Poincaré's nominalistic views regarding geometry are more definite primarily because he supplies us with more details. He tells us that geometry, too, "gives us a very convenient language," and that the formation of this language was suggested by all sorts of practical considerations and experiments connected with our ideas of space ([65], p. 43). He thought that we develop our ideas of space by investigating the relationships that obtain between "solid bodies," where our own bodies, straight edges, compasses, measuring instruments of all sorts, and telescopes, are classified as "solid bodies" ([67], p. 16-17). From the operationalist point of view, we get different definitions of distance, length, straight line, and the like, when we take different measuring procedures and measuring instruments as our standards. But since all our measuring instruments are imperfect, we must allow for the possibility of improving them. And since we do not wish to alter our ideas of space with each improvement and redefinition, we *idealize*: we construct a language in which we talk about ideal points, lines, planes, and figures, and this talk is similar to our talk about actual solid bodies in space.

> And then we shall say that geometry is the study of a set of laws hardly different from those which our instruments really obey but much more simple, laws which do not effectively govern any natural object but which can be conceived by the mind. In this sense, geometry is a convention, a sort of rough compromise between our love for simplicity and our desire not to go too far astray from what our instruments teach us. This convention defines both space and the perfect instrument ([67], pp. 17-18).

Experience, however, plays an important role in prompting and guiding us to construct this "language." Experience also prompts us to adopt this "language" over other choices: it is, for most purposes in everyday life, more convenient to use than other geometries ([66], pp. 70-71). But the theorems of geometry are not held to be experimental truths; the axioms are not synthetic-*a posteriori*. Nor did Poincaré think that the axioms are necessary truths; rather, he held that they are not truths at all but "definitions in disguise" of 'point', 'line', etc. ([66], p. 50).

Some may wonder how such a language could be so tremendously useful to scientists. The above quotation hints at an answer. We have a language in which we talk about certain "ideal" entities that have make-believe properties and relationships similar, in certain respects, to those of actual physical entities but far simpler and more easily described. The make-believe relationships are not relationships that we might discover in the physical universe—they are not given the necesssary operational definitions—although we do have in the back of our heads the similar physical relationships such as straight-ness, length, equidistance, and the like, that have been defined operationally. This make-believe world is given a far simpler, more precise, characterization than we can give of the real world, and we use this make-believe world as a kind of *standard of comparison* "to which we shall refer natural phenomena" ([66], p. 70).[4]

Poincaré provides us with examples that illustrate and clarify this view of geometry ([63]). Suppose, he tells us, we have two solid bodies, A and B, which are displaced with slight deformation. The relationships that obtain between A and B are extremely complicated; but we introduce the ideal entities A' and B', so-called *rigid bodies*, for which the laws of relative displacement (geometrical laws) are very simple. We thus divide the one big problem of describ-ing the complex relationships that obtain between A and B into separate, smaller problems: How does A differ from A', B from B'? And how is A' related to B'? The latter question is relatively easy to answer, since the laws of displacement of these figures are simple, and it is answered by the geometer. On the other hand, we have chosen A' and B' to be similar to A and B respectively, so that we can, as Poincaré puts it,

> add that the body A, which always differs very little from A', dilates from the effect of heat and bends from the effect of elasticity. These dilations and flexions, just because they are very small, will be for our mind relatively easy to study. Just imagine to what complexities of language it would have been

---

[4] There is an obvious similarity between the view I attribute to Poincaré here and Hilbert's doctrine of ideal elements in mathematics. See Hilbert, [43].

> necessary to be resigned if we had wished to comprehend in the same enunciation the displacement of the solid, its dilatation and its flexure ? ([63], p. 125).

The following quotation illustrates still further the role that Poincaré attributes to geometry: "This language causes us to give the same name to things which resemble one another, and states analogies which it does not allow us to forget. . . . it is the analogy with what is simple that enables us to understand what is complex." ([65], p. 43).

As I suggested above, Poincaré's views on arithmetic, analysis and set theory are more obscure. In these cases too, the mathematician supposedly constructs a language in which certain symbols only seem to denote independently existing entities; furthermore, it is suggested that numbers are merely symbols. "Kronecker," Poincaré tells us, "gives the name of incommensurable number to a simple symbol—that is to say, something very different from the idea we think we ought to have of a quantity which should be measurable and almost tangible" ([66], p. 20). According to Poincaré, the mathematical continuum, itself, is only a "system of symbols" ([66], p. 27).

As for the importance for the physicist of this "language" of mathematical analysis, Poincaré is more explicit. He claims, first of all, that the language enables the physicist to state empirical laws which he otherwise could not state: "Ordinary language is too poor, it is besides too vague, to express relations so delicate, so rich, and so precise" ([63], p. 76). Besides this, Poincaré also claims for the language an essential role in scientific discovery: it enables the scientist to see analogies which would be utterly beyond the discernment of a man completely lacking languages of this sort (such a man would not dream of "likening light to radiant heat") ([63], p. 77). Poincaré gave several examples to show how mathematical analogies may enable us to discern physical analogies, but I shall quote here only the following.

> The very same equation, that of Laplace, is met in the theory of Newtonian attraction, in that of the motion of liquids, in that of the electric potential, in that of magnetism, in that of the propagation of heat and in still many others. What is the result ? These theories seem images copied one from the other;

they are mutually illuminating, borrowing their language from each other; ask electricians if they do not felicitate themselves on having invented the phrase, flow of force, suggested by hydrodynamics and the theory of heat ([63], p. 79).

Thus, in speaking of mathematical analysis, Poincaré says: "It can give to the physicist only a convenient language; is this not a mediocre service, which, strictly speaking, could be done without...? Far from it; without this language most of the intimate analogies of things would have remained forever unknown to us" ([63], p. 13).

When it is said that mathematics provides physicists with a convenient language or that physics speaks the language of mathematics, I believe the speaker has in mind primarily the fact that the physicist makes use of the notation, symbolism, and especially the *concepts* of mathematics in formulating his laws, in describing the physical world, and in representing physical states and processes.[5] However, it does seem to me misleading to say, as Poincaré says above, that mathematics can give to the physicist *only* a language; for this suggests that the "truths" or theorems of mathematics can be of no use to the physicist. Surely, the mathematician's theorems, no less than his concepts, are invaluable to the physicist. One could argue, as did Wittgenstein, that making use of the concepts of mathematics involves making use of the theorems of mathematics—that the theorems are, themselves, part of the "conceptual machinery" the physicist makes use of in using mathematics. But to make this vague idea at all plausible would require a much fuller discussion than I care to indulge in at this point.[6]

Given Poincaré's views on geometry, the reader might suppose that he regarded statements of arithmetic and set theory to be, like those of Euclidean geometry, neither true nor false. But, as I said before, Poincaré defended Kant's thesis that there are synthetic *a priori* true arithmetical statements. Poincaré did not, moreover, treat set theory as a mere game played with symbols, nor did he picture set theory as simply consisting of a formal language containing primitive terms that are defined by the axioms. For example,

[5] Cf. Wigner [120], p. 130.
[6] Cf. Chihara [14].

one of his objections to Zermelo's set theory was that the axioms did not seem to him to be true ([67], pp. 58-60). For Poincaré, set theory is concerned with classifications of things, and he felt that any solution of the paradoxes should take account of the nature of this activity of classifying.

Unfortunately, many aspects of Poincaré's views on the nature of sets are obscure. Even if it makes sense to say, and even if it is true to say, "the mathematical continuum is only a system of symbols," and "numbers are only symbols," this does not decide the question, "Are classes of numbers only symbols too?" Given Poincaré's other philosophical beliefs, one would expect Poincaré to give an affirmative answer. Poincaré's nominalism certainly suggests as much. But nowhere does he attempt to provide an actual "reduction" of class talk into symbol talk. No doubt, this is a weakness in Poincaré's philosophy of mathematics; but I shall not pursue this difficulty here since in a later chapter I shall show how such a reduction can be carried out in accordance with the philosophical principles that are extracted in this chapter.

3.3 *Infinity*. In the previous chapter, we examined reasons for holding that there are certain nonphysical, nonspatial, abstract entities, which mathematicians study, called sets. Once one accepts such a position, it would be natural to hold that there are infinitely many, indeed nondenumerably many, such entities; this would be to accept what Poincaré called the 'actual infinite'. Belief in "actual infinities" is so closely tied to belief in the actual existence of sets that it is not surprising to find Poincaré including both beliefs in his characterization of the Cantoreans or Platonists; and at times, it is not clear whether he even distinguished Platonism in the sense of the previous chapter from belief in the actual infinite (see [67], p. 73). Not surprisingly, Poincaré rejects the belief that there actually exists an infinite number of entities of any kind as superstitious and unscientific. One sometimes gets the impression from the writings of some logicians that Poincaré rejected only certain sorts of actual completed infinities (see Feferman [27], p. 2). But this is clearly not the case. He does not say "There is no actual infinity save that of the natural numbers"; on the contrary, he tells us "There is no actual infinity" ([65], p. 195; also [67], p. 47).

Rejection of the actual infinite is, of course, not a new idea: it is clearly found in some of the ancient Greeks. Even the position he chooses—the doctrine of the potential infinite—is at least as old as Aristotle. But despite this rich heritage, Poincaré's own view of infinity is obscure. He describes his "pre-Cantorean" view in these words: "Mathematical infinity was only a quantity susceptible of growing beyond all limit; it was a variable quantity of which it could not be said that it *had passed*, but only that it *would pass*, all limits" ([65], p. 143). From this quotation, one might gather that Poincaré was primarily thinking of the use of such expressions as 'infinity' and '∞' in connection with functions and limits. Thus,

$$\lim_{x \to b} f(x) = \infty$$

does not say that the function, f(x), takes the value ∞ for argument b: it merely says that for every positive number B, there is a number δ such that the value of the function is greater than or equal to B for every argument x satisfying the condition

$$0 < |x - b| < \delta.$$

Clearly, in such statements, there is no need to *refer* to an infinite number or an infinite value (cf. [67], p. 66). However, even Poincaré refers to the class of natural numbers; and we surely do not wish to say that this set contains only finitely many members. So if the set is, in some sense, *infinite*, can we analyze its infinity into a statement to the effect that the quantity of its elements is a "variable quantity" growing beyond all limits? Let us turn to the following statement for enlightenment: "There is no actual infinity, and when we speak of an infinite collection, we understand a collection to which we can add new elements unceasingly (similar to a subscription list which would never end, waiting for new subscribers)" ([67], p. 47). Here Poincaré reiterates his view that no set (not even the set of natural numbers), should be regarded as actually infinite. If we take him literally, it would seem that, on his view, sets are really finite, but somehow growing without finite limit. But does such a view make sense? My first reaction is to say, "It doesn't make obvious sense." If the set of natural numbers is only a finite but potentially limitless set, how many members does it now have? And if the set of natural numbers is growing in membership, how fast does it grow? If these questions make no sense, why not? Obviously to understand Poincaré's doctrine of the potential infinite, we shall have to find some less literal interpretation of his views.

One way of interpreting Poincaré's statements about infinity immediately suggests itself—especially in view of the example of Russell's "no-class" theory, discussed in Chapter I. Perhaps Poincaré held that we ought to be able to *analyze* all statements about infinite sets into statements about finite sets to which we can add new elements unceasingly. Perhaps, in other words, Poincaré's doctrine of the "potential infinite" essentially boils down to a "no-infinity" theory. This interpretation gains in plausibility from the fact that Poincaré boldly adopted a "no-infinity" theory: he maintained that every statement about "infinity must be the translation, the precise statement of propositions concerning the finite" ([67], p. 63).

The justification he gives for this surprising position, however, is disappointing. He does not, as Russell did in the case of his "no-class" theory, show us how the relevant translations are to be actually carried out; he merely bases his justification on the verification principle of meaning: "But since verification can apply only to finite numbers, it follows that every theorem concerning infinite sets, or transfinite cardinals, or transfinite ordinals, etc., etc., can only be a concise manner of stating propositions about finite numbers. If it is otherwise, this theorem will not be verifiable, and if it is not verifiable, it will be meaningless" ([67], p. 62).

In response to this argument, a number of objections could be raised. First, one might object that the argument is obscure and unconvincing because Poincaré does not state clearly what a verification is. Second, one might ask: Why can only theorems about the finite be verified? I do not know why Poincaré was so confident that verifiable mathematical statements do not involve or "concern" infinite sets, numbers, and the rest: this is not, I believe, self-evident. Third, even granting Poincaré his point regarding the verifiability of only statements about the finite, many philosophers today would place little confidence in a position supported by so abused and so controversial a principle as the verification principle. In fact, showing that a particular philosophical justification rests on the verification principle is now regarded in certain circles as showing that the "justification" is no justification at all.

But despite these and other objections that can be raised against Poincaré's argument, there is something attractive about the position: even Platonists would welcome the availability of such translations. It should be recalled that some philosophers only accept Platonism after losing hope in the possibility of a nominalistic reduction (see chapter III). How disappointing it is, then, to find that Poincaré did not provide us with any method for translating the meaningful statements concerning infinite sets and numbers into statements about finite sets and numbers.

One might take the attitude that a method of effecting such a finitary translation is unnecessary on the grounds that by 'meaningful mathematical theorem', Poincaré just meant "theorem translatable into one concerning the finite": it would be simply *analytic*, to use the traditional category that every meaningful mathematical theorem is translatable into a statement concerning the finite, so one would not have to show by actual translations that the thesis is true. Such a reply would be deeply unsatisfying for several reasons. It would trivialize Poincaré's claims to the point of irrelevance and insignificance. Besides this, it is clear that Poincaré applied the term 'meaningless' to statements that he thought should be excluded from mathematics. So one wants to have some idea of the consequences of accepting the "no-infinity" theory. In particular, one would like to know how much of mathematics would be "meaningful," that is, translatable into the finite. Now there is no doubt that Poincaré was willing to throw out as illogical or meaningless some parts of mathematics: the vicious-circle principle implies this. But who would follow a philosopher who thought practically all of mathematics should be discarded as meaningless? So I repeat: Poincaré does not show how we are to translate the mathematical theorems that he considered meaningful into statements about the finite, and this is no small defect of his "no-infinity" theory. However, I shall leave further discussion of this lacuna in Poincaré's philosophy of mathematics for a later chapter, where an actual method will be supplied for translating theorems about infinite sets into statements involving only finitely many things.

There is another aspect of Poincaré's position regarding infinity that calls for some discussion. In a number of places, Poincaré says that infinite collections are to be understood in terms of the possibility of constructing (or "creating") as many elements of the collection as we wish (cf. [67], p. 72). This, of course, is one reason one wants to attribute the doctrine of the potential infinite to Poincaré. Now some unsympathetic Platonist might object: "Well, so long as we don't *wish* to construct very many natural numbers, Poincaré ought to regard the set of natural numbers less than a billion as being infinite." This silly objection needs no reply, but it raises a related objection which is more interesting and considerably more penetrating. This objection, which hinges on the tricky notion of *possibility*, was anticipated by Poincaré in connection with his thesis that in mathematics one should consider only objects which *can be* defined in a finite number of words. Poincaré observed that no living person can possibly utter more than a billion words in his lifetime; yet even he did not think that we ought to exclude from mathematics objects whose definitions contain a billion and one words. The reason he gives for this is: "However talkative a man may be, mankind will be still more talkative and, since we do not know how long mankind will last, we cannot limit beforehand the field of its investigations." ([67], pp. 66-67) Now if we allow this sort of "idealization," why not go a step further and reason in terms of some superman who can define objects using an infinite number of words in a finite length of time?[7] Poincaré's answer is not satisfactory: he simply asserts that the pragmatists "refuse to argue on the hypothesis of some infinitely talkative divinity capable of thinking of an infinite number of words in a finite length of time" ([67], p. 67). But behind this refusal to reason from the hypothesis of the infinitely talkative god there do seem to be some plausible intuitions. I sympathize with those who feel that the impossibility of uttering (even in the sense of saying *to oneself*) an infinite number of words in a finite amount of time is a stronger kind of impossibility than that

[7] Cf. C. Parson, [59], p. 202.

of uttering a billion words in a lifetime, and yet I do not know how to make such feelings or intuitions at all precise. One wants to say that the former, and not the latter, is a *conceptual* impossibility, except that no one has succeeded in giving an adequate definition of 'conceptual impossibility'.

Many philosophers have argued that performing an infinite number of distinct acts, where saying a word to oneself would be considered a distinct act, is a *logical* impossibility, and have attempted to *prove* that the hypothesis that some being has succeeded in performing such an act leads to an outright contradiction. So far as I know, all such attempts have been failures.[8] Some philosophers have argued on the other side claiming that it is only physically or "medically" impossible to perform such infinite acts in a finite amount of time. Taking his cue from Zeno, Russell argued that it is *logically* possible for some super-being to perform such acts, for example, by saying to himself the first natural number at exactly one half minute after midnight, the second natural number at exactly three quarters of a minute after midnight, and in general, the nth natural number at exactly $(2^n - 1)/2^n$ th of a minute after midnight; by continuing this until exactly one minute after midnight, he would have succeeded in uttering to himself an infinite number of words in a finite amount of time. The trouble with this argument is that someone genuinely skeptical about the logical or conceptual possibility of such "infinite acts" can reply: "*If* it were logically possible to continue in the above way until one minute after midnight, then I agree it would be logically possible to perform an infinite number of acts in a finite amount of time—but what makes you think that's logically possible?"

The weakness can be made more evident by considering a slight variation on Russell's argument. One might argue that it is logically (or perhaps conceptually) possible that someone might have counted the natural numbers in reverse order and in a finite amount of time: he simply counted the number one at exactly half a minute after midnight, after having counted the number two at exactly one quarter of a minute after midnight, and in general, after having counted the

[8] See Chihara [15].

number n at exactly $(\frac{1}{2})^{nth}$ of a minute after midnight. Here again, I think that anyone initially skeptical about the conclusion of the argument will be skeptical about the logical possibility of someone's having carried out the above directions ("How did he even get started?")

A closely related argument for the logical possibility of such infinite acts makes use of Zeno's famous Paradox of Achilles. Suppose that Achilles travels from some point in space, which for reference purposes we shall call '0', to another point which we shall call '1'. Clearly, before traversing this whole distance, he must have first travelled half the distance. We can say that he travelled from 0 to $\frac{1}{2}$. Again before traversing the rest of the distance, he must have first travelled half the remaining distance, and so on *ad infinitum*. So in traveling from 0 to 1, Achilles must have travelled from 0 to 1/2, 1/2 to 3/4, 3/4 to 7/8, and so on *ad nauseum*. And if this is possible, then it is surely also logically possible to utter an infinite number of words in a finite amount of time. Can we not conceive of Zeus saying to himself "one" when Achilles traverses the first sub-interval, "two" when Achilles traverses the second sub-interval, and in general "n" when Achilles traverses the nth sub-interval, so that when Achilles arrives at his destination, Zeus will have counted all the natural numbers?

I do not believe that Poincaré ever addressed himself specifically to these questions (at least in print), but given his general philosophical views on mathematics and science we can imagine him replying in the following manner.

"Your description of Achilles' journey suggests to me that you are not talking about real things at all but idealized entities, mathematical points, lines, and intervals, which do not *exist* in the ordinary sense of the term. If, however, you are speaking of a conceivable journey in real physical space, then one can ask for an explication of what one means when one says "Achilles travelled from point a to b," that is, one can ask for the defining operations, tests, or criteria by which one is to determine when something travels from one point to another. Now no matter what operations are specified, using range finders, telescopes, interferometers, or even more sophisticated instruments, there will always be a limit to what can be meaningfully measured. So if, in the sentence 'Achilles must have travelled from 0 to 1/2, 1/2 to 3/4, 3/4 to 7/8, . . .', the ' . . . ' means 'and so on *ad infinitum*', I do not admit the truth of the sentence since, in my view, eventually you will have sentences like 'Achilles travelled from $1/2^{10^{10}}$ to $1/(2^{10^{10}} + 1)$' which can be seen to be meaningless once the defining operations are specified. I admit that someday even more accurate measuring devices may be developed in terms of which one could give sense to some of these sentences, but this would not essentially alter the situation since there would still be a limit to what could be measured and ascertained. (I am not claiming that there are specific limits to what humans can achieve in this direction—I just know that there will always be limits.)"[9]

This reply could be contested on various grounds, but since it would take us too far afield to pursue the question in detail, I shall stop here.

3.4 *Mathematical Induction*. According to Poincaré, the entities to be studied in mathematics are supposedly only those that are "constructed" by some definition. Now given that we are to form collections by "successive additions of new members" and even taking into account the fact that we can contruct "new objects by combining old objects," one may still wonder how one could ever obtain *infinite* sets in this manner. Furthermore one might wonder how any sort of general theory could be developed from such procedures. Poincaré evidently thought that mathematicians could extend their theories from the finite to the infinite by means of inductive definitions and proofs by mathematical induction— something he called 'reasoning by recurrence', which for him was "the only instrument which enables us to pass from the finite to the infinite" ([66], p. 11). As is so often the case, Poincaré did not

---

[9] The position I attribute to Poincaré, here, is similar to that espoused by Black where he claims that "common-sense language does not permit of reference to the *indefinitely* small" ([6], p. 126) and suggests that we should avoid the "assumption that each distinguishable item of the mathematical description must be in one-to-one correspondence with a distinguishable item of physical reality" (p. 125n). For some critical comments on Black's position, see Chihara [15].

provide us with an abundance of details, but there is no doubt that he thought "reasoning by recurrence" was mathematical reasoning *par excellence*. He was wholly unsympathetic with attempts to show that the validity of mathematical induction was deducible from the definition of 'natural number' (cf. Parsons, [59]). As I said before, Poincaré argued that mathematical induction can be justified neither by logic alone nor by experiment and yet is known to be valid by some sort of "intuition." Poincaré's discussion of this intuition is sketchy and incomplete, but in his writings there is the suggestion that our appeal to and acceptance of mathematical induction is connected with an insight we have into the operations of our own minds, especially the operation of performing "the same act" an indefinite number of times. This suggestion is connected with Poincaré's ontology: the synthetic *a priori* intuition is made possible by the fact that the mathematician, unlike the physicist, is dealing with his own mental or intellectual constructions and not things "external to him." I shall attempt to explicate this point of view later on in more detail.

3.5 *Poincaré's rejection of the nondenumerable*. Ordinarily one proves Cantor's theorem that the set of real numbers is nondenumerable by making use of impredicative specifications. In Chapter I, I mentioned that Russell was able to prove Cantor's theorem only by appealing to the axiom of reducibility, thus apparently deviating from his own vicious-circle principle. Poincaré, however, was more faithful to his principles: he rejected Cantor's proof on the grounds that impredicative specifications were used ([67], p. 61). Poincaré also denied the existence of nondenumerable sets and cardinal numbers greater than $\aleph_0$ ([67], p. 69). Of course, he pretty much committed himself to this course when he maintained that in mathematics one should consider as existing only objects which can be defined in a finite number of words. Poincaré saw that any set of finite sequences of French words, for example, must be denumerable, so that if there were nondenumerable sets, it would follow that some objects are not definable by a finite sequence of French words (cf. [67], pp. 61-62).

Although Poincaré rejected Cantor's theorem, he did allow that there was something true in the theorem. Suppose, he tells us, that we have defined some real numbers, the totality of which we shall call 'R', and also a law of correspondence, L, that is one-one between the members of R and the natural numbers; then Cantor has shown that we can always "disrupt this correspondence" in the sense that we can define a real number that does not correspond by L to any natural number (although, of course, this new real number would not be a member of R). So the only meaning Poincaré's "pragmatists" attach to the statement 'the power of the continuum is not the power of the integers', is that it is impossible to construct a set of real numbers and a law of correspondence (one-one between the set and the integers) that could not be disrupted in the above manner ([67], p. 68).[10]

4. A Reexamination of Poincaré's Rejection of Impredicative Definitions

In "The Logicist's Foundations of Mathematics," Carnap considers an example of an impredicatively defined "concept," the property of inductiveness, which is defined thus:

> x is inductive if and only if every hereditary property possessed by 0 is also possessed by x.

And he suggests that those philosophers who think that this definition is circular come to this belief because they reason as follows: to determine whether some number, say three, is inductive, it is necessary for us first to determine whether every property that is hereditary and possessed by zero is also possessed by three; so, in particular, it is necessary first to determine whether the property of inductiveness is possessed by three (this is essentially the very example Poincaré considers in [65], p. 191). The circularity of impredicative

---

[10] In [64], p. 196, Poincaré writes: "*Il est impossible de trouver une formule définissant en un nombre fini de mots une relation entre un nombre réel et un nombre entier et qui soit telle que tout nombre réel définissable en un nombre fini de mots corresponde à un nombre entier en vertu de cette formule.* Quelle que soit cette formule, on pourra toujours définir en un nombre fini de mots un nombre réel que cette formule ne fait correspondre à aucun nombre entier. Voilà ce que Cantor démontre et voilà ce qu'on entend quand on dit que la puissance du continu n'est pas celle de l'ensemble des entiers."

definitions resides, on this view, in the fact that to *determine* whether the definition is satisfied it is necessary to determine first whether the definition is satisfied. Carnap then replies to this bit of reasoning by arguing that the verification of a universal statement does not, in general, consist in examining individual cases, so the circularity is only apparent.

We saw in Chapter I that Russell did not argue for the vicious-circle principle in this way. Is there no more to Poincaré's rejection of impredicative definitions than what is indicated above? Let us investigate further.

We are now in a better position to discuss Poincaré's reasons for rejecting the sort of impredicative definitions that Russell rejected. Poincaré argued, it should be recalled, that if we define X by postulating that X is related in such and such a way to all the members of G and that X is itself a member of G, our definition is viciously circular. He reasoned that one could not define X without knowing all the members of G and hence X itself. To this we could reply that the definition does not presuppose that we literally know all the members of G, as the example of the tallest living man brings out. But one feature of the tallest man example should be noted: the definition of 'the tallest living man' in no sense creates or constructs the tallest living man; it merely singles out one living man as the tallest. On the other hand, it is clear that Poincaré was concerned in the present context only with definitions that he considered essentially *creative*, that is, definitions that enable one to refer to some new mathematical entity. This is why he says: "Knowledge of the genus does not result in your knowing all its members; it merely provides you with the possibility of constructing them all, or rather of constructing as many of them as you may wish. They will exist only after they have been constructed; that is, after they have been defined; X exists only by virtue of its definition" ([67], pp. 70-71). Here I should like to make three brief points. First, although most readers will have some intuitive notion of what 'a new mathematical entity' means, the phrase admittedly needs clarification. The following discussion may help a little, and the point will be taken up in more detail in a later chapter after we have developed some "machinery" for discussing the notion with more precision. Second, what Poincaré seems to be discussing here are mathematical theories in which true statements are made. Evidently, for the case of Euclidean geometry, the axioms of which Poincaré regarded as definitions in disguise, a different tack would be required. Third, at this point in the argument, Poincaré was describing the situation from his own operationalistic, "pragmatic" viewpoint, and he was not trying to convince the confirmed Platonist. It is clear that he had begun to view the dispute over the acceptability of impredicative definitions and specifications as one small, but intense, battle in a "global conflict" between two opposing philosophical views of mathematics. In order to understand Poincaré's reasoning, I suggest that we try to view Poincaré's arguments from the *inside*, so to speak, instead of trying to fit his statements into the Platonic mold of contemporary set theory or model theory.

The mathematician, according to Poincaré, constructs "languages." Just how this "construction" is supposed to take place, he did not make very clear. However, as Poincaré viewed the situation, the rules of these "languages" are such that many mathematicians regard certain mathematical symbols as denoting or referring to objects, and since these symbols evidently do not denote objects locatable in space, some come to believe that the symbols refer to nonspatial, abstract entities. Poincaré held that these beliefs are misleading, since they lead to the Platonic view, in which mathematics is thought to be a kind of physics of a suprasensible world. He also thought mathematicians are misled by these views into thinking a "creative definition" merely specifies which of the already existing mathematical objects some symbol is to denote. This is the source of the controversy over impredicative definitions, according to Poincaré. The Platonist allows impredicative definitions because he does not consider these definitions to be truly creative: he thinks the impredicative definition of X merely singles out one of the already existing members of G to be called 'X'. From Poincaré's "pragmatic" standpoint, however, this conception of pre-existing mathematical objects is simply nonsense: there do not exist both the symbols and the abstract entities denoted by the symbols; there are only the symbols, some of which we treat as if they referred to objects. Thus, when Poincaré says "They will exist only after they have been constructed; that is, after they have been defined, it would seem that he is not suggesting that the mathematical objects spring into existence when they are defined—I should think this would have been nonsensical to Poincaré ([67], pp. 70-71).

What he did have in mind I only dimly comprehend. However, I shall attempt to give here a *rough* explanation of Poincaré's reasoning. (I do not claim that my account would stand up under searching criticism or that it can be made precise in terms intelligible to present-day mathematical logicians.) Basically, the underlying idea seems to be that, in the context under discussion, the question of the existence of some mathematical entity must, in the final analysis, be a question of whether the "language" includes some symbol with the appropriate property. For Poincaré, the power of the mathematician to "create" entities boils down to a power to introduce new symbols into his language *via* definitions. Of course, this creative power was thought to be limited by a condition of adequacy: the creative definition must not destroy the system by a contradiction. So, given that a creative definition had been given, Poincaré felt that one could determine if the mathematical entity so defined existed simply by ascertaining whether the definition was consistent. I believe that some such consideration as this lies behind Poincaré's dictum that 'exist' has a different sense in mathematics from that found in ordinary life and that it signifies only freedom from contradiction. If so, it would be reasonable to infer that Poincaré did not think 'exist' in mathematics is synonymous with 'is free from contradiction' (synonymy is too strong a relation)—a conclusion that fits well with our preliminary thoughts on the subject. This interpretation also accords with our earlier conclusion that Poincaré was not attempting to give an explication of what 'exist' means in all mathematical contexts. Furthermore, it explains why he sometimes stated his dictum in terms of the *definition* of the entity in question. It also explains why Poincaré held that a set exists only after it has been defined and that it exists by virtue of its definition. One can see, to some extent, why he would not distinguish "constructing" a set from defining it. Poincaré's thesis regarding mathematical existence, then, is really a thesis about the "entities" that *are to be regarded as existing* in a mathematical system—it is a thesis about what entities one can, in a manner of speaking, "refer to," "talk about," "quantify over," and "define other symbols in terms of"; and the thesis is: they are the entities that have been (adequately) defined.

The position sketched here is connected with one of Poincaré's early comments on the set-theoretical paradoxes. "For my part," he said, "I think . . . that the important thing is never to introduce any entities but such as can be completely defined in a finite number of words" ([65], p. 45). This tentative idea was retained and developed, so that by the time he wrote the *Last Essays*, he was willing to make the stronger affirmation: "Is it possible to reason about objects which cannot be defined in a finite number of words? Is it possible even to speak of them and know what we are talking about and be saying other than empty words? Or, on the contrary, must they be regarded as inconceivable? As for me, I do not hesitate to reply that they are mere nothingness" (p. 60). Poincaré's position on set theory had solidified into one opposing the Cantorean view that he had previously described in these words: "One of the characteristic features of Cantorism is that, instead of rising to the general by erecting more and more complicated constructions, and defining by construction, it starts with the *genus supremum* and only defines, as the scholastics would have said, *per genus proximum et differentiam specificam*" ([65], p. 44). Clearly Poincaré would have rejected the present-day method of developing set theory by laying down axioms as to what sets exist. He thought set theory should be constructive: sets should be "introduced" by definitions into the system; and no sets should be taken as existing that had not been defined. One would rise to the general by erecting more and more complicated constructions: "A collection is formed by the successive additions of new members; we can construct new objects by combining old objects, then with these new objects construct newer ones" ([67], p. 67).

Given these philosophical beliefs, it is easy to see how one might adopt some form of the vicious-circle principle. One might reason that if some set X is to be defined in terms of the members of G, then these members of G must *exist* (that is, must have already been defined), so X cannot be one of these members. Thus, it would seem that Poincaré's philosophical beliefs regarding mathematical

existence, far from being inconsistent with his banning of impredicative definitions, form part of the very foundation of his vicious-
circle principle. Thus, when Poincaré wrote, "It is not possible
to define X without knowing all the members of the series G, and
consequently without knowing X, which is one of the members,"
what he must have been thinking is that the definition makes sense
only if there is some fixed totality consisting of all the members of G
and hence only if all the members of G, including X itself, had already
been defined. The latter is ruled out since the situation under consideration is supposedly that in which a "new entity" is being defined.

In Chapter I, we saw that in adopting his vicious-circle principle,
Russell was faced with serious problems in trying to reconstruct
mathematics within his system. Not surprisingly, Poincaré was
faced with similar problems. Poincaré, like Russell, did not wish to
be in the position of having to reject huge sections of classical
mathematics. It was generally accepted by mathematicians of Poincaré's time that one could prove that every algebraic equation
$F(x) = 0$ has a root by proving that the greatest lower bound of
the set of values of $|F(x)|$ belongs to this set and that the greatest
lower bound $= 0$. Since the definition of the greatest lower bound of
the set of values of $|F(x)|$ is impredicative, it would seem that the
rejection of impredicative definitions results in the rejection of a
proof admitted as valid by all classical mathematicians ([64], p. 199).
Poincaré suggested that the classical proof could be made acceptable
by replacing the impredicative definition with the definition of the
greatest lower bound e, of E, the set of values of $|F(y)|$, where y
ranges over only those numbers whose real and imaginary parts are
rational. One can then show that for some number r, $|F(r)| = e$,
and $e = 0$.

Notice that his procedure is in accord with the above principle of
constructing sets: only previously constructed sets are used in
defining the elements of new sets. Thus the rationals can all be
defined without referring to the set of all rationals. Having constructed the rationals, one can then construct the numbers whose
real and imaginary parts are rational, which yields a new set R.
Then, making use of the algebraic formula $F(y)$ and the previously
constructed set R, one can define the elements of E. Finally with E

constructed, one can define the greatest lower bound of E. The definition of e poses no danger of "disrupting" any of the above sets since they have all been previously defined.[11]

It is frequently said that ontology has no practical consequences. From the above discussion, it would seem that a philosopher's ontological views can have profound implications not only for those attempting to characterize the nature of mathematics, but even for the practicing mathematician. From a rejection of the Platonist's ontology, Poincaré came to advocate, in effect, a radical revision of actual mathematical practice. There were two stages in Poincaré's reasoning: first there was a rejection of the Platonist's picture of pre-existing mathematical entities waiting to be specified and studied; secondly, there was the creation of an alternative construc-tivistic view, which yielded as a consequence some kind of vicious-circle principle. However, much of Poincaré's reasoning remains unclear. For example, how are we to understand the puzzling process by which the mathematician's definitions "create" new entities?

---

[11] In [27], S. Feferman characterizes the "original sense of predicativity." He notes, quite correctly, that both Poincaré and Russell focused their attention on the role of impredicative definitions in the paradoxes. But he goes on to say "The more thoroughgoing critics, such as Weyl, rejected their use throughout mathematics" ([27], p. 3), implying that Poincaré, not being as thoroughgoing as Weyl, did not reject their use throughout mathematics. Whether this im-plication accurately applies to Russell is perhaps mooted by Russell's acceptance of the axiom of reducibility, but this is surely not a just characterization of Poincaré's attitude toward impredicative definitions. In another place, Feferman claims that "we can never speak sensibly (in the predicative conception) of the 'totality' of all sets as a 'completed totality' but only as a *potential totality* whose full content is never fully grasped but only realized in stages" ([27], p. 2). Here again, this description fits Russell's philosophical ideas much better than Poincaré's. Although Russell, unlike Poincaré, saw nothing intrinsically wrong with the notion of a completed infinite totality, he did think it was nonsense to speak of "all sets" or "the totality of all sets" (as we saw in Chapter I), so one might very well say that Russell thought it was nonsense to speak of the "totality of all sets" as a completed totality. Poincaré, on the other hand, thought that there were no completed totalities at all: not just the totality of all sets, but even the totality of natural numbers, was regarded as being a potential totality. So Feferman's description of the predicative conception is misleading if it is taken to be a characterization of Poincaré's philosophical beliefs as well as of Russell's.

And in what sense can a mathematician "refer to", "talk about", or "quantify over" these created entities? How can we make sense of Poincaré's no-infinity theory? Such questions will be explored further in the next chapter.

CHAPTER V

A Predicative Alternative
to Quine's Platonism

The nominalist program seems already and painlessly achieved if Whitehead and Russell's elimination of classes by a theory of incomplete symbols is thought to bear. But it does not; it only eliminates classes in favor of attributes (Quine [81], p. 269n).

So long as 'propositional function' is thought of in the sense of 'matrix', such a construction would seem to serve its nominalistic objective; but actually Russell's construction involves use of 'ϕ', 'ψ', etc. in quantifiers, and hence calls for propositional functions in the sense rather of attributes (Quine [72], p. 22).

From the above quotations, it would seem that Quine allows that a nominalist can meet his argument for ontological Platonism by making the sort of "translation" that Russell's no-class theory provides, so long as the set-theoretical statements are translated into statements about matrices or open sentences rather than attributes. The question arises: Can we not provide such a translation of a system like *PM*? Evidently, Quine thinks no such translation is possible, since he says that the nominalist must restrict the mathematics in his science to such trivial portions as *very elementary arithmetic*. It will be the aim of this chapter to show that Quine is mistaken in thinking that such a translation is impossible and also to show how a nominalist (in the sense of an 'anti- (ontological) Platonist') can provide an alternative to Quine's view of mathematics. The position that emerges from this undertaking can be regarded as a natural development of the ideas of Russell and Poincaré.

Now what should be required of the no-class translation that the nominalist seeks? Obviously, the translation should at least preserve the theorems of the system. But must it also preserve the truths? If so, the demand would be that every sentence of the system that would be true (false) in the intended model (if there were such a thing) should get translated into a true (false) sentence about open sentences. Now Quine might insist that his proxy-function requirement also be satisfied by the translation. In Chapter III, I claimed that Russell's no-class theory did not satisfy this stringent demand. If I am correct on this point, Quine ought not demand so much, especially in view of the above quotation [81]. Quine could, of course, simply take back what he said. In any case, I do not wish to rest my case upon my criticisms of Quine's proxy-function requirement. For the sake of argument, I shall accept Quine's added requirement.

1. Wang's System Σ_ω

Our task, roughly speaking, is to provide a way of translating the statements of set theory into statements about open sentences so as to satisfy Quine's proxy-function requirement. In addition, the translation must be acceptable to an anti- (ontological) Platonist. For example, it must not presuppose some theory that requires quantification over abstract entities. But must we be able to translate all the sentences of all set theories? No. Recalling the structure of Quine's argument, it is clear that we need only concern ourselves with a system of set theory sufficient for the needs of empirical scientists. Unfortunately, what mathematical systems are sufficient for present-day science is not very clear. One system that has been put forward by Hao Wang as an attractive candidate is his Σ_ω. This system goes far beyond the trivial portions of mathematics, such as very elementary arithmetic, to which Quine restricts his nominalistic opponents. Wang even suggests that "classical analysis" would remain more or less intact in Σ_ω ([117], p. 643).[1] One reason for

---

[1] This suggestion has not yet been completely justified. For example, it is not obvious how measure theory is to be developed in Σ_ω. There are suggestions in Wang ([115], p. 569) that one might construct a substitute version of measure theory by substituting the notion of "relative indenumerability" for "absolute indenumerability." However, I have learned from Wang (personal communication dated July 8, 1970) that he never followed up this idea to see if it could be carried out in detail. It is worth noting, in this connection, that Paul Lorenzen has used a similar idea to define a nontrivial Lebesgue measure within a system that is regarded as similar to Wang's Σ family of set theories. (See Craig [23], p. 318 and Fraenkel & Bar-Hillel [29], pp. 158f). Skolem also indicated (in

considering the possibility of translating the sentences of Σ_ω into statements about open sentences is this: There are only denumerably many sets in the intuitive model of the system; consequently, one should be able to map the sets one-one onto a totality of open sentences. Another reason for looking at this set theory is the fact that it has been constructed to conform to the vicious-circle principle. In the preceding chapter, we saw that Poincaré's principle sprang from decidedly nominalistic attitudes. These facts give rise to the hope that an acceptable no-class translation of the system can be achieved.

Σ_ω belongs to a more powerful system Σ, a "constructive" set theory which is, strictly speaking, not a formal system at all (there being no effective way of giving all the primitive symbols of the system), but, as Hao Wang puts it, a "union" of formal systems Σ_α (where α is a "constructive ordinal") or a "recipe for making formal systems wherever an ordinal α is given" ([118], p. 593). Since, in an appendix, I shall discuss Σ_ω in some detail, I shall describe Σ only very generally and very informally.

Σ embodies Russell's ramified approach, with a number of important simplifications. First of all, the no-class theory is abandoned, the variables being regarded as simply ranging over *sets*. As in *PM*, the sets of Σ belong to *orders*, but the distinction of types within orders has been eliminated. Thus '$x \in x$' is not held to be meaningless in Wang's system. Furthermore, the orders are cumulative in the sense that a set of a given order also belongs to every higher order. At the lowest order, order 0, we have a denumerable totality of sets (the finite sets built out of the null set). Given the sets of order n, the sets of order $n + 1$ consist of the sets of order n and, in addition, the sets that can be specified by open sentences with bound variables that range, at most, over the sets of order n. It is this last feature, of course, which gives weight to Wang's claim that the sets of order n ($n > 0$) are constructed according to the vicious-circle principle.

---

[110], §15) how measure is developed within Lorenzen's system. My own preliminary investigations into the possibility of developing measure theory within one of Wang's sigma set theories suggest that it can be conveniently accomplished in Σ_{ω^2}. One of my students, Tom Schaffter, has been able to develop the measure theory of Lorenzen's book within Wang's system.

In Σ, there is no axiom of reducibility. Since this axiom seems to be so essential for the development of mathematics within *PM*, the reader may wonder how Wang can achieve so much in Σ without making use of some comparable axiom. Actually, Σ is a weaker set theory than *PM* (with the axiom of reducibility), and hence certain proofs which can be carried out in *PM* are not possible in Σ. But the authors of *PM* used the axiom of reducibility for certain purposes that can be achieved by means other than the appeal to such a strong axiom. For example, the axiom was used to show that their definition of identity had certain necessary properties. More specifically, it was used to show that if $x = y$, and $x \in z$, then $y \in z$ (no matter what the order of z). Wang is able to achieve this by adopting the above property as an *axiom* of his system. However, to have such an axiom, it is necessary to have variables that range over all the orders of the system.

This takes us to another important difference between Wang's system and Russell's. Unlike *PM*, Σ has transfinite orders. Thus order ω, the sets of Σ_ω, consists of the sets of finite order. With this added feature, one can have variables of order ω which range over all the orders of Σ_ω, and hence one can state the required axiom of identity.

Another result proved in *PM* by using the axiom of reducibility is the least upper bound theorem. We saw earlier that, within the ramified framework, given a bounded set x of real numbers of order n, the general specification that gives us the least upper bound of x defines a set of order $n + 1$. Of course, in *PM*, the need of ascending to a higher order is obviated by the axiom of reducibility, so that all the real numbers can be of a single order. In Σ_ω, a somewhat similar effect can be achieved as follows: The real numbers are defined as lower Dedekind cuts of fractions (which are sets of order 0). Consequently, there are real numbers of various orders. However, since every set of Σ_ω is a set of some finite order, and since every set of finite order is a set of order ω, all the real numbers are of the order ω. As for the least upper bound theorem, given a bounded set x of real numbers, x must be of some finite order, and hence all the elements of x will be of some finite order; so in specifying the least upper bound of x, we get a real number of higher finite order, but it is still of order ω. Thus, by utilizing variables of order ω, Wang is able to obviate the need to step up to higher orders in order to get least upper bounds.

However, the use of transfinite orders does not eliminate from the "analysis" of Σ_ω all the peculiarities of the stratification into orders that Russell was able to iron out with his axiom of reducibility. For example, in Σ_ω (and, for that matter, in the full system Σ) there is no set of all real numbers. Thus one cannot have functions defined over all the reals. It is easy to see why Cantor's proof of the inde-numerability of the reals cannot be carried out in Σ. Notice that the fact that Cantor's proof cannot be carried out in Σ gives some weight to Wang's claim that the system has been constructed so as to be in conformity with Poincaré's principle.

Having allowed transfinite orders, Wang can see no good reason for stopping at Σ_ω; hence we get $\Sigma_{\omega+1}$, $\Sigma_{\omega+2}$,... and in general Σ_α, for any "constructive ordinal" α. Unfortunately Wang ran into serious difficulty in attempting to say precisely what a constructive ordinal was. So the crucial question remains, "How far can one go?" Whatever else one may want to object to in Σ, it seems clear that until the above important question is answered, as Wang himself admits, we cannot regard Σ as an entirely satisfactory statement of predicative set theory.

However, we need not concern ourselves, here, with these problems of formalizing predicative reasoning. Let us concentrate on the problem at hand of translating the sentences of Σ_ω into statements about open-sentences.

2. The Construction of Some Ordinal Notation

We can all recognize and construct the following *primitive symbols:* The Arabic numerals

> 0, 1, 2, 3, 4, 5, 6, 7, 8, 9.
> The Greek letter 'ω'.
> The plus sign '$+$'.

It is assumed that we have learned and could formulate simple rules for constructing sequences of primitive symbols that are called 'Arabic natural numerals', that is, numerals in the Arabic decimal notation of the natural numbers. The ordinal numerals I shall need can then be given by the following rules:

(1) All Arabic natural numerals are ordinal numerals (these will be called 'finite ordinal numerals').

(2) 'ω' is an ordinal numeral.

(3) If n is a finite ordinal numeral, then $\ulcorner \omega + n \urcorner$ is an ordinal numeral.

The ordering of these ordinal numerals will be given in terms of certain well formed formulas defined as follows:

If n and m are ordinal numerals, then $\ulcorner n < m \urcorner$ is a well formed formula.

I shall now give "semantical rules" in terms of which one can classify a well formed formula as either true or false. In the following, instead of saying that a well formed formula is to be classified as true (false), I shall say simply that the sentence is true (false).

(1) If n and m are finite ordinal numerals, and n would be constructed before m in constructing the Arabic natural numerals according to the usual method (or rules), then $\ulcorner n < m \urcorner$ is true.

(2) If n is a finite ordinal numeral, and m is either 'ω' or is a numeral of the form $\ulcorner \omega + k \urcorner$, then $\ulcorner n < m \urcorner$ is true.

(3) $\ulcorner \omega < \omega + n \urcorner$ is true.

(4) If $\ulcorner n < m \urcorner$ is true, then $\ulcorner \omega + n < \omega + m \urcorner$ is true.

(5) All well formed formulas that are not true are false. We now have a natural ordering of our ordinal numerals; and we can say that n comes before m in this ordering if, and only if, $\ulcorner n < m \urcorner$ is true.

In constructing this ordinal notation, there is no need to commit oneself to abstract entities. We need not presuppose ordinal numbers for the numerals to denote. And we need not affirm the existence of totalities or sets. In fact, the above constructions would even satisfy Poincaré's finitistic attitudes, for we do not have to suppose that there actually exists an infinity of expressions or imagine that someone has actually performed an infinite sequence of distinct acts.

By the above method, ordinal numerals of the form

$$\omega^2 n + \omega m + 1$$

can be introduced, and the definition of the symbol '$<$' can be extended so as to encompass these numerals as well. Obviously, one can go much further, but for my purposes, these ordinals will be sufficient.

Later, I will prove some theorems using mathematical induction on the ordinals $\leqslant \omega^3$ (where 'ω^3' is an abbreviation for '$\omega^2\omega$'). It will be obvious that the results I obtain could also be obtained using only ordinary natural-number induction, but the use of the larger totality of ordinal numerals simplifies the exposition somewhat.

The construction of the no-class interpretation of Σ_ω will be quite similar to the above. I shall begin with a small list of primitive symbols and then provide a way of constructing open sentences from these symbols. I shall then construct "semantic definitions" that will explain what it means to say that one of these open sentences is true or false of one of these open sentences.

As an alternative to the system of natural numerals described above, one could use the sort of system suggested by Hilbert in [43], where sequences of strokes are used as the natural numbers:

$$|, \; ||, \; |||, \; \cdots \cdot$$

(Of course, I would regard the sequences of strokes as being numerals rather than numbers). This system of numerals has advantages, lending itself more directly to the sort of "justification" of rules of inference involving numerals which I discuss below.

The symbol '$<$' can be defined as follows: $\ulcorner a < b \urcorner$ is true if, and only if, a token of the same type as the latter can be constructed by appending a sequence of strokes to a token of the same type as the former. And we can say $\ulcorner a = Sb \urcorner$ is true if, and only if, a token of the same type as a can be constructed by appending a stroke to a token of the same type as b. The symbol '$+$' can be defined for contexts of the following sort:

$$a + b = c$$

by giving some such truth conditions as: the above is true if, and only if, a token of the same type as c can be constructed by appending a token of the same type as b to a token of the same type as a. (The above definitions are not meant to be complete, but are put forward only as indications of how one could proceed).

The main use to which I shall put these ordinal numerals can be illustrated by an example. The expressions of Σ_ω will be assigned numerals in various ways, each assignment being given by a simple effective rule. Now suppose each sentence of Σ_ω has been assigned some unique numeral by rule R. Suppose further that a certain formula φ containing one free variable 'x' is true of the numeral '|' (i.e. φ $x/$'|' is true, where φ $x/$'|' is the sentence that results from replacing all free occurrences of 'x' in φ by occurrences of the quote-name of '|'), and suppose that this is shown to be so. Suppose also that it is shown that if φ is true of a, then φ is also true of Sa. Then I would conclude that φ is true of all the natural numerals.

But what justifies this conclusion? One obvious way of responding to this question would be to cite a version of mathematical induction over these natural numerals. We certainly need some such rule of inference if we are to get any nontrivial results at all. It would seem that we need a principle of this sort to justify even the claim that some effective rule assigns a unique numeral to each sentence. But what *ultimately* justifies this use of induction? This, of course, is a profound and difficult question, which I shall not attempt to answer here. There are philosophers (like Poincaré) who feel that no logical justification of this principle is possible and that we know it to be valid on the basis of some sort of acquaintance with some facet of the operations of our minds. Without contradicting this position, I would claim that there are standard ways of bringing most people to accept this sort of inductive principle. For example, Parsons presents the following argument: Suppose we have proved both φ $x/$'|' and φ $x/a \to \varphi$ x/Sa. Then consider an arbitrary numeral b. Tokens of this type are constructed by starting with one stroke and successively appending another stroke, so we can convince ourselves of φ x/b by starting with φ $x/$'|', and making use of *modus ponens* and φ $x/a \to \varphi$ x/Sa at each succeeding step until φ x/b is proved ([60], p. 61). Parsons allows that there is an "air of circularity" to this reasoning. I agree, and for this reason I would not argue that the above considerations provide us with a *proof* (or "ultimate justification") of mathematical induction. However, it can be used to produce conviction in people or, to use Poincaré's way of speaking, to awaken a person's intuition.

Another way of bringing about acceptance of the principle is to appeal to some other basic principle such as the following form of *the least numeral principle:* If φ is true of some numeral, there is a least numeral of which φ is true. Then, if the antecedents of the inductive principle are shown to be satisfied, and φ is not true of some numeral b we can assert that there is a least numeral c of which $-\varphi$ is true. But since a token of the same type as c can be constructed by appending a stroke to some numeral d, we can assert: φ is true of d. Then we can use φ $x/d \rightarrow \varphi$ x/c and *modus ponens* to get a contradiction. Of course, the least numeral principle, itself, might be questioned, in which case, we could use some form of mathematical induction to bring about acceptance of that principle. But if both principles are questioned by the same person, obviously another route must be tried.

It is unlikely, however, that the ontological Platonists of the Quinian sort would fall into such a class. Indeed, the philosophers of mathematics who would most probably question the use of mathematical induction in the above way are the *extreme* finitists and *extreme* nominalists. Besides, it is easy to see how the sort of pragmatic justification that Quine, himself, accepts and puts forward can be given for accepting the above rules of inference.

3. *An Outline of the No-Class Translation*

The vocabulary of Σ_ω consists of the usual quantifiers, connectives, and parentheses of first-order logic. There are two predicate symbols: '$\in$', for membership, and '$=$', for identity. Every variable α_i is assigned some subscript i, which is either a finite ordinal numeral or 'ω'. The variable α_i will be said to be of *order i*. If ϕ is a formula of finite order and α is the only variable free in ϕ, then $\hat{\alpha}\phi$ is a constant, and α is the *argument variable* of the constant. Any variable or constant is a *term*. The (well formed) formulas of Σ_ω are formed from the predicate symbols and terms in the usual way. As is customary, I shall refer to formulas in which no free variable occurs as "*sentences.*"

In presenting the semantics of Σ_ω we assign orders to terms and formulas. These orders will be determined by syntactic properties of the expressions. Quantifier-free and constant-free formulas are assigned an order equal to the largest order of a variable occurring within them. Thus, such a formula will be of order zero if all of the variables occurring in it are of order zero.

The language of Σ_ω was devised with a particular interpretation in mind. I wish to consider interpretations of the language that satisfy certain conditions connecting the truth of sentences in one syntactic form with the truth of other sentences of a different syntactic form. These five conditions can be regarded as necessary conditions for the adequacy of an interpretation. The first two of these concern the predicate symbols:

(1) If $\alpha \in \hat{\beta}\phi$ is true, then $\phi \, \beta/\alpha$ is true (where $\phi \, \beta/\alpha$ is the result of replacing all free occurrences of β in ϕ by occurrences of α).

(2) $\alpha = \beta$ is true if, and only if, for every constant term γ, the sentence $(\gamma \in \alpha \leftrightarrow \gamma \in \beta)$ is true.

Consider now a constant of the form $\hat{\alpha}_0(\alpha_0 \neq \alpha_0)$. If β is a constant, and if $\beta \in \hat{\alpha}_0(\alpha_0 \neq \alpha_0)$ is true, so also is $\beta \neq \beta$. But by (2), $\beta = \beta$ is true since $(\gamma \in \beta \leftrightarrow \gamma \in \beta)$ is a tautology. Thus, $\beta \in \hat{\alpha}_0(\alpha_0 \neq \alpha_0)$ must be false. For this reason, terms of the form $\hat{\alpha}_0(\alpha_0 \neq \alpha_0)$ can be taken to denote the null-set. We assign order zero to the constants of the form $\hat{\alpha}_0(\alpha_0 \neq \alpha_0)$. If β and γ are constants of order zero, then we assign order zero to constants of the form $\hat{\alpha}_0(\alpha_0 \in \beta \lor \alpha_0 = \gamma)$.

We now assign the collection of sets denoted by constants of order zero, that is, the hereditarily finite sets, as the range of the variables of order zero. This determines the denotation of the rest of the constants which contain only order-zero variables (e.g., $\hat{\alpha}_0(\alpha_0 = \alpha_0)$ denotes the collection of hereditarily finite sets). We assign order one to these constants. We are now in a position to assign a range to the variables of order one, viz. the collection of those sets which are denoted by constants of order one. This in turn fixes the denotation of constants containing only order zero or order 1 terms. We proceed in this manner, for each finite ordinal n, to assign a range to variables of order n and then a denotation to the terms containing variables of order at most n.

I will now state the other three conditions of adequacy mentioned above:

(3) If the order of α is not greater than the order of β, and if $\phi \, \beta/\alpha$ is true, then $\alpha \in \hat{\beta}\phi$ is true.

(4) If the order of α is greater than the order of β, then the sentence $\alpha \in \hat{\beta}\phi$ is true if, and only if, there is a constant γ of order less than or equal to the order of β such that the sentences $\alpha = \gamma$ and $\gamma \in \hat{\beta}\phi$ are true.

(5) $(\exists\beta)\phi$ is true if, and only if, there is a constant α of order less than or equal to that of β such that $\phi \, \beta/\alpha$ is true.

The last condition restricts the interpretations we shall consider to those that are *complete interpretations* (in the sense of Mates [54], p. 57).

We have specified an order for all of the terms. We call an occurrence of a variable *open* if it is not in the scope of a circumflex variable. The order of a sentence is determined by its constants and open variables. If a sentence contains an order-ω variable, then the sentence is assigned order ω. Otherwise, the sentence will have the smallest finite order which is at least as large as the order of any constant occurring in it and is larger than the order of any open variable occurring in it. It is easy to see that the vicious-circle principle holds for this system.

The classical interpretation can now be given:

A. *Denotation of constants.*

    1. If α is of order zero, $\hat{\alpha}(\alpha \neq \alpha)$ denotes the null set.

    2. If $\hat{\alpha}(\alpha \in \beta \lor \alpha = \gamma)$ is a constant of order zero, then it denotes the set of all entities that are either members of β or are identical to γ (or both).

    3. If $\hat{\alpha}\phi$ is a constant, then it denotes the set of all entities of order less than or equal to that of α that satisfy ϕ.

B. *Interpretation of Predicates.*

    '$\in$' denotes the relation of membership.
    '$=$' denotes the relation of identity.

C. *Range of the Quantifiers.*

The variable α ranges over all sets denoted by a constant of order less than or equal to that of α. Thus, if α is of order ω, α ranges over all sets denoted by any constant.

In developing the semantics of Σ_ω I stated five necessary conditions for an adequate interpretation, which connect the truth of sentences of one syntactic form with the truth of sentences of a different syntactic form. We have already seen that these conditions determine the truth values of some sentences which are neither inconsistent nor valid. For example, we found that for any constant β, the sentence $\beta \in \hat{\alpha}_0(\alpha_0 \neq \alpha_0)$ must be false. In the appendix, I shall show that there is exactly one *normal assignment* of truth values to the sentences of Σ_ω in which all five of the conditions are satisfied, where an assignment of truth values to all the sentences is said to be "normal" if it assigns one and only one truth value to each sentence and also assigns truth values to molecular sentences in the way a standard truth function does. (For more on normal assignments, see Mates [54], p. 85).

One way in which a nominalist might proceed to "interpret" Σ_ω is by simply laying down truth-conditions which, in effect, provide a normal assignment of truth values to the sentences of Σ_ω. The truth-conditions can be regarded as providing us with a function, T, whose domain is the totality of sentences of Σ_ω and whose range is the totality containing just '0' and '1'. Thus, we could read 'ϕ is true' as saying "$T(\phi) = 0$" and 'φ is false' as saying "$T(\phi) = 1$". We can construct such a function by making use of the classical interpretation V: we could specify that $T(\phi) = 0$ if, and only if, ϕ is true under V, and $T(\phi) = 1$ if, and only if, ϕ is false under V. And we would be assured that this function would satisfy the five conditions of adequacy mentioned above. However, a nominalist would be precluded from proceeding in this fashion. If we wish to construct our mathematical theories without presupposing the existence of sets, we must not construct our interpretation of Σ_ω in terms of the sets of V.

There are various ways in which an acceptable nominalistic interpretation of Σ_ω might be given. I would not claim that the ones I give are the simplest possible or even the most natural. I can, however, provide motivation for some of the main features of the interpretations. First of all, I wanted to construct interpretations under which the sentences of the language are intuitively true or false and not merely assigned the numerals '1' or '0'. Secondly, I wanted to use the interpretations to gain some insights into the connection between the "no-class" theory and the vicious-circle principle: I wished to see, in terms of the interpretations, how and in what sense the "sets" of the system are constructed. Thus consider the sentence

> Sue is a member of the class of men who are more than five feet tall.

This seems to be a somewhat pompous way of saying:

> Sue is a man more than five feet tall.

Similarly, the sentence

> The class of humans is a subset of the class of animals.

seems to be a roundabout way of saying

> All humans are animals.

The above suggest that we might treat the sentences

$$\alpha \in \hat{\beta}\phi$$

as abbreviations for

$$\phi \, \beta/\alpha$$

For if we adopted such a convention, we would have:

$$\hat{x}Fx \subset \hat{x}Gx$$

is an abbreviation of

$$(y)(y \in \hat{x}Fx \rightarrow y \in \hat{x}Gx)$$

which is an abbreviation of

$$(y)(Fy \rightarrow Gy).$$

Basically, Russell's idea was to treat all statements of set theory in someway like that suggested above. Although Russell's no-class theory was defective in many respects, I believe the basic idea can be recaptured in a satisfactory theory.

Essentially, a set-theoretical statement can be taken to be a roundabout statement about open sentences (or what are also called 'sentence forms' by Mates in [1]). Thus, I shall construct the no-class theory so as to satisfy the following conditions:

(1) If $\hat{\alpha}\phi$ is a constant, then it will denote an open sentence called the '*correspondent* of $\hat{\alpha}\phi$', which with only slight modifications is ϕ. The notation '$C(\hat{\alpha}\phi)$' will be used to refer to the correspondent of $\hat{\alpha}\phi$.

(2) $\alpha \in \beta$ will be true if, and only if, $C(\beta)$ is true of $C(\alpha)$, where 'true of' and 'false of' have their customary sense: An open sentence ϕ with argument variable α is true of the open sentence ψ, which has a name β, if $\phi \; \alpha/\beta$ is true; ϕ is false of ψ if $\phi \; \alpha/\beta$ is false.

(3) If $\hat{\alpha}\phi$ and β are constants, where the order of $\beta \leqslant$ the order of α, then $C(\hat{\alpha}\phi)$ will be true of $C(\beta)$ if, and only if, $\phi \; \alpha/\beta$ is true. If the order of $\beta >$ the order of α, then $C(\hat{\alpha}\phi)$ will be true of $C(\beta)$ if, and only if, there is a constant γ of order $\leqslant$ the order of α such that the sentences $\beta = \gamma$ and $\phi \; \alpha/\gamma$ are both true.

Now I shall construct my interpretation of Σ_ω in such a way that correspondents of constants will be true of (or false of) correspondents of constants. If one proceeds in this way, it is easy to see that the correspondents will, in effect, get "extensions": each will separate a totality of open sentences into those it is true of and those it is false of. However, to keep to the basic idea of the vicious-circle principle, I require that each open sentence be constructed so as to satisfy the following additional conditions:

(4) For each open sentence constructed, a definite totality must be specified as its *argument range*. Each element of this argument range of which the open sentence is true will be said to belong to the *extension* of the open sentence.

(5) Each open sentence constructed must be well-defined over its argument range in the following sense: If ϕ is a member of the argument range of ψ, then ψ is either true of ϕ or false of ϕ (but not both).

(6) The open sentences must be constructed in stages in such a way that no open sentence will belong to its own argument range.

(7) No open sentence constructed at one stage will belong to the argument range of an open sentence constructed at an earlier stage.

Now since condition 6) will receive some slight modification, I should like to reexamine the vicious-circle paradoxes that gave rise to this condition. The vicious-circle paradox that is most relevant to my reconstruction of set theory along these no-class lines is the Grelling (or heterological) paradox, a version of which I give below.

We first define the open sentence 'x is heterological' thus: For every open sentence x, x satisfies 'x is heterological' if, and only if, x is not true of x. It then seems to follow that 'x is heterological' is heterological if, and only if, 'x is heterological' is not heterological.

Now condition (6) clearly precludes the heterological paradox from arising. But one wonders if the condition is not too strong. Obviously, much weaker restrictions will enable us to avoid this paradox. For example, we can simply preclude 'x is heterological' from being in its own argument range: it is not necessary that we preclude every open sentence from being in its own argument range.

J. Thomson has analyzed various "solutions" of the Grelling paradox and has concluded that they all "come to the same thing" ([114], p. 113). What they all come to, he says there, is this: 'x is heterological' is undefined for itself as argument. In the paper, the suggestion is made that we regard the above open sentence in this light. Later, he says: "I should still claim that the suggestion above that we regard "x is heterological" as undefined for itself as argument is simpler than any hierarchical account and is to this extent preferable" ([114], pp. 114-5). However, although Thomson's suggestion is simpler than Russell's "solution", it does not give us any general method of avoiding vicious-circle paradoxes, as does Russell's theory of types. Certainly, if we find an open sentence in our system with the unpleasant qualities of 'x is heterological', we can expunge it from our system, but we should like to proceed without any fear of such paradoxical open sentences cropping up. Russell's vicious-circle principle was formulated with the idea of guiding our construction of systems of propositional functions. Thomson's suggestion does not provide me with any guidelines for constructing my system of open sentences so as to avoid such ill-defined open sentences.

Let us reconsider an example from Chapter I, Section 6. Let α be the open sentence 'x contains (at least) three (English) words'. Now why cannot α fall within its own argument range? Here, there seems to be no danger of a vicious-circle paradox arising, for to determine whether α is true of β, we need only look at the syntactical features of β. To see if α is true of α, we need only count the English words that occur in α. In contrast to this example, to determine if 'x is heterological' is true of β, one must examine the semantical properties of β. This suggests that we can be confident of avoiding contradiction so long as we prevent the occurrence of the sort of "semantical looping" exemplified above. Thus we might allow an open sentence β to belong to its own argument range so long as (roughly) the truth conditions of β are such that to determine if β is true of γ one need consider not the semantical properties of γ, but only certain syntactical properties of open sentences together with the semantical properties of previously constructed open sentences. Thus, we can allow β to belong to its own argument range so long as

(A) an effective rule is specified which assigns to each argument γ a sentence $\phi(\gamma)$ that refers only to previously constructed open sentences such that β is true of γ if and only if $\phi(\gamma)$ is true.

To make sure that the definition of β will not lead us into paradox, we need only prove that for every γ in the argument range of β, $\phi(\gamma)$ is either true or false (but not both). Thus, we can restate condition (6) as follows:

(6) The open sentences must be constructed in stages in such a way that no open sentence will belong to its own argument range unless it is an open sentence β that satisfies clause (A).

It will be shown in the appendix how such a no-class interpretation of Σ_ω can be constructed. In addition to satisfying these six conditions mentioned above, the interpretation will have the following features:

Connectives:

The truth-functional connectives will be interpreted in the usual way.

Identity:

'$=$' will mean extensional identity, i.e., $\alpha = \beta$ will be true if, and only if, $C(\alpha)$ and $C(\beta)$ are true of the same open sentences.

Quantification:

$(\exists \alpha)\phi$ will be true if, and only if, there is a constant β of order less than or equal to that of α such that $\phi \ \alpha/\beta$ is true.

Let us call the Theory Σ_ω when interpreted in the above no-class manner S, and call it W when interpreted classically. Then it is easy to show that, by Quine's proxy-function criterion, the ontology of W can be reduced to the ontology of S. Furthermore, it can be argued that all the theorems of S are intuitively true. When we turn to proving that all the theorems of S are intuitively true, we could again make use of V. Since it is shown that a sentence of S is intuitively true if, and only if, the corresponding sentence of W is true, and since it can be seen that all the theorems of W are true, one can conclude that all the theorems of S are true. But a nominalist can no more justify his claim that his theorems are true by appealing to the truth of theorems of set theory than he can construct his interpretation by reference to the entities of set theory. For this reason, a more nominalistically acceptable proof of the intuitive truth of the theorems is constructed in the appendix.

4. Does the No-Class Theory Presuppose Quantification Over Abstract Entities?

Let us now turn to the theory S. The question that must now be explored is whether or not the theory presupposes quantification over abstract entities of some sort. Let us consider some objections that might be raised to my claim that the no-class interpretation I have constructed is indeed acceptable to a nominalist (or anti-[ontological] Platonist) who forswears quantification over abstract entities.

First of all, it might be argued against me that although I do not talk about sets or classes in constructing my interpretation, I do use the term 'totality', which seems to be a term used roughly to denote sets. I should like to point out that in constructing this no-class interpretation, I shall use 'totality' in a Pickwickean sense: the usual set-existence assumptions are not to be made in the case of totalities. First of all, I restrict the use of the term to "totalities of expressions". Secondly, I use the term only when an inductive or simple mechanical rule for constructing, one after another, the expressions that belong to the totality is either given or "implied" (such a statement can easily be devised given what has already been said), so that one can regard statements about a totality as statements about the results of constructing expressions in accordance with the statement of the rule. Thus,

(1) An expression b is said to "belong to a totality B" (or "be an element of a totality B") if b can be constructed in accordance with a statement of the rule that specifies the totality B.

(2) Totality A is identical to totality B if and only if each expression that is an element of A is an element of B and conversely.

In answer to the objection, then, one can say that although the term 'totality' is used in constructing the interpretation of Σ_ω, the existence of sets or classes in anything like the Platonic sense is not presupposed.

Now the reader may have noticed that in my reply to this objection, I spoke of *giving an inductive rule for constructing expressions;* I also said something about *acting in accordance with a statement of a rule.* This gives rise to a second objection. It would seem from the above that I am presupposing the existence of *rules*, and surely rules are abstract entities in the same boat as sets, classes, and functions. Thus, if I assert that I have given a rule for constructing certain sorts of expressions, I seem to be saying something that can be translated as follows: $(\exists x)(x$ is a rule & I have given $x)$. Similarly, if I say "S is a statement of a rule," then I seem to be saying "$(\exists x)$ (x is a rule & S states x)." Thus, I seem to be quantifying over rules and, to that extent, assuming that there are such entities, or at the very least, I *suggest* that there are such entities. However, it can be seen that for my purposes one can regard expressions like 'gave a rule', 'states a rule', 'is a statement of a rule', 'formulates a rule', as hyphenated expressions ('formulates-a-rule'), essentially single-word predicates, that do not involve quantification over anything. And it is not necessary in constructing my interpretation of Σ_ω to make statements that *require* quantification over rules.

Another similar objection can be stated as follows: In constructing the interpretation, I sometimes say such things as "for every finite ordinal," "If n is an ordinal $< \omega$," and so forth. It might seem reasonable to suppose that I presuppose at least the existence of ordinal numbers, and surely these are Platonic entities. My position is that wherever I speak of ordinals or ordinal numbers, one can translate the statement into one involving only *ordinal numerals* or expressions of certain sorts.

Reconsidering my interpretation of the quantifiers, it might be argued that Σ_ω is now committed to the existence of abstract entities. By 'constant' one can mean either type or token. However, if token is meant, what does it mean to say "There is a constant of such and such kind"? Is it being claimed that such a string of symbols actually appears somewhere? By that reading, many existential theorems of Σ_ω would be false. If, however, type is meant, then since a type seems to qualify as a universal, I seem to be committing myself to the existence of universals in asserting '$(\exists x_0)\, x_0 = x_0$'. To avoid these difficulties, we can regard such phrases as 'there is a constant of such and such kind' as a kind of Russellian incomplete symbol: sentences containing these phrases are abbreviations for sentences not containing them. To see how the translations would be made, the following should be noted: for each order j, one can specify a simple inductive rule for constructing all the constants of order j. Hence, given a sentence $(\exists \alpha)\phi$, one can specify an inductive rule for generating all the sentences of the form $\phi\, \alpha/\beta$, where β is a constant of the same order as α. $(\exists \alpha)\phi$ will then mean: If one were to follow this rule of construction without end, one would eventually construct a true sentence. One could also interpret the sentence to read: It is possible to construct a true sentence by following this rule of construction. The negation of the sentence, would then mean: If one were to follow the rule of construction without end, one would never construct a true sentence. Or, alternatively, it would mean: It is not possible to construct a true sentence by following this rule of construction.

5. *Poincaré's Views in the Light of the No-Class Theory*

Consider the statements:

The 3 level correspondent of α is true of the 2 level correspondent of β.

There is an entity of level 5 which is extensionally identical to the image of a 3 level correspondent of α.

It would seem that as a result of the definitions I gave earlier of the entities of level n, one can make statements about them, refer to them, and even quantify over them: in short, it would seem that one can talk as if one were talking about actually existing objects. Looked at in this way, the situation seems to be one in which we bring the entities into existence by means of definitions. So it is not hard to understand why someone like Poincaré might say that I constructed entities of my theory by means of definitions. This throws some light on Poincaré's metaphor of constructing sets by means of definitions. How, I asked, can sets spring into existence simply as a result of being defined? We can now see that the position is not so paradoxical after all. Within the framework of the no-class interpretation of Σ_ω, it is easy to see that the metaphor of constructing sets is apt, but what is more important, it is easy to see what is behind the metaphor.

At this point, I should like to return to a point I brought up in the previous chapter. Recall that in discussing Poincaré's arguments for rejecting impredicative definitions, I suggested that Poincaré was concerned with "creative definitions," that is, definitions of some "new entity." At that point in my exposition of Poincaré's philosophy of mathematics, I found it difficult to say what was meant by 'new entity'. However, in terms of the preceding constructions, it is easy enough to single out what I had in mind. The entities of my interpretation of Σ_ω are constructed in a step by step fashion so that, at any stage in the development, we can say what entities have already been defined and what entities are being defined (the notion of "new entity" being obviously relative to the particular stage in the process one is talking about). But "new entity" should be distinguished from "new set"; for once one grasps the interpretation I give to the sentences of Σ_ω, one can reasonably ask whether the "construction" (or defining) of some new entity brings a new set into the system. It can be seen that not every new entity results in a new set. (The introduction of $C_3(\hat{x}_2 \, (x_2 \neq x_2))$ does not bring a new set into the system.) As I mentioned before, I believe it is best to view Poincaré's rejection of impredicative definitions in terms of "new entity" rather than "new set."

This way of regarding the constructions of my no-class interpretation also throws light on Poincaré's vicious-circle principle, in so far as it provides us with insights into his reasons for rejecting impredicative specifications. We can appreciate more fully Poincaré's refusal to specify or define sets using quantification over entities that have not been defined. Viewing Poincaré's position in terms of the constructions outlined above, we arrive at a rationale for the vicious-circle principle that Gödel anticipated when he suggested that the vicious-circle principle applies if the entities involved are constructed by ourselves: "In this case there must clearly exist a definition (namely the description of the construction) which does not refer to a totality to which the object defined belongs, because the construction of a thing can certainly not be based on a totality of things to which the thing itself belongs" (Gödel [38], p. 136).

We can now see more clearly how to reconcile Poincaré's nominalism with his predicativism. His doctrine that 'exist' has a special sense in mathematics is not so puzzling when the quantifier is understood in the way described above. Certainly, the entities that are (apparently) referred to, named, and quantified over do not exist in any ordinary sense of the word. Furthermore, in order to quantify (in the above manner) over some totality, each entity in the totality must be defined first. And since it is reasonable to require that the relevant definitions be consistent, one can even make some sense of Poincaré's dictum: 'exist' in mathematics means "to be free from contradiction." Also, we can make better sense of his insistence that the mathematician does not deal with the physical world as the physicist does but instead constructs and studies systems of symbols and a kind of "language." (I shall discuss this thesis in more detail in a later section).

Now what light does the method of construction outlined here shed on Poincaré's views on infinity? First of all, Poincaré's no-infinity doctrine can be applied to S: One could argue that each statement about the infinite is translated into a statement about the finite, in so far as the *expressions* that are actually constructed (or need to be constructed) are finite in length and number. Poincaré's doctrine of the potential infinite also seems intelligible and reasonable within this framework. For no actual existing infinities are ever presupposed by the constructions or by the assertions of S. What are presupposed are methods of constructing ever expanding sequences of tokens (similar to Poincaré's subscription list), or potential infinities.

The methods used in constructing and reasoning about the no-class interpretation (in the appendix) might be called "finitary." Kleene says ([46], p. 63) that methods are called "finitary" if only intuitively conceivable objects and performable processes are employed. As I suggested above, I would claim that there is a sense in which the no-class theory deals only with intuitively conceivable objects (finite sequences of symbols from a finite alphabet) and requires only performable processes (if 'performable' is given the idealized sense usual in these mathematical contexts). Kleene goes on to say, however, that in finitary mathematics, "no infinite class is regarded as a completed whole."

Whether the no-class theory presupposes any completed infinite totalities may be somewhat controversial. It might be argued by intuitionists, for example, that in some of my proofs, I in effect make use of the law of excluded middle, and that this use presupposes a completed infinite totality. The point at issue can be illustrated by the following example: We have all learned a computational procedure for carrying out the decimal expansion of $\sqrt{2}$ to indefinitely many places. Now to assert 'If one were to carry out the decimal expansion without stopping, one would either get seven consecutive sevens in the expansion or never get seven consecutive sevens', does not appear to me to presuppose a completed infinite totality or to be meaningless. Thus, I am willing to assert such things, unlike the intuitionists. Roughly speaking, intuitionistic (mathematical) assertions are concerned not with mathematical truth but with decidability and verification. Even if one were to continue the decimal expansion of $\sqrt{2}$ without ever ending, at no moment in time would one have searched through the entire sequence, so the algorithm for carrying out the decimal expansion of $\sqrt{2}$ indefinitely does not provide us with an effective proceedure for deciding if one or the other disjunct is true. If one assumes that asserting the disjunction presupposes the hypothesis that one could actually complete the search through the entire expansion, then it might be thought that my "use of the law of excluded middle" presupposes a completed actual infinite. I would maintain however that the assertion of the disjunction does not require the possibility of completing such an infinite search, nor does it presuppose that we have an effective proceedure for deciding which of the disjuncts is true, for the connectives are not those of the intuitionist.

Actually, the situation is more complicated than I have indicated, and a fuller discussion is called for. When a philosopher claims that the law of excluded middle is not valid, it is frequently unclear what is being specifically denied. Is he denying that every statement (or proposition) is either true or false? Is he denying that if ϕ is a proposition, either ϕ or $-\phi$ is true? Or is he suggesting that some sentences which have been accepted as true because they seem to be instances of a certain tautological formula of the propositional calculus. ('$P \lor -P$') do not express genuine propositions? Or are not true? Or should not be asserted? As we shall see in the next section, the intuitionist's rejection of the law of excluded middle sometimes boils down to the latter. In the case of intuitionism, the situation is even more complicated because there are two formulas which can be said to be (or express) "the law of excluded middle": one from the classical propositional calculus and the other from the intuitionist's propositional calculus.

6. The Law of Excluded Middle and Constructivistic Interpretations of the Quantifiers

Brouwer once argued that the traditional principles of logic were developed as a result of investigations of finite systems. He allowed that these principles are perfectly valid for finite systems but went on to argue that they are not valid when applied to cases involving infinite totalities ([8], p. 336). Mathematical theories based upon these invalid principles are therefore "incorrect," according to Brouwer's analysis. Like Russell, Brouwer blamed the paradoxes on our logical principles. But he was even more radical than Russell in attacking such basic logical laws as the law of excluded middle.

To justify his claim that classical mathematical theories are indeed "incorrect" and founded upon invalid logical principles, Brouwer gave several "counter-examples" to well-known classical theorems. Let us dwell on one of these examples. Consider the sequence of rational numbers r_1, r_2, r_3,... where

$r_j =$ $(-\frac{1}{2})^j$ if seven consecutive sevens do not occur in the decimal expansion of pi carried to the jth place to the right of the decimal place;

$(-\frac{1}{2})^n$ if seven consecutive sevens occur in the decimal expansion of pi for the first time at exactly the nth place, $n \leqslant j$.

Let r be the real number defined by this sequence (i.e. the limit). Then, according to Brouwer, "none of the conditions $r = 0, r < 0$, or $r > 0$ holds" ([8], p. 337). Since the classical theorem "refuted" by this example is based upon the law of excluded middle, the example is taken as showing that the traditional law of logic is also incorrect.

I believe most traditional mathematicians do not find Brouwer's reasoning at all convincing. The classical view is expressed by Ramsey's remark: "The cases in which Brouwer thinks the Law of Excluded Middle false are ones in which, as I should say, we could not tell whether the proposition was true or false" ([93], p. 66). From Ramsey's point of view, we can say that, since it is not known whether there are seven consecutive sevens in the decimal expansion of pi, it is not known whether $r = 0$, $r < 0$, or $r > 0$. However, one of the three cases must hold.

Taking up the cause of traditional mathematics, Hilbert responded to Brouwer's remarkable claims with the words:

> The principle of excluded middle is not to be blamed in the least for the occurrence of the well-known paradoxes of set theory; rather, these paradoxes are due merely to the introduction of inadmissible and meaningless notions. ... Taking the principle of excluded middle from the mathematician would be the same, say, as proscribing the telescope to the astronomer or to the boxer the use of his fists ([44], p. 476).

Kreisel, commenting much later on the dispute between Hilbert and Brouwer, wrote: "It is not the restrictions imposed *by* intuitionism, but those *on* intuitionism which seem to constitute the most significant differences. Hilbert's own remarks on this opposition seem quite inept" ([8], p. 158). And in a footnote, he added: "Considering that the intended meaning of the intuitionistic disjunction is different from that of classical disjunction, the rejection of *tertium non datur* is much more like depriving non-commutative algebra of the rule $ab = ba$ than a boxer the use of his fists." But Kreisel was not entirely fair to Hilbert, in my opinion. It is clear from Brouwer's early writings that he was not merely claiming that the law of excluded middle does not hold in intuitionistic mathematics: he also claimed that classical mathematics contains many false theorems based upon invalid logical laws.

It is possible that Kreisel based his criticisms of Hilbert upon more recent writings of intuitionists, which contain more cautious criticisms of classical theorems. For example, Heyting does not claim that he has counter-examples to classical theorems; he only suggests that his rejection of the traditional approach to mathematics is based upon the fact that he cannot attach any clear sense to classical propositions ([42], p. 11). Now the reasons Heyting gives for not accepting certain theorems and logical laws that are the intuitionistic analogues of classical theorems and laws are generally clear. For example, he shows why

$$p \vee \neg p$$

is not a theorem of the intuitionistic propositional calculus. The intuitionistic logical connectives are explained in the following way ([42], p. 97-8):

$\vee$: One can assert $p \vee q$ if one can either assert p or assert q.

&: One can assert $p \mathbin{\&} q$ if one can assert p and assert q.

$\neg$: One can assert $\neg p$ if one possesses a construction which leads to a contradiction from the supposition that a proof of p was carried out.

Let 'A' be an abbreviation for the statement 'There are seven consecutive sevens in the decimal expansion of pi'. Then, to be able to assert

$$A \vee \neg A$$

either I must be able to assert A (which I cannot do since I have no proof of A) or I must be able to give a construction (or constructive proof) which leads from a proof of A to a contradiction (which I cannot do either). Hence, given Heyting's intuitionistic interpretation of the connectives, everyone would agree that one cannot assert

$$p \vee \neg p$$

for all propositions p.

At this point, it would seem that Heyting has made a significant retreat from the extravagant anti-classical position of the early Brouwer. At first sight, Heyting's position seems to be quite innocuous: His rejection of the law of excluded middle seems to involve nothing more radical than a reinterpretation of the logical connectives! But there is more to Heyting's rejection of classical logical laws than this. Consider his example of a definition which is acceptable to traditional mathematicians but is not acceptable to intuitionists:

$$l = \begin{cases} k, \text{ where } k \text{ is the greatest prime number having the} \\ \quad \text{property that } k - 2 \text{ is also a prime (if there is such} \\ \quad \text{a number);} \\ 1 \text{ if there is no such number.} \end{cases}$$

Heyting does not regard the above definition as legitimate because we have no method of calculating l ([42], p. 2). In this respect, the above definition contrasts sharply with the previous definition of Brouwer's. Now Heyting goes on to say that this rejection of the above definition presupposes the rejection of the law of excluded middle, "for if the sequence of twin primes were either finite or not finite . . . the above definition would define an integer." In this passage, Heyting is surely not claiming that intuitionists reject the intuitionistic analogue of the classical law of excluded middle. Evidently, he is claiming that intuitionists also reject the classical version. But if this is so, what are his grounds for this rejection? He claims that he cannot understand the classical theorem, "Either there exist finitely many twin primes or there do not exist finitely many twin primes." He argues that if 'there exist' is given the intuitionist interpretation, it is not legitimate to make this assertion; and if 'there exist' does not mean what intuitionists mean, "it must have some metaphysical meaning" ([42], p. 2).

Heyting's attitude toward existence statements in classical mathematics is not all that strange. It was argued in previous chapters that classical mathematics at least seems to be Platonic in character, abounding in assertions that seem to assert the existence of abstract entities. Being unable to attach a clear meaning to such statements as

'There are infinitely many twin primes', which would preserve the classical law of excluded middle, Heyting advocates adopting a constructivistic interpretation of the quantifiers. Thus, let $P(x)$ be a predicate of one variable x, x ranging over some intuitionistically acceptable totality Q. Heyting explains what is meant by '$(\exists x) P(x)$' by saying:

> $(\exists x) P(x)$ will be true if and only if an element a of Q for which $P(a)$ is true has actually been constructed.

If we take Heyting's words at face value, existential assertions in intuitionistic mathematics are ambiguous with respect to time in the way 'It is raining' is ambiguous. If at t_0, someone says "$(\exists x) P(x)$," when as a matter of fact no element a of Q has been constructed for which $P(a)$ is true, then the assertion is false. However, if at t_1, $t_1 > t_0$, the same sentence is uttered by the same person, and in the meantime he has come up with the required construction, what is asserted is true. (Cf. Heyting [42], pp. 2-3). That mathematical propositions change in truth value as time passes is, of course, paradoxical. The alternative seems to be that mathematical assertions of the above sort are simply ambiguous. One can avoid this troublesome feature by shifting from giving truth conditions for '$(\exists x) P(x)$' as Heyting does and instead giving assertability conditions (as he did in the case of the truth functional connectives). This might be done roughly as follows:

One can assert '$(\exists x) P(x)$' if one has a construction of a, an element of Q, and a proof that '$P(a)$' is true.

Now it is clear that I interpret neither the connectives nor the quantifiers in the way Heyting does. Hence, the fact that the law of excluded middle is incompatible with Heyting's intuitionistic interpretation of the logical constants does not preclude the law from being compatible with my interpretation of Σ_ω. This is not to say, however, that I can prove the validity of the law of excluded middle for my system. I can offer a sort of Russellian–Quinian argument for accepting the law, based upon "pragmatic" considerations. And I can appeal to intuition. Indeed, most people agree that if one were to follow the rules for constructing the decimal expansion of pi without end, either one would eventually construct seven consecutive sevens or one would never do so. However, such appeals to intuition may carry very little weight to an opposing philosopher. And in any case, some philosophers would regard such subjunctive conditional statements as too unclear in meaning to enable us to assert with any confidence that the statement is true. The corresponding modal statement, "Either it is possible to follow the rules for constructing the decimal expansion of pi and get seven consecutive sevens, or it is not possible," would undoubtedly be equally unacceptable to these philosophers. Still, it would be strange if such statements were meaningless. For if someday we should find seven consecutive sevens in carrying out the decimal expansion of pi, we would certainly want to say they are true.[2] In any case, we should consider the possibility that some of the statements of Σ_ω (under my interpretation) are so unclear in sense that the law of excluded middle does not obtain in the system. I shall take this point up in a later section.

7. How the No-class Theory can be Applied

I do not wish to leave the reader with the idea that I believe I have refuted Quine's argument for ontological Platonism. Actually, I see no reason why a nominalist should be required to refute the argument. The principal questions that should be considered, as I see it, are: "Which of the ontological alternatives is the more plausible?" "And which seems to provide the more fruitful line of research?"

Let us once more reconsider the reasoning that led Quine to espouse ontological Platonism. The nominalist, supposedly, must renounce all bound variables for abstract entities that he cannot explain away by paraphrases—unless he is willing to deny that his "platonic" assertions are true. But if the nominalist does deny that

[2] According to G. E. Moore, Wittgenstein once argued that the sentence 'There are three consecutive sevens in the decimal expansion of pi' is nonsense. But having affirmed this position, he then claimed that if someone carried out a decimal expansion of pi for ten years and actually found three consecutive sevens, this would prove that there were three consecutive sevens in "a ten year expansion of pi"! (Moore [56], p. 302). Evidently, Wittgenstein eventually came to admit that the above sentence about pi does have sense, although a "very curious" one (p. 303).

some of his mathematical assertions are true, he is precluded from giving the most straightforward and (so it would be argued) plausible explanation of the usefulness of mathematical theories in the empirical sciences, namely the explanation that the mathematical theory is useful because it is true. From these considerations, it would seem that the main theoretical advantage of ontological Platonism lies in its ability to explain the usefulness of mathematics. (At this point we may ask: What genuine explanatory power does the postulation of sets have, other than this?) The Quinian approach to the justification of Platonism is to be contrasted with the Gödelian approach which tries to find the explanatory value of ontological Platonism primarily in its explanation of mathematical intuition: It is in its use in explaining "applications of mathematics" that Quine finds the principal explanatory value of ontological Platonism. Now the nominalist cannot give the Platonist's explanation of the usefulness of mathematics, but he is certainly not prevented from giving any explanation of it, as I shall argue in this section.

Can a nominalist actually apply Σ_ω in empirical contexts when the system is given the above no-class interpretation? The following examples will illustrate one way in which this no-class theory could be used by the empirical scientist. Let us imagine a scientist analysing the flow of heat in a slab of homogeneous material as follows: The slab is described as a set of ordered triples of real numbers bounded by the planes $x = 0$ and $x = \text{pi}$. It is assumed that the initial temperature of the slab is given by some function $u = f(x)$, the values of which depend only on the distances from the faces. In addition, certain other assumptions are thought to be reasonable: it is assumed that $f(x)$ is sectionally continuous in the interval $(0, \text{pi})$ and has one-sided derivatives at all interior points of that interval. Certain other boundary conditions are assumed to hold. Now the heat equation

$$\frac{\partial u}{\partial t} = K \frac{\partial^2 u}{\partial x^2} \ (0 < x < \text{pi}, t > 0)$$

is an idealized mathematical representation of the flux of temperature which has been found to agree closely with experimental data. Clearly, the situation has been "idealized." For example, the actual dimensions of the slab only approximate those given by the mathematical representation: under magnification, the edges of the slab can be seen to be rough and jagged, the sides have pits, the corners are rounded. But the scientist will expect some small discrepancies to arise from these idealizations and will take account of them. Now the problem is to find a function that satisfies the heat equation and the boundary conditions. At this point, the physicist can make use of the mathematician's work. Using the results of classical analysis, it can be shown that the series

$$\sum_1^\infty b_n\, e^{-n^2 K t} \sin nx$$

satisfies all the given conditions.[3] Theoretically, the physicist can determine, by using this function, the temperature at all points in the slab at every instant.

Now consider a much simpler example. Suppose that a projectile is shot into a gigantic vacuum chamber and that a scientist knows the muzzle velocity and the angle from the horizontal at which the projectile enters the chamber. As in the previous example, this scientist "idealizes" the situation, representing the projectile as being subjected to only the force of gravity inside the chamber. He then makes use of known empirical relationships ($F = ma$) and empirically determined facts (the force of gravity at that elevation is such and such) in calculating the apogee of the path of the projectile. The reasoning involves the use of elementary calculus. Let us consider how the no-class Σ_ω might be used in place of the usual classical mathematics in this situation. We can regard the open sentence

The projectile is n feet from the floor of the chamber at time t

as determining a vague or "fuzzy" set of ordered pairs of numbers. In calculating the apogee with the usual classical systems, one ordinarily identifies this vague set with some precise set describable in the mathematical theory. It is at that point that the scientist makes

---

[3] See Churchill, [20], pp. 102 f.

use of the sort of "idealization" that Duhem emphasized in [25].[4] However, we could use some precise "set" from Σ_ω instead of the classical set (in which case we would be using an open sentence rather than a set in our calculation). Similarly, the "extensions" of such open sentences as

The vertical velocity of the projectile at time t is x feet per second

The vertical acceleration of the projectile at time t is x feet per second per second

can be regarded as the rough counterparts of extensions of certain open sentences of the no-class theory. The mathematical reasoning could then proceed in Σ_ω much as it does in a classical system.

Clearly, the reasoning of the first example can be carried through in a similar manner by using Σ_ω. All the equations of the example could be interpreted to be about open sentences instead of sets, so that the theorems of Σ_ω that are analogous to the classical ones could be used to provide the required information to the scientist.

There are, of course, differences between the functions of Σ_ω and the usual classical functions. For example, in Σ_ω one cannot have a function defined over all the real numbers: each real function is only defined over real numbers of a certain finite order. But it is hard to see how these differences could lead to any incorrect empirical predictions or to erroneous scientific conclusions. I am reminded of Poincaré's remark:

Now the numbers the physicist measures by experiment are never known except approximately; and besides, any function always differs as little as you choose from a discontinuous function, and at the same time it differs as little as you choose from a continuous function. The physicist may, therefore, at will suppose that the function studied is continuous, or that it is discontinuous; that it has or has not a derivative; and may do so without fear of ever being contradicted, either by

[4] Cf. Duhem's comment: "What the physicist states as the result of an experiment is not the recital of observed facts, but the interpretation and the transposing of these facts into the ideal, abstract, symbolic world created by the theories he regards as established." [25], p. 159.

present experience or by any future experiment. We see that with such liberty he makes sport of difficulties which stop the analyst ([63], p 83).

Even if Poincaré exaggerated the freedom with which physicists can operate, surely mathematicians have long noticed the sort of thing Poincaré had in mind. Of course, looked at from the above point of view, this "freedom" need not be "lack of rigor", as some mathematicians humorously describe it.

One way, then, in which the no-class Σ_ω can be applied is outlined by the following schema:

(a) Appropriate open sentences are constructed ('The projectile is n feet from the ground at time t'), certain substitutional sentences of which are true or approximately true ('The projectile is 10.7 feet from the ground at 6.8 seconds passed 5 p.m.').

(b) The open sentences are regarded as determining sets (or, perhaps, "fuzzy sets"), and these sets are regarded as being identical with (or approximately identical with) certain sharply defined sets of Σ_ω.

(c) The theorems of Σ_ω provide the scientist with information about these sets, which is then used to supply information about the empirical situation.

Now in step (b) of the above, one finds that process of simplification and approximation known as "idealization." Scientists consciously make idealizations and are generally aware of the respects in which, and the extent to which, they have idealized the actual situation. Duhem describes an incident which illustrates this fact ([25]). During an experiment, the French scientist, Regnault, corrected a reading which his assistant had taken from a manometer. According to Duhem, the correction was not the expression of a lack of confidence in the powers of observation of his assistant; rather it was the result of a complex process of reasoning. In the first place, Regnault "idealized" the situation in which he was working by representing the *actual* manometer, which consists of glass tubes containing mercury, as an *ideal* one containing "a perfect fluid." It was in terms of this ideal manometer that Regnault theorized, applying the laws of physics and calculating *as if* his manometer were this ideal one. However, finding that his idealization had over-simplified the situation so as to yield significant distortions, he was forced to idealize the real manometer in a slightly more complicated but more accurate way, and in this way, he produced a correction. Thus, Regnault first represented the manometer as having an incompressible fluid, each point in the fluid having the same temperature and each point on its free surfaces being subjected to an atmospheric pressure independent of its height. Then after realizing that his idealization would result in significant discrepancies, Regnault changed his representation of the manometer to that of one containing a compressible fluid. He also allowed variations in temperature in the manometer and changes in the barometric pressure on the free surfaces of the fluid.

Clearly, scientists do take account of the fact that they have idealized the actual situation when they apply their theories. A scientist might expect his Fourier-series solution to the boundary-value problem discussed in the first example of this section to give the distribution of temperature with a reasonable degree of accuracy as one moved from centimeter to centimeter inside the slab. However, few would expect such an analysis of temperature to reflect the differences in temperature inside the atoms of the slab which one would expect from an analysis of the structure and nature of atoms.

In view of the fact that Σ_ω can be used in the above way, it is not stretching things too far, I believe, to say that the system of open sentences about which Σ_ω is a theory provides scientists with a conceptual or linguistic tool for describing and representing physical states, processes, and interactions. One might even say that the system enlarges the physicist's language—which, after all, is not so far from Poincaré's doctrine that the mathematician provides the physicist with a language. Where Poincaré seems to have gone wrong is in suggesting that the mathematician *only* gives the physicist a language. For he seems not to have given sufficient weight to the mathematician's theories. The theory, Σ_ω, should not be identified either with the language of the theory or with the linguistic entities (the open sentences) that prove to be so useful to the physicist in representing physical events. The mathematical theory gives the physicist genuine information—information that can be translated into predictions of verifiable physical events and that could lead to machines not working, bridges collapsing, and even stronger expectations being unfulfilled if it is incorrect.

8. *Some Objections Considered*

In this concluding section, I shall take up several objections to the view developed in this chapter and present some replies to them.

8.1 It might be suggested that I have provided only a sketch of a nominalistic theory of mathematics and that the platonic view should be accepted until it is shown in detail how the anti-(ontological) Platonist can account for all of the applications of mathematics in the empirical sciences without presupposing abstract entities. I would agree that the position I have presented has not been fully developed and that many details need to be worked out. But is it the case that we have two competing theories, one of which has been worked out in detail and found to be adequate and the other of which has only been worked out in outline? On the contrary, the Quine–Berry explanation that mathematics is useful to the scientist because it is a true description of the universe of sets is itself only an outline of an explanation: We are by no means given a detailed explanation of how mathematics is applied in specific cases (such as the boundary-value example) and of why, in these cases, mathematics proves to be so useful to scientists. And as I mentioned in Chapter III, much of Quine's philosophy of science is only programatic.

8.2 Let us reconsider Quine's objections to the use of subjunctive conditionals and modal terms in science. His thesis is: All traits of reality worthy of the name can be set down in his canonical notation. Since there are obvious advantages to using such an extensional language of science, Quine concludes that we ought to reconstruct our sciences in his strict notation and eschew the use of subjective conditionals and modal terms.

Now it should be noted that, despite the nonstandard interpretation of the quantifiers, the formal language of Σ_ω has the clean and simple structure of Quine's canonical grammar and hence has many of the attractive features of his "language of science." However, I certainly would not claim that the sentences of the no-class Σ_ω express "traits of reality worthy of the name." Perhaps Quine would then claim that such sentences do not express genuine "scientific truths." I see no reason for contesting this point either. The important question is whether or not the anti-(ontological) Platonist can use this system in his scientific work. Here, I would argue that, by using Σ_ω in the way I have indicated above, nominalists (in the sense in which I am using this term) can have scientific theories that include substantially more mathematics than very elementary arithmetic.

It is tempting to attribute to Quine's overall view of science advantages that scientific theories would possess if they were reconstructed in Quine's canonical notation. It should be emphasized that Quine's own theory of science is not expressed in his canonical notation or even in terms of concepts that Quine finds acceptable from the scientific point of view. He has recently argued that the subjective conditional belongs to a family of disreputable notions, each of which is definable or explicable in terms of the other members of this family, but no one of which can be defined in a more satisfactory way, say, in terms of acceptable scientific concepts ([92], p. 129). (Cf. Quine's attitude toward the analyticity family of terms). This family includes, besides the subjunctive conditional, the notions of *disposition*, *similarity*, *kind* and *cause*. One interesting feature of Quine's view is this: although he regards these notions as scientifically disreputable, he admits that they are "practically indispensible." He says that they are "crucial to all learning, and central in particular to the process of inductive generalization and prediction which are the very life of science" ([92], p. 133). In general, it is only when a particular branch of science has matured and developed to a high degree, Quine tells us, that its dispositional terms and subjunctive conditionals become "superfluous." Evidently, Quine's own scientific views have not yet reached this point of development, for he frequently makes use of the notion of disposition in stating his own theory of human knowledge. Hence, although the existence of sets is required by Quine's general view of science and mathematics, it is not true that he has expressed this view in the sort of extensional language he advocates for science and free of such disreputable notions as dispositions and subjunctive conditionals. In this respect then, Quine's platonic view is not superior to the nominalistic one I have sketched in this chapter.

Still, we should reconsider the doubts regarding subjunctive conditionals (and modal terms) that we raised earlier: Are the subjunctive conditionals, into which the sentences of Σ_ω are translated, meaningful? Are they true or false? As I said earlier, I have no doubt that in some sense they are meaningful. That we understand such statements as 'If one were to carry out, correctly, the decimal expansion of *pi* without ever stopping, one would either construct seven consecutive sevens or never construct seven consecutive sevens' is indicated by the fact that we all know what would verify the statement and we know what sorts of things would refute the statement (a deduction of a contradiction from the assumption that someone had correctly carried out an expansion of *pi* which contained seven consecutive sevens would certainly refute the statement). However, let us suppose, for the sake of argument, that some of the subjunctive conditional statements of the language of Σ_ω are neither true nor false. Would this make the system unusable? Would the anti-(ontological) Platonist be forced to restrict his science to very elementary arithmetic? Not at all. For what is clearly essential to the sorts of "applications" of the no-class theory discussed in section 5 is that there be accepted procedures and techniques for objectively and intelligibly classifying its statements (not necessarily all) as 'true' or 'false'. The subjunctive statements I have been discussing all involve a multitude of rules and techniques we have mastered. We know how to follow these rules and apply the techniques, so that even an un-mathematical novice can, with little or no prompting, determine the truth or falsity of statements of the no-class theory. Even if there are some "undecidable statements," this would not make the system unusable for such empirical purposes, nor would it especially bother a physicist.

8.3 Brouwer's criticism of classical mathematics is open to the following reply: If classical analysis is an "incorrect theory" containing many false theorems (as Brouwer claimed [8]), why has it been so successful and so fruitful in the empirical sciences? A similar objection might be raised against the view put forward in this chapter. If platonic mathematical theories are not literally true, why have they proved to be so useful in science? This objection poses less of a problem for the anti-(ontological) Platonist than it does for the intuitionist, since the analysis of Σ_ω is more like classical analysis than is intuitionistic analysis. Thus, the nominalist could say that the mathematical theories that are so useful in science, such as classical analysis, can be approximated by theories constructable within the no-class Σ_ω. He could then argue (although details would have to be supplied) that the differences between the two versions are not such as to lead to significant differences when they are "applied" in the empirical sciences.

8.4 The following sort of response to the position developed in this chapter was once suggested to me by Hilary Putnam: Let us grant, for the sake of argument, that Σ_ω is sufficient for the scientific theories of today. But what about future science? Who knows what sort of mathematics may be needed twenty years from now? Is it not absurd to limit scientists to predicative mathematics because of nominalistic qualms?

Such an objection suggests that I should clarify my position further. I should emphasize that I am not suggesting that we limit empirical scientists to some brand of mathematics. I have not argued in this essay, as did Poincaré and Russell, that impredicative mathematics is inherently unscientific. Even though the no-class alternative to Platonism I have sketched here clearly owes much to the work of Poincaré, Russell, and Wang, there is nothing in the doctrine that requires accepting the *arguments* of these predicativists that supposedly show that the set theories which violate the vicious-circle principle are unintelligible, unsound, or illogical. Indeed, the position of this chapter is compatible with accepting the mythological approach to platonic systems of mathematics described in Chapter II. What I have suggested is that if Σ_ω is sufficient for present-day science, then Quinian considerations do not compel us to postulate the existence of abstract entities *at this time*. If science should some day presuppose the truth of a mathematical system that extends beyond predicative systems, or if predicative systems should prove to be insufficient for the needs of scientists even today, then perhaps we shall have good reason for adopting the Quinian ontology. In that event, Quine's arguments may persuade more philosophers than they do now.

8.5 It might be argued that my no-class theory is not faithful to the Poincaré-Russell vicious-circle principle, since I make use of inductive definitions in constructing the interpretation. It is some-times thought that the use of inductive definitions presupposes a violation of the spirit, if not the letter, of the vicious-circle principle, because "when inductive definitions are converted into explicit ones by the Frege-Dedekind method, the results are definitely impredica-tive" (Wang [117], p. 644).

Now Poincaré was not reluctant to use inductive definitions. As I noted earlier, he held that it is only through inductive definitions and the principle of mathematical induction that we can "pass from the finite to the infinite." It is clear that Poincaré did not take induc-tive definitions to involve a violation of his version of the vicious-circle principle. Russell, on the other hand, felt some difficulties in trying to justify the use of induction. I think it is a mistake to look for a difference of vicious-circle principles to explain this difference of attitudes toward induction. Basically, this difference arose out of a significant difference of attitudes toward the foundations of mathe-matics. Russell's problems with induction arose out of his "logicism"; more specifically, out of his attempt to justify the use of inductive definitions and the principle of mathematical induction from the "logical" axioms of *PM*. Poincaré, on the other hand, did not regard the method of induction as needing some more ultimate justification.

The no-class interpretation of this chapter is much closer, in spirit, to Poincaré's views. The basic insights upon which it proceeds involve laying down effective rules of construction, and reasoning about the results of applying these rules. Inductive definitions and mathematical induction are basic to this reasoning, and no attempt is made to base these on set-theoretical principles. On the contrary, set theory is based on this reasoning.

8.6 My no-class interpretation involves interpreting the quantifiers in a nonstandard way. Hence, one cannot apply Quine's criterion of ontological commitment to a theory so interpreted; *a fortiori*, one cannot say that the no-class theory *S* is not ontologically com-mitted to abstract entities (Cf. Parsons [60], pp. 162-3).

I raise this objection at the end because it allows me to finish this essay with a brief summary of my response to Quine's argument for ontological Platonism. Recall that in Chapter III, I claimed to find a number of defects in Quine's argument. For example, I found fault with his criterion of ontological commitment and gave reasons for questioning his criterion of ontological reduction. However, I was able to formulate an argument for ontological Platonism that seemed to capture the main ideas of Quine's argument but did not depend upon accepting the various Quinian doctrines I found questionable. In this chapter, I have been arguing along two lines. On the one hand, I have continued to examine and criticize Quine's own position, insofar as it is discernable in his writings. Thus, showing that the ontology of W is reducible, by Quine's own proxy-function criterion, to the ontology of S (when the quantifiers are interpreted in the standard way) was primarily aimed at some things Quine has said in print. But on the other hand, I have been concerned with the reformulated Quinian argument, which does not depend for its force on the specific doctrines put forward by Quine. And it is this argument that prompted me to give the nonstandard interpretations to the quantifiers in constructing the no-class set theory. The Quinian argument does not depend upon Quine's defective criterion of ontological commitment, but it does demand of the nominalist an explanation of the existential statements of the mathematical system used in his empirical sciences. In this chapter, I have indicated one way in which those philosophers who are skeptical of the ontological claims of the Platonist might reply to this demand.

Appendix

1. *Terms*

a. *Variables*: The italicized lower case letters

$$u, v, w, x, y, z,$$

with subscripts and with or without superscripts 0, 1, 2,..., ω.

b. *Constants*: If φ is a formula containing no variable subscripted ω and containing free occurrences of only one variable α, then $\hat{\alpha}\varphi$ is a constant.

2. *Formulas*

a. *Atomic*: If α and β are terms, then $\alpha \in \beta$ and $\alpha = \beta$ are atomic formulas.

b. *Molecular*: If φ and ψ are formulas, then $-\varphi$, $(\varphi \ \& \ \psi)$, $(\varphi \lor \psi)$, $(\varphi \to \psi)$, and $(\varphi \leftrightarrow \psi)$ are molecular formulas.

c. *Quantificational*: If φ is a formula and α is a variable, then $(\exists\alpha)\varphi$ is a quantificational formula.

3. *The Order Function $\mathcal{O}$*

a. *Variables*: The order of a variable is the ordinal denoted by its subscript, i.e. $\mathcal{O}(\alpha_j) = j$.

b. *Formulas and Constants of Order* 0:

(i) If α is a variable of order zero, then the formula $\alpha \neq \alpha$ is a *basic formula*.

(ii) If φ is a *basic formula* containing free occurrences of only one variable α, then $\mathcal{O}(\hat{\alpha}\varphi) = 0$.

213

(iii) If α and β are constants of order zero, γ is a variable of order zero, then the formula $(\gamma \in \alpha \vee \gamma = \beta)$ is a *basic formula*.

c. *Constants of Order Greater Than Zero:* If $\hat{\alpha}\varphi$ is a constant and φ is not basic, then $\mathcal{O}(\hat{\alpha}\varphi) = \max\{\mathcal{O}(\alpha) + 1, \mathcal{O}(\varphi)\}$.

d. *Other Formulas:*

(i) $\mathcal{O}(\alpha \in \beta) = \mathcal{O}(\alpha = \beta) = \max\{\mathcal{O}(\alpha), \mathcal{O}(\beta)\}$.

(ii) $\mathcal{O}(\varphi) = \max\{\mathcal{O}(\psi) : \psi$ is a truth functional component of $\varphi\}$.

(iii) $\mathcal{O}((\exists\alpha)\varphi) = \max\{\mathcal{O}(\alpha) + 1, \mathcal{O}(\varphi)\}$ if $\mathcal{O}(\alpha) < \omega$
$\qquad\qquad\quad = \omega$ if $\mathcal{O}(\alpha) = \omega$.

4. *Abbreviation*

The Universal Quantifier: $(\alpha)\varphi$ is an abbreviation for $-(\exists\alpha) - \varphi$.

5. *The Nesting Function $\mathcal{N}$*

a. *Terms:*

(i) *Variables:* $\mathcal{N}(\alpha) = 0$.

(ii) *Constants:* $\mathcal{N}(\hat{\alpha}\varphi) = \mathcal{N}(\varphi) + 1$ if $\mathcal{O}(\varphi) = \mathcal{O}(\hat{\alpha}\varphi)$;
$\qquad\qquad\qquad\qquad = 0$ otherwise.

b. *Formulas:*

$\mathcal{N}(\varphi) = \max\{\mathcal{N}(\alpha) : \alpha$ is a constant occurring in φ and $\mathcal{O}(\alpha) = \mathcal{O}(\varphi)\} \cup \{0\}$.

6. *The Length Function $\mathcal{L}$*

a. *Atomic Formulas:*

$\mathcal{L}(\alpha \in \beta) = 0$ if $\mathcal{O}(\alpha) < \mathcal{O}(\beta)$ or
$\qquad\qquad\qquad$ if $\mathcal{O}(\alpha) = \mathcal{O}(\beta) = 0$ and $\mathcal{N}(\alpha) < \mathcal{N}(\beta)$.
$\qquad\qquad = 4$ otherwise.

$\mathcal{L}(\alpha = \beta) = 2$.

b. *Molecular Formulas:*

$\mathcal{L}(\varphi) = \max\{\mathcal{L}(\psi) : \psi$ is a truth functional component of φ, $\mathcal{O}(\psi) = \mathcal{O}(\varphi)$, and $\mathcal{N}(\psi) = \mathcal{N}(\varphi)\} \cup \{0\}$.

c. *Quantificational Formulas:*

$\mathcal{L}((\exists\alpha)\varphi) = \mathcal{L}(\varphi) + 1$.

d. *Terms:*

$\mathcal{L}(\alpha) = 0$.

7. *The Degree Function $\mathscr{D}$ for Terms and Formulas*

$\mathscr{D}(\varphi) = \omega^2 \cdot \mathcal{O}(\varphi) + \omega \cdot \mathcal{N}(\varphi) + \mathscr{L}(\varphi).$

8. *The Necessary Conditions for an Adequate Interpretation of Σ_ω*

(1) If $\alpha \in \hat{\beta}\varphi$ is true, then $\varphi\,\beta/\alpha$ is true.

(2) $\alpha = \beta$ is true iff for every constant γ, $(\gamma \in \alpha \leftrightarrow \gamma \in \beta)$ is true.

(3) If $\mathcal{O}(\alpha) \leqslant \mathcal{O}(\beta)$ and $\varphi\,\beta/\alpha$ is true, then $\alpha \in \hat{\beta}\varphi$ is true.

(4) If $\mathcal{O}(\alpha) > \mathcal{O}(\beta)$, then $\alpha \in \hat{\beta}\varphi$ is true iff for some constant γ of order less than or equal to $\mathcal{O}(\beta)$, both $\alpha = \gamma$ and $\gamma \in \hat{\beta}\varphi$ are true.

(5) $(\exists\alpha)\varphi$ is true iff for some constant β of order less than or equal to $\mathcal{O}(\alpha)$, $\varphi\,\alpha/\beta$ is true.

Definition: A constant of order zero is *fundamental* if the only variable that occurs in it is 'x_0'.

Lemma 0.1.1: The relation denoted by '$=$' is an equivalence relation under any adequate interpretation.

Lemma 0.1.2: Under any adequate interpretation, for every constant α of order zero, there is a fundamental constant β such that $\alpha = \beta$ is true and $\mathcal{N}(\beta) = \mathcal{N}(\alpha)$.

Lemma 0.1.3: Under any adequate interpretation, for constants α and β of order zero, $\alpha \in \beta$ is true iff there is a fundamental constant γ such that $\mathcal{N}(\gamma) < \mathcal{N}(\beta)$ and $(\gamma \in \beta\ \&\ \gamma = \alpha)$ is true.

Proofs: 0.1.1 follows from condition (2). 0.1.2 follows from conditions (1), (2), and (3). The proof is by induction on $\mathcal{N}(\alpha)$. To prove 0.1.3, let us first assume that $\alpha \in \beta$ is true. If $\mathcal{N}(\alpha) < \mathcal{N}(\beta)$, then the conclusion we want follows from 0.1.2. So assume otherwise. If β is of the form $\hat{\delta}(\delta \neq \delta)$, where $\mathcal{O}(\delta) = 0$, then $\alpha \in \beta$ is false. Hence β must be of the form $\hat{\delta}(\delta \in \zeta \vee \delta = \eta)$. We now prove what we want by course of value induction on $\mathcal{N}(\beta)$. By condition (1), $(\alpha \in \zeta \vee \alpha = \eta)$ must be true. If $\alpha \in \zeta$ is true, then by the induction hypothesis we get what we want. If $\alpha = \eta$ is true, then by 0.1.1, 0.1.2 (applied to η), and condition (3) we arrive at the desired conclusion. The other direction is proved in a straightforward way by induction on the *index* of ϕ, where β is $\hat{\delta}\phi$. (The index of ϕ

is the number of occurrences of connectives and quantifiers in ϕ).

Lemma 0.2: If α is a term of order zero, then there are only a finite number of fundamental constants β such that $\mathcal{N}(\beta) \leqslant \mathcal{N}(\alpha)$.

Proof: Use induction on $\mathcal{N}(\alpha)$.

Definition: In view of Lemma 0.2, one can make the following definitions. If ϕ is a formula containing free occurrences of only one variable α, then $\bigvee_n \phi$ is the disjunction of all substitution instances $\phi \, \alpha/\beta$, where β is a fundamental constant of nesting less than n. $\bigwedge_n \varphi$ is the conjunction of these.

Definition: A *normal assignment function* is a function from the sentences of Σ_ω into $\{0, 1\}$, the values of which, for molecular sentences, are determined by the appropriate truth function of its values for the non-molecular components (under the convention: 0 is true, 1 is false). (See Mates [54] p. 85).

Definition: I divide the non-molecular sentences into nine disjoint classes. For each of these classes, I provide a clause which either gives a value of a normal assignment function T for sentences in this class or connects a value of T for sentences in this class with the value of T for sentences in another class. I shall refer to these nine clauses as *truth conditions*.

Sentences of Order 0

1. $\alpha = \beta$, where $\mathcal{N}(\alpha) = \mathcal{N}(\beta) = 1$: $T(\alpha = \beta) = 0$.
2. $\hat{\alpha}\varphi = \hat{\beta}\psi$, where $\max\{\mathcal{N}(\hat{\alpha}\varphi), \mathcal{N}(\hat{\beta}\psi)\} > 1$: $T(\hat{\alpha}\varphi = \hat{\beta}\psi) = T(\bigwedge_n (\varphi \, \alpha/\gamma \leftrightarrow \psi \, \beta/\gamma))$ where $n = \mathcal{N}(\hat{\alpha}\varphi = \hat{\beta}\psi)$ and γ is the first variable of order zero not occurring in either φ or ψ.
3. $\alpha \in \beta$, where $\mathcal{N}(\beta) = 1$: $T(\alpha \in \beta) = 1$.
4. $\alpha \in \hat{\beta}\varphi$, where $\mathcal{N}(\hat{\beta}\varphi) > 1$, $\mathcal{N}(\alpha) < \mathcal{N}(\hat{\beta}\varphi)$: $T(\alpha \in \hat{\beta}\varphi) = T(\varphi \, \beta/\alpha)$.
5. $\alpha \in \beta$, where $\mathcal{N}(\beta) > 1$, $\mathcal{N}(\alpha) \geqslant \mathcal{N}(\beta)$: $T(\alpha \in \beta) = T(\bigvee_n (\gamma \in \beta \, \& \, \gamma = \alpha))$, where $n = \mathcal{N}(\beta)$ and γ is the first variable of order zero.

Sentences of Order Greater than Zero

6. $\alpha \in \hat{\beta}\phi$, where $\mathcal{O}(\alpha) \leqslant \mathcal{O}(\beta)$: $T(\alpha \in \hat{\beta}\phi) = T(\phi \, \beta/\alpha)$.

7. $\alpha \in \hat{\beta}\phi$, where $\mathcal{O}(\alpha) > \mathcal{O}(\beta)$: $T(\alpha \in \hat{\beta}\phi) = T((\exists\gamma)(\phi\,\beta/\gamma\,\&\,\gamma = \alpha))$ where γ is the first variable of order equal to $\mathcal{O}(\beta)$ that does not occur in either α or ϕ.

3. $\hat{\alpha}\phi = \hat{\beta}\psi$, where $\mathcal{O}(\hat{\alpha}\phi = \hat{\beta}\psi) = n + 1$: $T(\hat{\alpha}\phi = \hat{\beta}\psi) = T((\gamma)(\gamma \in \hat{\alpha}\phi \leftrightarrow \gamma \in \hat{\beta}\psi))$ where γ is the variable consisting of 'x' with the numeral denoting n as subscript.

9. $(\exists\alpha)\phi$: $T((\exists\alpha)\phi) = \min\{T(\phi\,\alpha/\beta) : \mathcal{O}(\beta) \leqslant \mathcal{O}(\alpha)\}$.

Theorem 1: There is exactly one normal assignment function which satisfies the above truth conditions.

Lemma 1.1: If ϕ is a formula containing a free occurrence of a variable α, $\mathcal{O}(\alpha) < \mathcal{O}(\phi)$, and γ is a constant of order less than the order of ϕ, then $\mathcal{D}(\phi) = \mathcal{D}(\phi\,\alpha/\gamma)$.

Proof: By straightforward induction on the index of formulas.

Lemma 1.2: In each of the nine truth conditions except 1 and 3, any sentence appearing on the left has a larger degree than the corresponding sentences appearing on the right.

Lemma 1.2.1: If α is a variable, ψ is a formula and β is a term such that $\mathcal{O}(\beta) \leqslant \mathcal{O}(\alpha)$, then $\mathcal{O}(\psi\,\alpha/\beta) \leqslant \mathcal{O}(\psi)$.

Lemma 1.2.2: If α is a free variable in a formula ψ, then $\mathcal{O}(\psi) \geqslant \mathcal{O}(\alpha)$.

Lemma 1.2.3: If α is a variable and ψ is a formula such that $\mathcal{O}(\psi) > \mathcal{O}(\alpha)$, and β is a term such that $\mathcal{O}(\beta) \leqslant \mathcal{O}(\alpha)$, then $\mathcal{O}(\psi\,\alpha/\beta) = \mathcal{O}(\psi)$.

Lemma 1.2.4: If ψ is a formula, α, β are variables, and $\mathcal{O}(\alpha) = \mathcal{O}(\beta)$, then $\mathcal{D}(\psi\,\alpha/\beta) = \mathcal{D}(\psi)$.

Lemma 1.2.5: If ψ is a formula containing no variable of order ω, then $\mathcal{O}(\psi) < \omega$. Hence $\mathcal{O}(\alpha) < \omega$, if α is a constant.

Remark: Lemmas 1.2.1–1.2.5 can be proved in each case by induction on the index of the formula ψ. *Lemmas* 1.2.1 and 1.2.3 are used in checking *Clause* 6.

Proof of Lemma 1.2: By examination of the nine clauses, the above can be easily checked. I shall examine three of the clauses.

Clause 5: $T(\alpha \in \beta) = T(V_n\,(\gamma \in \beta\,\&\,\gamma = \alpha))$.

If δ is a fundamental constant such that $\mathcal{N}(\delta) <$

$\mathcal{N}(\beta)$, then $\mathcal{N}(\delta \in \beta \ \& \ \delta = \alpha) = \mathcal{N}(\alpha \in \beta)$ and $\mathcal{L}(\alpha \in \beta) = 4$, which is greater than $\mathcal{L}\ (\delta \in \beta) = 0$ and $\mathcal{L}(\delta = \alpha) = 2$.

Clause 7: $T(\alpha \in \hat{\beta}\phi) = T((\exists \gamma)(\phi \ \beta/\gamma \ \& \ \gamma = \alpha))$.

(1) $\mathcal{O}(\alpha \in \hat{\beta}\phi) = \max\{\mathcal{O}(\alpha), \mathcal{O}(\phi)\}$;
$\mathcal{O}((\exists \gamma)(\phi \ \beta/\gamma \ \& \ \gamma = \alpha)) = \max\{\mathcal{O}(\alpha), \mathcal{O}(\phi \ \beta/\gamma)\}$.

By *Lemma* 1.2.4, $\mathcal{O}(\alpha \in \hat{\beta}\phi) = \mathcal{O}((\exists \gamma)(\phi \ \beta/\gamma \ \& \ \gamma = \alpha))$.

(2) If $\mathcal{O}(\alpha) < \mathcal{O}(\hat{\beta}\phi)$, then $\mathcal{N}(\alpha \in \hat{\beta}\phi) = 1 + \mathcal{N}(\phi)$, and $\mathcal{N}((\exists \gamma)(\phi \ \beta/\gamma \ \& \ \gamma = \alpha)) = \mathcal{N}(\phi \ \beta/\gamma)$. Hence, by *Lemma* 1.2.4, we are done. If $\mathcal{O}(\alpha) > \mathcal{O}(\hat{\beta}\phi)$, then $\mathcal{N}(\alpha \in \hat{\beta}\phi) = \mathcal{N}(\alpha) = \mathcal{N}((\exists \gamma)(\phi \ \beta/\gamma \ \& \ \gamma = \alpha))$. If $\mathcal{O}(\alpha) = \mathcal{O}(\hat{\beta}\phi)$, then either $\mathcal{O}(\hat{\beta}\phi) > \mathcal{O}(\phi)$ or $\mathcal{O}(\hat{\beta}\phi) = \mathcal{O}(\phi)$. Assume the former. Then $\mathcal{N}(\alpha \in \hat{\beta}\phi) = \mathcal{N}(\alpha) = \mathcal{N}((\exists \gamma)(\phi \ \beta/\gamma \ \& \ \gamma = \alpha))$. Assume the latter. Then $\mathcal{N}(\alpha \in \hat{\beta}\phi) = \max\{\mathcal{N}(\alpha), 1 + \mathcal{N}(\phi)\}$, and $\mathcal{N}((\exists \gamma)(\phi \ \beta/\gamma \ \& \ \gamma = \alpha)) = \max\{\mathcal{N}(\alpha), \mathcal{N}(\phi \ \beta/\gamma)\}$. By *Lemma* 1.2.4, $\mathcal{N}(\alpha \in \hat{\beta}\phi) \geqslant \mathcal{N}((\exists \gamma)(\phi \ \beta/\gamma \ \& \ \gamma = \alpha))$.

(3) We need consider only the case in which $\mathcal{N}(\alpha \in \hat{\beta}\phi) = \mathcal{N}((\exists \gamma)(\phi \ \beta/\gamma \ \& \ \gamma = \alpha))$. Since $\mathcal{O}(\alpha) > \mathcal{O}(\beta)$, $\mathcal{O}(\alpha) > 0$. From (2), $\mathcal{O}(\alpha) \geqslant \mathcal{O}(\hat{\beta}\phi)$. Hence $\mathcal{L}(\alpha \in \hat{\beta}\phi) = 4$. If $\mathcal{O}(\alpha) > \mathcal{O}(\phi)$, $\mathcal{L}(\phi \ \beta/\gamma \ \& \ \gamma = \alpha) = \mathcal{L}(\gamma = \alpha) = 2$. If $\mathcal{O}(\alpha) = \mathcal{O}(\phi)$, then $\mathcal{O}(\phi) = \mathcal{O}(\hat{\beta}\phi)$. Hence $\mathcal{N}(\hat{\beta}\phi) = 1 + \mathcal{N}(\phi)$. If $\mathcal{N}(\phi) \geqslant \mathcal{N}(\alpha)$, then $\mathcal{N}(\hat{\beta}\phi) > \mathcal{N}(\alpha)$ and hence $\mathcal{N}(\alpha \in \hat{\beta}\phi) \neq \mathcal{N}((\exists \gamma)(\phi \ \beta/\gamma \ \& \ \gamma = \alpha))$, which is impossible. Hence $\mathcal{N}(\phi) < \mathcal{N}(\alpha)$. Then $\mathcal{L}(\phi \ \beta/\gamma \ \& \ \gamma = \alpha) = \mathcal{L}(\gamma = \alpha) = 2$, since $\mathcal{N}(\phi) = \mathcal{N}(\phi \ \beta/\gamma)$ by *Lemma* 1.2.4. Thus $\mathcal{L}((\exists \gamma)(\phi \ \beta/\gamma \ \& \ \gamma = \alpha)) = 3$.

Clause 9: $T((\exists \alpha)\phi) = \min\{T(\phi \ \alpha/\beta) : \mathcal{O}(\beta) \leqslant \mathcal{O}(\alpha)\}$.

By *Lemma* 1.2.2, $\mathcal{O}(\phi) \geqslant \mathcal{O}(\alpha)$. If $\mathcal{O}(\phi) > \mathcal{O}(\alpha)$, then since $\mathcal{O}(\beta) \leqslant \mathcal{O}(\alpha)$, by *Lemma* 1.1, $\mathcal{D}(\phi) = \mathcal{D}(\phi \ \alpha/\beta)$. Hence $\mathcal{D}((\exists \alpha)\phi) \geqslant \mathcal{D}(\phi) + 1 > \mathcal{D}(\phi \ \alpha/\beta)$. If $\mathcal{O}(\phi) = \mathcal{O}(\alpha)$, then either $\mathcal{O}(\alpha) < \omega$ or $\mathcal{O}(\alpha) = \omega$. Assume the former. Then $\mathcal{O}((\exists \alpha)\phi) = \mathcal{O}(\alpha) + 1$. Since by *Lemma* 1.2.1, $\mathcal{O}(\phi) \geqslant \mathcal{O}(\phi \ \alpha/\beta)$, $\mathcal{O}((\exists \alpha)\phi) > \mathcal{O}(\alpha) \geqslant \mathcal{O}(\phi \ \alpha/\beta)$, and hence $\mathcal{D}((\exists \alpha)\phi) > \mathcal{D}(\phi \ \alpha/\beta)$. Suppose $\mathcal{O}(\alpha) = \omega$. Then $\mathcal{O}((\exists \alpha)\phi) = \omega$. If $\mathcal{O}(\phi \ \alpha/\beta) < \omega$, we are done. If $\mathcal{O}(\phi \ \alpha/\beta) = \omega$, then $\mathcal{N}((\exists \alpha)\phi) = \mathcal{N}(\phi \ \alpha/\beta) = 0$, since no constant is of order ω (*Lemma* 1.2.5).

By induction on the index of ϕ, we can prove that $\mathscr{L}(\phi \; \alpha/\beta) \leqslant \mathscr{L}(\phi)$.

Proof of Theorem 1: Let Γ be the collection of non-molecular sentences for which the truth conditions do not determine exactly one value. Suppose Γ is non-empty. Then Γ contains a sentence ϕ such that no sentence in Γ has a degree smaller than ϕ and ϕ falls under exactly one of the nine clauses. But in each case the truth conditions provide a unique value of $T(\phi)$ either directly or in terms of sentences of degree smaller than that of ϕ for which a unique value is given. This contradicts the above. Hence Γ is empty.

Definition: The unique normal assignment function satisfying the above nine truth conditions will be referred to as '$\mathscr{T}$'.

Discussion: The statement of *Theorem* 1 is a little misleading, especially since, from the set-theoretical point of view, the theorem asserts the *existence* of a set of a certain sort. Also from this point of view, what was proved was only that all normal assignment functions satisfying the nine truth conditions are identical; it was never proved that there is such a set. Strictly speaking, the nominalistic position taken in this book does not allow one to make any genuine assertions of the existence of sets. Hence, it will have to be shown how, and in what sense, the nominalist can assert the existence of the function $\mathscr{T}$. This will be done shortly as follows: I shall specify a "no-class" interpretation of the language of Σ_ω that is compatible with my nominalistic position. Under this interpretation (assuming that certain sorts of subjunctive or modal statements have truth values) each sentence of the language has a (unique) truth value. Since the truth functional connectives are interpreted in the standard way, one determines the truth value of a molecular sentence ϕ in the way a Platonist would determine the value of a normal assignment function for argument ϕ. It will be shown that under this interpretation, the nine truth conditions are satisfied. Hence, the "no-class" interpretation, in effect, provides us with the normal assignment function $\mathscr{T}$.

In the following discussion, it will be convenient to continue to use the Platonic mode of speech. Thus, I shall speak of the function $\mathscr{T}$ rather than use clumsy and wordy circumlocutions involving subjunctive conditionals and phrases like 'the value a Platonist would assign to $\mathcal{T}$'. I shall do this primarily for the sake of conciseness but also to make the development of the theory more perspicuous and more comparable to traditional ways of developing such theories. I have already made use of Platonic ways of speaking. For example, clause (9) of the truth conditions is stated in terms of a one- or two-element set. To state the condition in a way compatible with my nominalistic position, I would use either the modal or subjunctive method of translation described in Chapter V, section 4. Of course, if one rejected the very meaningfulness of such sentences as

It is possible to follow rule R and construct a sentence $\phi \, \alpha/\beta$ that is true.

or if one questioned the assumption that such sentences are either true or false, then one would also, no doubt, question *Theorem* 1. I should also mention here that the "no-class" interpretation to be constructed presupposes not only the meaningfulness of subjunctive or modal statements but also an intuitive notion of truth.

Theorem 2: Any normal assignment function $\mathcal{T}'$ satisfying the five necessary conditions for an adequate interpretation of Σ_ω must be identical to $\mathcal{T}$.

Proof: By examining each of the nine truth conditions, it can be seen that $\mathcal{T}'$ must assign the same values to sentences as does $\mathcal{T}$. For example:

Clause 7: $\mathcal{T}'(\alpha \in \hat{\beta}\phi) = 0$ iff $\mathcal{T}'(\gamma \in \hat{\beta}\phi \,\&\, \gamma = \alpha) = 0$ for some constant γ of order less than or equal to that of β (by necessary condition (4)). By necessary conditions (1) and (3), iff $\mathcal{T}'(\phi \, \beta/\gamma \,\&\, \gamma = \alpha) = 0$ for some constant γ of order less than or equal to that of β. By necessary condition (5) iff $\mathcal{T}'((\exists\delta)(\phi \, \beta/\delta \,\&\, \delta = \alpha)) = 0$ where δ is the first variable of order equal to $\mathcal{O}(\beta)$ that does not occur in ϕ or α.

Note: In proving that $\mathcal{T}'$ assigns the same values to the sentences described by *Clause* 2 as does $\mathcal{T}$, I make use of *Lemmas* 0.1.1, 0.1.2, and 0.1.3.

Theorem 3: $\mathcal{T}$ satisfies the five necessary conditions.

Definitions: If α is a constant of order zero, then $f(\alpha)$ is the fundamental constant which results from replacing all occurrences of variables in α by occurrences of the variable 'x_0'. Thus, $\mathcal{N}(\alpha) = \mathcal{N}(f(\alpha))$.

Lemma 3.1: If $\mathcal{O}(\alpha) = \mathcal{O}(\hat{\beta}\phi) = 0$, then

(a) $\mathcal{T}(\hat{\beta}\phi = f(\alpha)) = \mathcal{T}(\hat{\beta}\phi = \alpha)$

(b) $\mathcal{T}(\hat{\beta}\phi \in f(\alpha)) = \mathcal{T}(\hat{\beta}\phi \in \alpha)$.

Proof: By induction on $\mathcal{N}(\alpha)$.

1. *Assume* $\mathcal{N}(\alpha) = 1$. Then (b) follows by *Clause* 3. And if $\mathcal{N}(\hat{\beta}\phi) = 1$, then (a) follows by *Clause* 1. If $\mathcal{N}(\hat{\beta}\phi) > 1$, then $\mathcal{T}(\hat{\beta}\phi) = \alpha) = 0$ iff for every fundamental constant γ having nesting $< \mathcal{N}(\hat{\beta}\phi)$, $\mathcal{T}(\phi \, \beta/\gamma) = 1$; and hence iff $\mathcal{T}(\hat{\beta}\phi = f(\alpha)) = 0$.

2. *Assume* $\mathcal{N}(\alpha) > 1$. Then α has the form $\hat{\gamma}(\gamma \in \delta \lor \gamma = \delta')$, and $f(\alpha) = \hat{x}_0(x_0 \in f(\delta) \lor x_0 = f(\delta'))$. By the inductive hypothesis, for every constant γ of order zero, $\mathcal{T}(\gamma \in \delta) = \mathcal{T}(\gamma \in f(\delta))$ and $\mathcal{T}(\gamma = \delta') = \mathcal{T}(\gamma = f(\delta'))$. By *Clause* 2, $\mathcal{T}(\hat{\beta}\phi = \alpha) = \mathcal{T}(\hat{\beta}\phi = f(\alpha))$, so (a) holds. Now if $\mathcal{N}(\hat{\beta}\phi) < \mathcal{N}(\alpha)$, then (b) holds by *Clause* 4. If $\mathcal{N}(\hat{\beta}\phi) \geqslant \mathcal{N}(\alpha)$, then (b) holds by *Clause* 5.

Lemma 3.2: If $\mathcal{O}(\alpha) = \mathcal{O}(\beta) = 0$, then $\mathcal{T}(\alpha \in \beta) = \mathcal{T}(f(\alpha) \in \beta)$.

Proof: By induction on $\mathcal{N}(\beta)$.

1. *Assume* $\mathcal{N}(\beta) = 1$. Then the above holds by *Clause* 3.

2. *Assume* $\mathcal{N}(\beta) > 1$. Then β is of the form $\hat{\gamma}(\gamma \in \delta \lor \gamma = \delta')$. If $\mathcal{N}(\alpha) < \mathcal{N}(\beta)$, then $\mathcal{T}(\alpha \in \beta) = \mathcal{T}(\alpha \in \delta \lor \alpha = \delta')$, and $\mathcal{T}(f(\alpha) \in \beta) = \mathcal{T}(f(\alpha) \in \delta \lor f(\alpha) = \delta')$. By the inductive hypothesis, $\mathcal{T}(\alpha \in \delta) = \mathcal{T}(f(\alpha) \in \delta)$. By *Lemma* 3.1, $\mathcal{T}(\alpha = \delta') = \mathcal{T}(f(\alpha) = \delta')$. Hence $\mathcal{T}(\alpha \in \beta) = \mathcal{T}(f(\alpha) \in \beta)$. If $\mathcal{N}(\alpha) \geqslant \mathcal{N}(\beta)$, then $\mathcal{T}(\alpha \in \beta) = \mathcal{T}(f(\alpha) \in \beta)$ by *Clause* 5 and *Lemma* 3.1.

Definition: If α and β are terms or formulas, then $\alpha < \beta$ iff $\mathcal{O}(\alpha) < \mathcal{O}(\beta)$ or $\mathcal{O}(\alpha) = \mathcal{O}(\beta) = 0$ and $\mathcal{D}(\alpha) < \mathcal{D}(\beta)$. If γ is the constant $\hat{\alpha}\phi$, then $\mathcal{P}(\gamma) = \mathcal{O}(\alpha)$, where $\mathcal{P}(\gamma)$ is said to be the "position of γ."

Lemma 3.3.1: $\mathcal{T}(\alpha = \beta) = 0$ iff $\mathcal{T}(\gamma \in \alpha \leftrightarrow \gamma \in \beta) = 0$ for every constant $\gamma < (\alpha = \beta)$.

Lemma 3.3.2: If $\mathcal{T}(\alpha \in \beta) = 0$, then $\mathcal{T}(\gamma \in \beta \;\&\; \gamma = \alpha) = 0$ for some constant γ, where $\gamma < \beta$, $\gamma \leqslant \alpha$, and $\mathcal{O}(\gamma) \leqslant \mathcal{P}(\beta)$.

Proof: 3.3.1: from *Clauses* 1, 2, 8 and *Lemma* 3.2.

       3.3.2: from *Clauses* 3, 4, 5, 6 and 7.

Lemma 3.4: For all constants α, β, γ, if $\mathcal{T}(\alpha = \beta) = 0$, then $\mathcal{T}(\gamma \in \alpha \leftrightarrow \gamma \in \beta) = 0$.

Proof: By induction on $\mathcal{D}(\gamma)$.

1. *Assume* $\mathcal{D}(\gamma) = \omega$. Then $\gamma < (\alpha = \beta)$, so it holds by *Lemma* 3.3.1.

2. *Assume* that for every constant δ, such that $\mathcal{D}(\delta) < \mathcal{D}(\gamma)$, the lemma holds. Suppose that α and β are constants and that $\mathcal{T}(\alpha = \beta) = 0$. If $\gamma < (\alpha = \beta)$, then $\mathcal{T}(\gamma \in \alpha \leftrightarrow \gamma \in \beta) = 0$ by *Lemma* 3.3.1. If γ is not $< (\alpha = \beta)$, then suppose $\mathcal{T}(\gamma \in \alpha) = 0$. I shall argue that $\mathcal{T}(\gamma \in \beta) = 0$.

(a) By *Lemma* 3.3.2, $\mathcal{T}(\delta \in \alpha \;\&\; \delta = \gamma) = 0$ for some $\delta < \alpha$. (Hence $\delta < \gamma$).

(b) By the inductive hypothesis, $\mathcal{T}(\delta \in \beta) = 0$. Hence by *Lemma* 3.3.2, $\mathcal{T}(\rho \in \beta \;\&\; \rho = \delta) = 0$ for some $\rho \leqslant \delta$, where $\mathcal{O}(\rho) \leqslant \mathcal{P}(\beta)$.

(c) Since $\mathcal{T}(\delta = \gamma) = 0$ and $\mathcal{T}(\rho = \delta) = 0$, $\mathcal{T}(\mu \in \delta \leftrightarrow \mu \in \gamma) = 0$ and $\mathcal{T}(\mu \in \rho \leftrightarrow \mu \in \delta) = 0$ for every constant $\mu < \gamma$, by the inductive hypothesis.

(d) Hence, for every constant $\mu < \gamma$, $\mathcal{T}(\mu \in \rho \leftrightarrow \mu \in \gamma) = 0$. Thus, by *Lemma* 3.3.1, $\mathcal{T}(\rho = \gamma) = 0$.

(e) Hence $\mathcal{T}(\rho \in \beta \;\&\; \rho = \gamma) = 0$ for some constant ρ such that $\mathcal{O}(\rho) \leqslant \mathcal{P}(\beta)$. By *Clauses* 5 and 7, $\mathcal{T}(\gamma \in \beta) = 0$, since γ is not $< (\alpha = \beta)$ and $\mathcal{D}(\beta) = \omega$ is impossible by the assumptions $\mathcal{T}(\alpha = \beta) = 0$ and $\mathcal{T}(\gamma \in \alpha) = 0$. Thus, if $\mathcal{T}(\gamma \in \alpha) = 0$, then $\mathcal{T}(\gamma \in \beta) = 0$. Similarly, if $\mathcal{T}(\gamma \in \beta) = 0$, then $\mathcal{T}(\gamma \in \alpha) = 0$.

Corollary: $\mathcal{T}(\alpha = \alpha) = 0$.

       If $\mathcal{T}(\alpha = \beta) = 0$, then $\mathcal{T}(\beta = \alpha) = 0$.

       If $\mathcal{T}(\alpha = \beta) = 0$ and $\mathcal{T}(\beta = \gamma) = 0$, then $\mathcal{T}(\alpha = \gamma) = 0$.

Definition: An occurrence of a constant is *free* if it is not within the scope of a circumflex variable.

Lemma 3.5: If ϕ' is the result of replacing a free occurrence of the constant α in the sentence ϕ with a constant β, then $\mathcal{T}(\alpha = \beta \rightarrow (\phi \leftrightarrow \phi')) = 0$.

Proof: By induction on the index of ϕ.

1. If ϕ is an *atomic* sentence of the form $\alpha = \gamma$, then the lemma holds by the corollary to *Lemma* 3.4.

2. If ϕ is an *atomic* sentence of the form $\gamma \in \alpha$, then the lemma holds by *Lemma* 3.4.

3. If ϕ is an *atomic* sentence of the form $\alpha \in \hat{\gamma}\psi$, then assume $\mathcal{T}(\alpha \in \hat{\gamma}\psi) = 0$. By *Lemma* 3.3.2, $\mathcal{T}(\delta \in \hat{\gamma}\psi \,\&\, \alpha = \delta) = 0$ for some δ having order $\leqslant \mathcal{O}(\gamma)$. Hence $\mathcal{T}(\delta \in \hat{\gamma}\psi \,\&\, \beta = \delta) = 0$, by the corollary to *Lemma* 3.4. If $\mathcal{O}(\beta) > \mathcal{O}(\gamma)$, then $\mathcal{T}(\beta \in \hat{\gamma}\psi) = 0$ by *Clauses* 6, 7 and 9. If $\mathcal{O}(\beta) \leqslant \mathcal{O}(\gamma)$, then by *Clause* 6, $\mathcal{T}(\delta \in \hat{\gamma}\psi) = \mathcal{T}(\psi\,\gamma/\delta)$ and $\mathcal{T}(\beta \in \hat{\gamma}\psi) = \mathcal{T}(\psi\,\gamma/\beta)$. By the inductive hypothesis, $\mathcal{T}(\psi\,\gamma/\delta) = \mathcal{T}(\psi\,\gamma/\beta)$. Hence $\mathcal{T}(\beta \in \hat{\gamma}\psi) = 0$. By a similar argument, if $\mathcal{T}(\beta \in \hat{\gamma}\psi) = 0$, then $\mathcal{T}(\alpha \in \hat{\gamma}\psi) = 0$.

4. If ϕ is *molecular*, then if the lemma holds for the non-molecular components, it holds for ϕ.

5. ϕ is *quantificational:* $\phi = (\exists\delta)\psi$. Let $\phi' = (\exists\delta)\psi'$. Suppose $\mathcal{T}(\phi) = 0$. Then for some constant γ, $\mathcal{O}(\gamma) \leqslant \mathcal{O}(\delta)$, $\mathcal{T}(\psi\,\delta/\gamma) = 0$. By the induction hypothesis, $\mathcal{T}(\psi'\,\delta/\gamma \leftrightarrow \psi\,\delta/\gamma) = 0$. Hence $\mathcal{T}(\psi'\,\delta/\gamma) = 0$. Hence $\mathcal{T}(\phi') = 0$ by truth condition 9. Similarly, if $\mathcal{T}(\phi') = 0$, then $\mathcal{T}(\phi) = 0$.

Lemma 3.6: If $\mathcal{T}(\alpha \in \hat{\beta}\phi) = 0$, then $\mathcal{T}(\phi\,\beta/\alpha) = 0$.

Proof: Consider each of the possible cases in which $\mathcal{T}(\alpha \in \hat{\beta}\phi) = 0$.

Clause 3: Trivial.

Clause 4: Trivial.

Clause 5: If $\mathcal{T}(\alpha \in \hat{\beta}\phi) = 0$, then for some fundamental constant γ such that $\mathcal{N}(\gamma) < \mathcal{N}(\hat{\beta}\phi)$, $\mathcal{T}(\gamma \in \hat{\beta}\phi) = 0$ and $\mathcal{T}(\gamma = \alpha) = 0$. Then $\mathcal{T}(\phi\,\beta/\gamma) = 0$ by *Clause* 4. Hence $\mathcal{T}(\phi\,\beta/\alpha) = 0$, by *Lemma* 3.5.

Clause 6: Trivial.

Clause 7: Again use *Lemma* 3.5.

Lemma 3.7: If $\mathcal{O}(\alpha) = \mathcal{O}(\hat{\beta}\phi) = 0$ and $\mathcal{T}(\phi \, \beta/\alpha) = 0$, then $\mathcal{T}(\alpha \in \hat{\beta}\phi) = 0$.

Proof: We can assume $\mathcal{N}(\alpha) \geqslant \mathcal{N}(\hat{\beta}\phi)$ since otherwise the lemma holds by *Clause* 4. Now ϕ is of the form ($\beta \in \delta \vee \beta = \delta'$); so $\mathcal{T}(\alpha \in \delta \vee \alpha = \delta') = 0$. If $\mathcal{T}(\alpha = \delta') = 0$, then since $\mathcal{T}(\delta' \in \hat{\beta}\phi) = 0$, we have $\mathcal{T}(\alpha \in \hat{\beta}\phi) = 0$ by *Lemma* 3.5. If $\mathcal{T}(\alpha \in \delta) = 0$, then since $\mathcal{N}(\alpha) > \mathcal{N}(\delta)$, we can use *Clause* 5, to assert that there is a constant μ, such that $\mathcal{N}(\mu) < \mathcal{N}(\delta)$ and $\mathcal{T}(\mu \in \delta \,\&\, \alpha = \mu) = 0$. So by *Clause* 4, $\mathcal{T}(\mu \in \hat{\beta}\phi) = 0$. By *Lemma* 3.5, $\mathcal{T}(\alpha \in \hat{\beta}\phi) = 0$.

Proof of Theorem 3: Check each of the five necessary conditions. The theorem follows almost immediately from lemmas.

Corollary: There is a unique normal assignment function that satisfies the five necessary conditions.

The Logical Calculus of Σ_ω

1. *Logical Axioms:*

Every tautologically valid formula is an axiom.

2. *Rules of Inference:*

(a) *Modus Ponens*

(b) If β is a term, α is a variable, $\mathcal{O}(\beta) = \mathcal{O}(\alpha)$, and if ($\phi \vee \psi \, \alpha/\beta$) is derivable, then ($\phi \vee (\exists\alpha)\psi$) is derivable.

(c) If α is a variable that does not occur free in ϕ, and if ($\psi \rightarrow \phi$) is derivable, then (($\exists\alpha)\psi \rightarrow \phi$) is derivable.

3. (*Non-Logical*) *Axioms:*

(1) *Identity:*

If α, β, γ are variables, $\mathcal{O}(\gamma) \geqslant \max\{\mathcal{O}(\alpha), \mathcal{O}(\beta)\}$, then ($\alpha = \beta \,\& \alpha \in \gamma) \rightarrow \beta \in \gamma$ is an axiom.

(2) *Summation:*

If $\mathcal{O}(\alpha) < \mathcal{O}(\beta) = \omega$, then $(\alpha)(\exists\beta)(\beta = \alpha)$ is an axiom.

(3) *Abstraction:*

If α and β are variables of the same order, α does not occur in ϕ, then $\alpha \in \hat{\beta}\phi \leftrightarrow \phi \, \beta/\alpha$ is an axiom.

(4) *Pair set:*

If α, β, γ, δ are variables of order ω, then $(\exists\alpha)(\beta)(\beta \in \alpha \leftrightarrow (\beta = \gamma \vee \beta = \delta))$ is an axiom.

(5) *Extensionality:*

If α and γ are variables of order k(k $= 0$ or ω), β is a variable of order $\leqslant$ k, and $\gamma \neq \alpha$, β, then $\alpha = \beta \leftrightarrow (\gamma)(\gamma \in \alpha \leftrightarrow \gamma \in \beta)$ and $\beta = \alpha \leftrightarrow (\gamma)(\gamma \in \alpha \leftrightarrow \gamma \in \beta)$ are axioms. If α is a variable of finite order k(k $\neq 0$), β is a variable of order $\leqslant$ k, and γ is a variable different from β of order k $- 1$, then $\alpha = \beta \leftrightarrow (\gamma)(\gamma \in \alpha \leftrightarrow \gamma \in \beta)$ and $\beta = \alpha \leftrightarrow (\gamma)(\gamma \in \alpha \leftrightarrow \gamma \in \beta)$ are axioms.

(6) *Foundation:*

If α, β, γ are variables of order $n \leqslant \omega$, then $(\exists\alpha)(\alpha \in \beta) \rightarrow (\exists\alpha)(\alpha \in \beta \,\&\, (\gamma) - (\gamma \in \alpha \,\&\, \gamma \in \beta))$ is an axiom.

(7) *Bounded Order:*

If α, β, γ are variables, $\mathcal{O}(\alpha) > \mathcal{O}(\beta) = \mathcal{O}(\gamma) = 0$, then $(\alpha \in \beta \rightarrow (\exists\gamma)\gamma = \alpha)$ is an axiom. If α, β, γ are variables, $\mathcal{O}(\alpha) \geqslant \mathcal{O}(\beta) = \mathcal{O}(\gamma) + 1$, then $(\alpha \in \beta \rightarrow (\exists\gamma)\gamma = \alpha)$ is an axiom.

Remarks on the axiom of Limitation:

To state this axiom, it is necessary to develop first the theory of natural numbers and then show that it is possible to enumerate all the sets of order ω required by the above axioms. The axiom of limitation then states, in effect, that the enumerated sets are all sets of order ω. However, since the required enumerating function is of order $\omega + 2$ (see Wang [118], pp. 602f.), this axiom cannot even be stated in Σ_ω. To avoid such difficulties (and others) one can replace the axiom with rules of inference which imply that any set of order ω is also of finite order (details to be presented elsewhere). An alternative approach is to add such axioms as *Intersection* and :

(8′) *Union:*

If α, β, γ, δ are variables of order ω, then $(\exists\alpha)(\beta)(\beta \in \alpha \leftrightarrow (\exists\gamma)(\beta \in \gamma \,\&\, \gamma \in \delta))$ is an axiom.

Remarks: Some of the nonlogical axioms are open formulas (formulas that are not sentences). Let us say that an open formula is true if, and only if, its universal closure is true, that is, let us extend the function $\mathscr{T}$ in such a way that, for every open formula ϕ, if ϕ' is its universal closure, $\mathscr{T}(\phi) = \mathscr{T}(\phi')$.

4. *Theorems of Σ_ω :*

ϕ is a theorem if ϕ is an axiom or is derivable from the axioms using the rules of inference.

Theorem 4: If Γ is a set of true sentences (i.e. if $\phi \in \Gamma$, then $\mathscr{T}(\phi) = 0$) and if ψ is derivable from Γ, then $\mathscr{T}(\psi) = 0$.

Proof: By straightforward examination of the rules of inference.

Theorem 5: If ϕ' is the result of replacing occurrences of the constant α in ϕ with the constant β, then $\mathscr{T}(\alpha = \beta \to (\phi \leftrightarrow \phi')) = 0$.

Proof: In view of *Lemma* 3.5, we need only consider the case in which a non-free occurrence of α is replaced by β. Suppose α occurs in the constant $\hat{\gamma}\psi$ but free in ψ. Then it is easy to show that for every constant δ, $\mathscr{T}(\delta \in \hat{\gamma}\psi \leftrightarrow \delta \in \hat{\gamma}\psi') = 0$. For if $\mathcal{O}(\delta) > \mathcal{O}(\gamma)$, look at necessary condition (4) and use *Lemma* 3.5. If $\mathcal{O}(\delta) \leqslant \mathcal{O}(\gamma)$, use *Lemma* 3.5 and necessary conditions (1) and (3). We can thus conclude $\mathscr{T}(\hat{\gamma}\psi = \hat{\gamma}\psi') = 0$. By using this result and *Lemma* 3.5 repeatedly, we get the above results.

Corollary: If ϕ is one of the usual axioms of identity, then $\mathscr{T}(\phi) = 0$.

Theorem 6: If ϕ is a non-logical axiom then $\mathscr{T}(\phi) = 0$.

Proof: Examine each of the axioms.

1. *Identity:* An immediate consequence of *Lemma* 3.5.

2. *Summation:* Obvious, given the corollary of *Lemma* 3.4 and the truth conditions.

3. *Abstraction:* Follows from truth condition (6).

4. *Pair Set:* Trivial.

5. *Extensionality:* Obvious, given the truth conditions (especially (8)) and *Lemma* 3.4.

6. *Foundation:* Suppose β is a constant of order $\leqslant n$, and suppose $\mathscr{T}(\alpha \in \beta) = 0$ for some constant α of order at most n. Then there must be some constant μ of least degree such that

$\mathscr{T}(\mu \in \beta) = 0$. Suppose there is a constant λ such that $\mathscr{T}(\lambda \in \mu) = 0$. Then there is a constant ζ such that $\mathscr{T}(\zeta = \lambda) = 0$ and $\mathscr{D}(\zeta) < \mathscr{D}(\mu)$. Hence $\mathscr{T}(\zeta \in \beta) = 1$, and hence $\mathscr{T}(\lambda \in \beta) = 1$. We can conclude $\mathscr{T}((\exists\alpha)(\alpha \in \beta \,\&\, (\gamma) - (\gamma \in \alpha \,\&\, \gamma \in \beta))) = 0$, where $\mathcal{O}(\alpha) = n$, $\mathcal{O}(\gamma) = n$.

7. *Bounded Order:* Trivial.

8'. *Union:* Obvious.

(Note: the axiom of *Limitation* will be discussed later.)

The No-Class Interpretation

I. *The First Hierarchy*

Definitions of the entities of finite layers:

1. Layer 0 consists of exactly one entity, viz. '*'.

2. If $\hat{\alpha}\phi$ is a constant of order 0, nesting n, then ϕ is an entity of layer n (or n layer entity).

3. If ϕ is an entity of layer n, $0 < n < \omega$, then the configuration consisting of 'I' immediately followed by ϕ flanked by parentheses is an entity of layer $n + 1$ and is called the $n + 1$ layer image of ϕ.

4. If ϕ is the $n + 1$ layer image of ψ and ψ is the n layer image of χ, then ϕ is the $n + 1$ layer image of χ.

Remark: If ϕ is an image of ψ, then for some open sentence χ, ϕ is an image of χ. Also, every entity of layer n, $n \neq 0$, is either an open sentence or an image of an open sentence.

5. If ϕ is an entity of layer k, and ψ is the $k + m$ layer image of ϕ, $0 < m$, then the configuration consisting of 'I' with subscript m immediately followed by ϕ flanked with parentheses will be used to denote ψ. By this convention $I_m(\phi) = \underbrace{I(I(I \ldots (I(\phi)) \ldots))}_{m}$ and $I_n(I_m(\phi)) = I_{n+m}(\phi)$, where $0 < m, n < \omega$ and ϕ is any entity of finite layer except '*'.

Definition of correspondents of constants of order 0:

1. If $\mathcal{N}(\hat{\alpha}\phi) = n$, then $C_n(\hat{\alpha}\phi)$, the n layer correspondent of $\hat{\alpha}\phi$, is ϕ.

2. If $\mathcal{N}(\hat{\alpha}\phi) = n$, $n < m < \omega$, then $C_m(\hat{\alpha}\phi) = I_{m-n}(\phi)$.

Notational Conventions:

1. Greek letters (except '∈') with subscripts function as variables ranging over totalities of entities of the first hierarchy. The subscript indicates the layer over which the variable is to range. Such a variable with subscript n ranges over the entities of layer n and is called a variable of layer n.

2. If A is a variable of layer n, then A flanked by parentheses is to read

for an entity A

and the configuration consisting of '(∃' followed by A and ')' is to read

for some entity A.

3. The configuration consisting of '∈' with subscript n flanked by Greek letters is an abbreviation for the configuration one obtains by giving the first Greek letter subscript $n - 1$ and the second n. Similarly, the configuration consisting of '∼' with subscript n flanked by Greek letters is an abbreviation for the configuration one obtains by giving the letters subscript n. This convention will be carried over to the case in which '∈' (or '∼') with subscript n is flanked by any two symbols which refer to entities of the appropriate layers. Thus '$I(\phi) \in_n C(\alpha)$' is an abbreviation for '$I_1(\phi_{n-2}) \in_n C_n(\alpha)$'.

4. A Greek letter (other than '∈') occurring in a single context with different subscripts will denote different level correspondents of the same constant. Hence, if both 'ϕ_n' and 'ϕ_{n+j}' appear in a sentence, then 'ϕ_{n+j}' will denote the $n + j$ layer image of the entity denoted by 'ϕ_n'.

5. The connectives '&', '∨', '→', and '↔' will be used with their customary truth-functional definitions.

6. The above conventions are to be extended in the obvious way (*mutatis mutandis*) as new entities are defined.

Definitions of '$\in_n$' and '$\sim_n$' for $0 < n < \omega$:

1. If ϕ_n is an open sentence and if
$n = 1$, then $\psi \in_1 \phi$ iff '$*$' $\neq$ '$*$';

$n > 1$, then ϕ_n is of the form $(\gamma \in \alpha \vee \gamma = \beta)$, and $\psi \in_n \phi$ iff $(\psi \in_n C(\alpha) \vee \psi \sim_{n-1} C(\beta))$.

If ϕ_n is an image, then $\psi \in_n \phi$ iff $(\exists \delta_{n-2})(\psi \sim_{n-1} \delta \And \delta \in_{n-1} \phi)$.

2. $\phi \sim_n \pi$ iff $(\psi_{n-1})(\psi \in_n \phi \leftrightarrow \psi \in_n \pi)$.

Definition of $\mathscr{R}(\phi_n)$, the rank of an entity of layer $n(n > 0)$:

$\mathscr{R}(\phi_n) = n$ if ϕ_n is an open sentence,

$\qquad k$ if $\phi_n = I_{n-k}(\psi_k)$, where ψ_k is an open sentence.

Properties of entities of finite layers:

In this section, it is to be understood that

1. $0 < n < \omega$ and $0 \leqslant j < \omega$;

2. in the case of the lemmas that follow (and also the lemmas that occur in the following sections), if the statement of a lemma consists of a formula with free variables, it is the closure of the formula that is intended.

Lemma 7.1: $(\phi \sim_n \psi \And \psi \in_{n+1} \pi) \to \phi \in_{n+1} \pi$
Proof: Trivial.

Lemma 7.2: $\psi \in_{n+1} \phi \to \psi \in_{n+j+1} \phi$
Proof: By induction on j.

Lemma 7.3: $\psi \notin_{n+1} \phi \to \psi \notin_{n+2} \phi$
Proof: By induction on n.

Lemma 7.4: $\psi \in_{n+1} \phi \leftrightarrow \psi \in_{n+j+1} \phi$
Proof: By induction on j (using *Lemmas* 7.1 and 7.3).

Lemma 7.5: $\psi \sim_n \phi \leftrightarrow \psi \sim_{n+j} \phi$
Proof: By induction on j (using *Lemma* 7.4).

Lemma 7.6: If $\mathscr{R}(\phi_n) = k$, $k < n$, and $\psi \in_n \phi$, then for some δ_{n-1}, $\psi \sim_{n-1} \delta$ and $\delta \in_k \phi$.
Proof: This is easily proved from the preceding lemmas (noting that if $\psi \in_n \phi$, then $1 < k$).

Definition of the ω layer image of an n layer entity $(0 < n < \omega)$:

1. If $\mathscr{R}(\phi_n) = n$, then the configuration consisting of 'I_ω' immediately followed by ϕ_n flanked by parentheses is the ω layer image of ϕ_n.

2. If $\mathscr{R}(\phi_n) = k$ and $k < n$, then the ω layer image of ϕ_k is the ω layer image of ϕ_n .

Remark: In extending notational convention 3 to cover '$\in_\omega$' and '$\sim_\omega$', clearly '$\phi \in_\omega \psi$' is to be an abbreviation for '$\phi_\omega \in_\omega \psi_\omega$' and not for '$\phi_{\omega-1} \in_\omega \psi_\omega$', and '$\phi \sim_\omega \psi$' is to be an abbreviation for '$\phi_\omega \sim_\omega \psi_\omega$'.

Definitions:

1. The entities of layer ω are the ω layer images defined above and nothing else.

2. $C_\omega(\hat{\alpha}\phi)$, the ω layer correspondent of a constant $\hat{\alpha}\phi$ of order 0, is the ω layer image of ϕ.

3. $\psi \in_\omega \phi$ iff for some n, $1 < n < \omega$, $\psi \in_n \phi$.

4. $\psi \sim_\omega \phi$ iff $(\pi_\omega)(\pi \in_\omega \psi \leftrightarrow \pi \in_\omega \phi)$.

Properties of ω layer entities:

No proofs are given since the lemmas follow easily from the previous ones.

Lemma 7.7: $\phi \in_n \psi \leftrightarrow \phi \in_\omega \psi$, $1 < n < \omega$.

Lemma 7.8: $\phi \sim_n \psi \leftrightarrow \phi \sim_\omega \psi$, $0 < n < \omega$.

Lemma 7.9: $(\phi \sim_\omega \psi \ \& \ \phi \in_\omega \pi) \rightarrow \psi \in_\omega \pi$.

Lemma 7.10: If $\mathscr{R}(\phi_n) = k$, $k \leqslant n$, then $\psi \in_\omega \phi$ iff for some m, $0 < m < \omega$, $(\exists \pi_m)(\psi \sim_m \pi \ \& \ \pi \in_k \phi)$.

II. *The Second Hierarchy*

Definitions of the entities of finite levels:

1. Level 0 consists of exactly the ω-layer entities (of the first hierarchy). An entity of level 0 is called an open sentence of level 0.

2. If $\hat{\alpha}\phi$ is a constant of order n, $0 < n$, then ϕ is an entity of level n. (Obviously, ϕ is an open sentence of level n).

3. If ϕ is an entity of level n, $0 \leqslant n < \omega$, then the configuration consisting of '$\mathscr{I}$' immediately followed by ϕ flanked by parentheses is an entity of level $n + 1$, and is called the $n + 1$ level image of ϕ.

4. If ϕ is the $n + 1$ level image of ψ and ψ is the n level image of χ, then ϕ is the $n + 1$ level image of χ.

5. As before, '$\mathscr{I}_m(\phi)$' will denote the $m + k$ level image of ϕ, if ϕ is an entity of level k. So we have $\mathscr{I}_m(\mathscr{I}_n(\phi)) = \mathscr{I}_{m+n}(\phi)$, $0 < m, n < \omega$.

Definition of the finite level correspondents of a constant $\hat{\alpha}\phi$:

1. If $\mathcal{O}(\hat{\alpha}\phi) = 0$, $C_0(\hat{\alpha}\phi)$, the 0 level correspondent of $\hat{\alpha}\phi$, is $C_\omega(\hat{\alpha}\phi)$.

2. If $\mathcal{O}(\hat{\alpha}\phi) = n$, $0 < n$, then $C_n(\hat{\alpha}\phi) = \phi$.

3. If $\mathcal{O}(\hat{\alpha}\phi) = m$, and $m < k < \omega$, then $C_k(\hat{\alpha}\phi) = \mathscr{I}_{k-m}(\phi)$.

Definition of the rank of an entity of finite level:

If $\phi = C_n(\alpha)$, where α is a constant, then the rank of ϕ, $\mathscr{R}(\phi)$, $= \mathcal{O}(\alpha)$.

Note: Every entity of finite level is a correspondent of some constant.

Notational Convention: I shall write '$\langle \in \rangle_0$' instead of '$\in_\omega$' and '$\langle \sim \rangle_0$' instead of '$\sim_\omega$'.

Definition of '$\langle \in \rangle_n$', '$\langle \sim \rangle_n$', '$\langle \sigma \rangle_m$' (*where σ is a (closed) sentence and $0 < n < \omega$, $0 \leqslant \mathcal{O}(\sigma) \leqslant m < \omega$*):

1. $\phi \langle \sim \rangle_n \psi$ iff $(\pi_{n-1})(\pi \langle \in \rangle_n \phi \leftrightarrow \pi \langle \in \rangle_n \psi)$.

2. If ϕ is an image of level n, and if $n = 1$, then $\psi \langle \in \rangle_n \phi$ iff $\psi \langle \in \rangle_0 \phi$; if $n > 1$, then $\psi \langle \in \rangle_n \phi$ iff $(\exists \pi_{n-2})(\psi \langle \sim \rangle_{n-1} \pi \ \& \ \pi \langle \in \rangle_{n-1} \phi)$.

3. $\langle \sigma \rangle_m$

    (i) *atomic:*

        (a) σ is $\alpha \in \beta$: if $\mathcal{O}(\sigma) = 0$, then $\langle \alpha \in \beta \rangle_0$ iff $C(\alpha) \langle \in \rangle_0 C(\beta)$; if $\mathcal{O}(\sigma) = n$, then $\langle \alpha \in \beta \rangle_n$ iff $(\exists \delta_{n-1})(C(\alpha) \langle \sim \rangle_n \delta \ \& \ \delta \langle \in \rangle_n C(\beta))$.

        (b) σ is $\alpha = \beta$: if $\mathcal{O}(\sigma) = 0$, $\langle \alpha = \beta \rangle_0$ iff $C(\alpha) \langle \sim \rangle_0 C(\beta)$; if $\mathcal{O}(\sigma) = n$, $\langle \alpha = \beta \rangle_n$ iff $C(\alpha) \langle \sim \rangle_n C(\beta)$.

    (ii) *molecular:* ($\mathcal{O}(\sigma) = m$):

σ is $-\phi$: $\langle -\phi \rangle_m$ iff not $\langle \phi \rangle_m$;

σ is $(\phi \vee \psi)$: $\langle (\phi \vee \psi) \rangle_m$ iff either $\langle \phi \rangle_m$ or $\langle \psi \rangle_m$;

σ is $(\phi \ \& \ \psi)$: $\langle (\phi \ \& \ \psi) \rangle_m$ iff $\langle \phi \rangle_m$ and $\langle \psi \rangle_m$;

σ is $(\phi \rightarrow \psi)$: $\langle (\phi \rightarrow \psi) \rangle_m$ iff not $\langle \phi \rangle_m$ or $\langle \psi \rangle_m$;

σ is $(\phi \leftrightarrow \psi)$: $\langle (\phi \leftrightarrow \psi) \rangle_m$ iff $\langle (\phi \rightarrow \psi) \rangle_m$ and $\langle (\psi \rightarrow \phi) \rangle_m$.

(iii) *quantificational:*

σ is $(\exists \alpha)\phi$, $\mathcal{O}(\sigma) = n$: $\langle (\exists \alpha)\phi \rangle_n$ iff there is a constant β such that $\mathcal{O}(\beta) = \mathcal{O}(\alpha)$ and $\langle \phi \, \alpha/\beta \rangle_n$.

(Note: By *Lemma* 1.2.1, $\mathcal{O}(\phi \, \alpha/\beta) \leqslant n$).

(iv) If $\mathcal{O}(\sigma) = n$ and $n < m$, $\langle \sigma \rangle_m$ iff $\langle \sigma \rangle_n$.

4. If $\hat{\alpha}\phi$ is a constant of order n, ψ an entity of level $n - 1$, then $\psi \langle \in \rangle_n C(\hat{\alpha}\phi)$ iff there is a constant β such that $\mathcal{O}(\beta) = \mathcal{O}(\alpha)$, $\psi \langle \sim \rangle_{n-1} C(\beta)$ and $\langle \phi \, \alpha/\beta \rangle_n$.

Remark: It is easily verified that in the definitions of '$\langle \in \rangle_n$', '$\langle \sim \rangle_n$', and '$\langle \sigma \rangle_m$', only "previously constructed entities" are presupposed (to use Poincaré's terminology).

Properties of entities of finite level:

In the following lemmas, $0 \leqslant n, j < \omega$.

Lemma 7.11: $(\phi \langle \sim \rangle_n \psi \, \& \, \phi \langle \in \rangle_{n+1} \pi) \rightarrow \psi \langle \in \rangle_{n+1} \pi$.

Lemma 7.12: $\phi \langle \in \rangle_n \psi \rightarrow \phi \langle \in \rangle_{n+j} \psi$.

Lemma 7.13: $\phi \langle \notin \rangle_n \psi \rightarrow \phi \langle \notin \rangle_{n+1} \psi$.

Lemma 7.14: $\phi \langle \in \rangle_n \psi \leftrightarrow \phi \langle \in \rangle_{n+j} \psi$.

Lemma 7.15: $\phi \langle \sim \rangle_n \psi \leftrightarrow \phi \langle \sim \rangle_{n+j} \psi$.

Lemma 7.16: If $\mathcal{R}(\phi_n) = k$, $0 \leqslant k < n$, and $\pi \langle \in \rangle_n \phi$, then there is a ψ_{n-1} such that $\psi \langle \sim \rangle_{n-1} \pi$ and $\psi \langle \in \rangle_k \phi$.

Definition of images of level ω:

ω level images are constructed in the way the ω layer images were constructed except that '$\mathcal{I}_\omega$' is used instead of 'I_ω'.

Definitions:

1. Every ω level image is an entity of level ω and nothing else is.

2. If α is a constant of order n, $C_\omega(\alpha) = \mathcal{I}_\omega(C_n(\alpha))$.

3. If α is a constant of order n and $C_\omega(\alpha) = \phi_\omega$, then $\mathcal{R}(\phi_\omega) = n$.

4. $\phi \langle \in \rangle_\omega \psi$ iff $\phi \langle \in \rangle_n \psi$ for some $n < \omega$.

5. $\phi \langle \sim \rangle_\omega \psi$ iff $(\pi_\omega)(\pi \langle \in \rangle_\omega \phi \leftrightarrow \pi \langle \in \rangle_\omega \psi)$.

Properties of entities of level ω:

In the following, $0 \leqslant n < \omega$; they can be easily proved.

Lemma 7.17: $\phi \langle \in \rangle_n \psi \leftrightarrow \phi \langle \in \rangle_\omega \psi$.

Lemma 7.18: $\phi \langle \sim \rangle_n \psi \leftrightarrow \phi \langle \sim \rangle_\omega \psi$.

Lemma 7.19: $(\phi \langle \sim \rangle_\omega \psi \,\&\, \phi \langle \in \rangle_\omega \pi) \rightarrow \psi \langle \in \rangle_\omega \pi$.

Lemma 7.20: If $\mathcal{R}(\phi_\omega) = k$, $0 \leqslant k < \omega$, then $\psi \langle \in \rangle_\omega \phi$ iff for some $m < \omega$, $(\exists \pi_m)(\psi \langle \sim \rangle_m \pi \,\&\, \pi \langle \in \rangle_k \phi)$.

Definition of $\langle \sigma \rangle_\omega$ (where σ is a (closed) sentence):

1. If σ is $\alpha \in \beta$, then $\langle \sigma \rangle_\omega$ iff $C(\alpha) \langle \in \rangle_\omega C(\beta)$.

2. If σ is $\alpha = \beta$, then $\langle \sigma \rangle_\omega$ iff $C(\alpha) \langle \sim \rangle_\omega C(\beta)$.

3. If σ is molecular, $\langle \sigma \rangle_\omega$ is defined in the usual way.

4. If σ is $(\exists \alpha)\phi$, and $\mathcal{O}(\alpha) < \omega$, then $\langle \sigma \rangle_\omega$ iff there is a constant β of order $\mathcal{O}(\alpha)$ such that $\langle \phi \, \alpha/\beta \rangle_\omega$.

5. If σ is $(\exists \alpha)\phi$, and $\mathcal{O}(\alpha) = \omega$, then $\langle \sigma \rangle_\omega$ iff there is a constant β such that $\langle \phi \, \alpha/\beta \rangle_\omega$.

Theorem 7: If σ is a (closed) sentence, and $\mathcal{O}(\sigma) = n$, $n \leqslant \omega$, then $\langle \sigma \rangle_n$ iff $\langle \sigma \rangle_\omega$.

Proof: By induction on the *free index* of σ, where the *free index* of σ is the number of occurrences of connectives and free occurrences of quantifiers in σ. (An occurrence of a quantifier is *free* if it is not within the scope of a circumflex variable.)

Theorem 8: If σ is a (closed) sentence, then $\langle \sigma \rangle_\omega$ iff $\mathcal{T}(\sigma) = 0$.

Proof: This is easily proved by checking the nine truth conditions.

Corollary: If ϕ is a theorem of Σ_ω, then $\langle \phi \rangle_\omega$.

Proof: This is an immediate consequence of *Theorems* 4, 6 and 8.

Discussion: The above construction makes it clear that the axiom of *Limitation* is satisfied by the model. Since the only open sentences we construct are those required by the *Abstraction* axiom, it is clear that the interpretation was tailor-made to satisfy the axiom. Of course, from the Platonic point of view, it is obvious that the above model satisfies what is intended by the axiom of *Limitation*, even though the axiom cannot be stated in Σ_ω.

An Open-Sentence Interpretation of Σ_ω

In the following, I shall show how to construct two hierarchies which will "mirror" the previously defined hierarchies and in which the only entities required (except for the asterisk) will be open sentences. The semantical features of this system will be derived from the intuitive notion of truth. In defining this system, I shall again make use of the platonic mode of speech (speaking of functions and sets) in order to simplify the exposition. However, it will be easy to see how the whole construction could be carried out without references to such entities as functions and sets.

The function E

The 1-1 function E defined below is from the set of entities of the previously defined hierarchies onto the set of new entities that will constitute the two new hierarchies. *E preserves the positions and titles of entities* in the following sense: (1) If ϕ is an entity of layer (or level) m, $m \leqslant \omega$, of the previous hierarchies, then $E(\phi)$ is an entity of layer (or level) m of the new hierarchies. (2) If ϕ is the m layer (or level) correspondent of α in the previous hierarchies, then $E(\phi)$ is the m layer (or level) correspondent of α in the new hierarchies. (3) If ϕ is the m layer (or level) image of ψ in the previous hierarchies, then $E(\phi)$ is the m layer (or level) image of $E(\psi)$ in the new hierarchies.

I. *The First Hierarchy*

I.1 If ϕ is a 0 layer entity, $E(\phi) = \phi$.

I.2 If ϕ is a 1 layer entity, say $\alpha \neq \alpha$, then $E(\phi) =$

  α is not identical to α.

I.3 If ϕ is the open sentence of layer n, $1 < n < \omega$, $(\alpha \in \beta \lor \alpha = \gamma)$, then $E(\phi) =$

  The n layer correspondent of β is true of α or the $n - 1$ layer correspondent of γ is extensionally identical to α.

I.4 If ϕ is a 1 layer entity, say $\alpha \neq \alpha$, then $E(I(\phi)) =$

  α is not extensionally identical to α.

I.5 If ϕ, ψ are entities of layer n, $n - 1$ respectively, $2 < n < \omega$, and $\phi = \mathrm{I}(\psi)$, then $E(\phi) =$

> x is extensionally identical to the $n - 1$ layer image of an $n - 2$ layer entity of which A is true

where the quote name of $E(\psi)$ occurs in place of 'A'.

I.6 If ϕ is an entity of layer ω, say $\mathrm{I}_\omega(\psi)$, then $E(\phi) =$

> For some n, $1 < n < \omega$, the n layer image of A is true of some $n - 1$ layer entity of which x is the ω layer image

where the quote name of $E(\psi)$ occurs in place of 'A'.

Definitions (these definitions are relevant to both the first and second hierarchies):

1. If α is a constant of order 0, nesting n, then the m layer correspondent of α, $n \leqslant m \leqslant \omega$, is $E(C_m(\alpha))$. If α is a constant of order n, $0 < n$, then the m level correspondent of α, $n \leqslant m \leqslant \omega$, is $E(C_m(\alpha))$.

2. 'True of' and 'false of' will be defined in such a way that ϕ will be true (false) of ψ only if ϕ and ψ are entities of the appropriate layers (levels). Thus, if ϕ, ψ are entities in the range of E of layer (level) n, $n - 1$ respectively, $0 < n < \omega$, then ϕ is *true (false) of* ψ iff the sentence obtained from ϕ by replacing all free occurrences of the free variable by the quote name of ψ is true (false). (Note: every open sentence in the range of E contains exactly one free variable.)

3. If ϕ, ψ are entities in the range of E of layer (level) n, $0 < n < \omega$, then ϕ is *extensionally identical* to ψ iff for any entity δ of the $n - 1$ layer (level), ϕ is true of δ iff ψ is.

4. For entities in the range of E of layer (level) ω, 'true of', 'false of', and 'extensionally identical' are defined as above except all the entities involved are of layer (level) ω.

Remark 1: It is clear that 'true of', 'false of', and 'extensionally identical', are given their usual meanings except for one slight difference: an argument variable of an open sentence is to be regarded as ranging over a domain (or argument range); so the open sentence can be true (false) of only those open sentences in this domain.

Remark 2: It is also clear that E preserves the relations $\in_n$ and $\sim_n$, $0 < n \leqslant \omega$, in the following sense: for any entities ϕ, ψ in the domain of E, $\phi \in_n \psi$ iff $E(\psi)$ is true of $E(\phi)$, and $\phi \sim_n \psi$ iff $E(\phi)$ is extensionally identical to $E(\psi)$. Indeed, the aim of preserving $\in_n$ and $\sim_n$ guided the construction of the open sentences in the range of E. All the relevant semantical properties (*Lemmas* 7.1–7.10) of the entities of the First Hierarchy are thus preserved. It is also clear that the First Hierarchy is *well defined* in the following sense: for any entities ϕ, ψ of layer m, $m - 1$ respectively, $0 < m < \omega$, either ϕ is true of ψ or ϕ is false of ψ, and similarly, *mutatis mutandis*, for the ω layer case. The reader can easily verify that the semantical properties of the entities of the Second Hierarchy defined below are also preserved and that the Second Hierarchy is also *well defined* (in the analogous sense).

II. *The Second Hierarchy*

II.1 If ϕ is an open sentence of level n, $0 < n < \omega$, and α is the variable that occurs free in ϕ, then $E(\phi) =$

> There is a constant of the same order as
> B such that x is extensionally identical to
> the $n - 1$ level correspondent of the constant
> and the sentence obtained by replacing all
> free occurrences of B in A by occurrences of the
> constant is true

where the quote names of ϕ and α occur in place of 'A' and 'B' respectively.

II.2 If ϕ is an entity of level 1 and $\phi = \mathscr{I}(\psi)$, then $E(\phi) =$

> A is true of x

where the quote name of $E(\psi)$ occurs in place of 'A'.

II.3 If ϕ is an entity of level n, $1 < n < \omega$, and $\phi = \mathscr{I}(\psi)$, then $E(\phi) =$

> x is extensionally identical to the
> $n - 1$ level image of an $n - 2$ level entity
> of which A is true

where the quote name of $E(\psi)$ occurs in place of 'A'.

II.4 If ϕ is an entity of level ω, then ϕ is the ω level correspondent of a constant α of some finite order m, and then $E(\phi) =$

> For some n, $0 < n < \omega$, the n level image
> of A is true of some $n - 1$ level entity of
> which x is the ω level image

where the quote-name of $E(C_m(\alpha))$ occurs in place of 'A'.

Remark: Note that entities of level 0 are open sentences and hence possess ω level images. The function E is defined by I.1–I.6 and II.1–II.4.

The Interpretation of the Constants and Primitive Symbols of Σ_ω :

(In the following, σ will always be a [closed] sentence of Σ_ω).

1. $\in$

   If σ is $\alpha \in \beta$ and $\mathcal{O}(\sigma) = 0$, then σ is to be interpreted: the 0 level correspondent of β is true of the 0 level correspondent of α.

   If σ is $\alpha \in \beta$ and $\mathcal{O}(\sigma) = n > 0$, then σ is to be interpreted: the n level correspondent of α is extensionally identical to the n level image of an $n - 1$ level entity of which the n level correspondent of β is true.

2. $=$

   If σ is $\alpha = \beta$ and $\mathcal{O}(\sigma) = n$, $0 \leqslant n < \omega$, then σ is interpreted: the n level correspondent of α is extensionally identical to the n level correspondent of β.

3. *Logical Connectives*

   These are interpreted in the usual way.

4. *Quantifiers*

   If σ is $(\exists \alpha)\phi$ and $\mathcal{O}(\alpha) < \omega$, then σ is interpreted: there is a constant β such that $\mathcal{O}(\beta) = \mathcal{O}(\alpha)$ and $\phi \, \alpha/\beta$ is true.

   If σ is $(\exists \alpha)\phi$ and $\mathcal{O}(\alpha) = \omega$, then σ is interpreted: there is a constant β such that $\phi \, \alpha/\beta$ is true.

Remark: The above, in effect, assigns denotations to occurrences of constants in sentences and gives meaning to occurrences of the primitive symbols in sentences. The interpretation is quite non-standard in so far as the denotation of an occurrence of a constant and the meaning of an occurrence of '∈' depend upon their respective "sentential contextual surroundings." For example, the denotion of the first occurrence of the constant α in the sentence $(\alpha \in \beta \,\&\, \gamma \in \alpha)$ may be different from the denotation of the second occurrence. Because the interpretation has such features, it is unclear how one could apply Quine's criterion of ontological reduction to reduce some theory to Σ_ω interpreted in the above way. Thus, I shall provide another open-sentence interpretation of Σ_ω which will be based upon the above system and its semantical features but which will be closer to the standard sort of interpretation given to the first-order languages. However, the importance of the above interpretation is indicated by the following:

Notational Convention: I shall use the notation

$$\langle \sigma \rangle_{s'}$$

to refer to a (closed) sentence, σ, of the language of Σ_ω interpreted in the above manner.

Theorem 9: If σ is a (closed) sentence of Σ_ω, then

$$\langle \sigma \rangle_\omega \text{ iff } \langle \sigma \rangle_{s'} \text{ is true; and}$$
$$\langle -\sigma \rangle_\omega \text{ iff } \langle \sigma \rangle_{s'} \text{ is false.}$$

Proof: The proof is straightforward and left as an exercise for the reader.

The Standard Open-Sentence Interpretation of Σ_ω:

1. *Denotations of constants*
If α is a constant, then α is to denote $E(C_\omega(\alpha))$.

2. '∈' is to mean: *satisfies*
(where ϕ *satisfies* ψ iff ψ is true of ϕ).

3. '=' is to mean: *extensionally identical to.*

4. $(\exists \alpha)\phi$ is to mean: there is a constant β such that $\mathcal{O}(\beta) \leqslant \mathcal{O}(\alpha)$ and $\phi \,\alpha/\beta$ is true.

Notational Convention: I shall use the notation

$$\langle \sigma \rangle_s$$

to refer to a (closed) sentence, σ, of the language of Σ_ω interpreted in the above standard manner.

Theorem 10: If σ is a (closed) sentence of Σ_ω, then $\langle\sigma\rangle_{s'}$ is true iff $\langle\sigma\rangle_s$ is true; and $\langle\sigma\rangle_{s'}$ is false iff $\langle\sigma\rangle_s$ is false.

Proof: The proof is also straightforward.

Discussion: The theory S (discussed in Chapter V) is Σ_ω interpreted in the above standard manner. It follows almost directly from earlier theorems that the nine truth conditions are satisfied under this interpretation and that if σ is a theorem of Σ_ω then $\langle\sigma\rangle_s$ is true. The interpretation of Σ_ω which results in the theory S can be seen to be a realization of Russell's no-class idea: statements about sets, under analysis, turn out to be statements about propositional functions ($=$ open sentences) and the membership relation among sets is analyzed in terms of the satisfaction relation among open sentences. This no-class interpretation can also be seen to be a development of Poincare's nominalistic predicativism (see Chapter V).

For some purposes, say of developing such parts of analysis as measure theory, it may be useful for the nominalist to have an interpreted no-class set theory higher in the Σ hierarchy than Σ_ω. However, the above no-class interpretation can be easily extended to higher orders. Thus, by constructing a third hierarchy along the lines the second hierarchy was constructed, we can get a no-class interpretation of $\Sigma_{\omega 2}$.

Theorem 11: Using Quine's criterion of ontological reduction, the ontology of W (Σ_ω interpreted classically) can be reduced to that of S.

Proof: One can specify an effective method for well-ordering the constants of Σ_ω. One can then specify the proxy-function f as follows:

If $\alpha \in$ the domain of W, then $f(\alpha) = E(C_\omega(\beta))$, where β

is the first (in the above ordering) constant denoting α.

The function g can then be specified:

$g('\in') = $ 'x satisfies y'

$g('=') = $ 'x is extensionally identical to y'.

From *Theorems* 1, 8–10, we have:

$\langle \alpha, \beta \rangle \in$ the set assigned to '$\in$' by the classical interpretation iff $f(\alpha)$ satisfies $f(\beta)$;

$\langle \alpha, \beta \rangle \in$ the set assigned to '$=$' by the classical interpretation iff $f(\alpha)$ is extensionally identical to $f(\beta)$.

Bibliographical References

[1] Alston, W. P. "Ontological Commitment," Benacerraf and Putnam [2], pp. 249-257. Originally published in *Philosophical Studies* 9 (1958), pp. 8-17.

[2] Benacerraf, Paul, and Hilary Putnam. *Philosophy of Mathematics: Selected Readings*. Englewood Cliffs, New Jersey: Prentice-Hall, 1964.

[3] Bernays, Paul. "On Platonism in Mathematics," Benacerraf and Putnam, pp. 274-86. Translated from the French by C. D. Parsons from *L'Enseignement Mathématique* 34 (1935), pp. 52-69.

[4] Berry, George. "Logic with Platonism," Davidson and Hintikka [24]. Originally published in *Synthèse* 19 (1968), pp. 215-249.

[5] Beth, E. W. *The Foundation of Mathematics*. Amsterdam: North-Holland, 1959.

[6] Black, Max. "Is Achilles Still Running?" *Problems of Analysis*. Ithaca, New York: Cornell University Press, 1954, pp. 109-126.

[7] ———. *The Nature of Mathematics*, Paterson, New Jersey: Littlefield, Adams, 1959.

[8] Brouwer, L. E. J. "On the Significance of the Principle of Excluded Middle in Mathematics, Especially in Function Theory," Heijenoort [41], pp. 334-41. Translated into English by Stefan Bauer-Mengelberg and J. Van Heijenoort from *Journal für die reine und angewandte Mathematik* 154 (1923), pp. 1-7.

[9] Carnap, Rudolph. "The Logicist Foundations of Mathematics," Benacerraf and Putnam [2], pp. 31-41. Translated into English by E. Putnam and G. J. Massey from *Erkenntnis* 2 (1931), pp. 91-121.

[10] ———. "Empiricism, Semantics and Ontology," Benacerraf and Putnam [2], pp. 233-248. Reprinted with modification from *Revue Internationale de Philosophie* 4 (1950), pp. 20-40.

[11] ———. *The Logical Syntax of Language*. Translated by A. Smeaton. Paterson, New Jersey: Littlefield, Adams, 1959; first

published in English by Routledge and Kegan Paul, London, 1937.

[12] Cartwright. Richard. "Ontology and the Theory of Meaning," *Philosophy of Science* 21 (1954), pp. 316-25.

[13] Chateaubriand, Oswaldo. *Ontic Commitment, Ontological Reduction, and Ontology*. (Ph.D. thesis, University of California, Berkeley 1971).

[14] Chihara, C. S. "Mathematical Discovery and Concept Formation," *Philosophical Review* 72 (1963), pp. 17-34.

[15] ———. "On the Possibility of Completing an Infinite Process," *Philosophical Review* 74 (1965), pp. 74-87.

[16] ———. "Our Ontological Commitment to Universals," *Noûs* 2 (1968), pp. 25-46.

[17] Church, Alonzo. "Ontological Commitment," *Journal of Philosophy* 55 (1958), pp. 1008-1014.

[18] ———. Review of Copi [22], *Journal of Symbolic Logic* 16 (1951), pp. 154-155.

[19] Chomsky, Noam, and Israel Scheffler. "What Is Said to Be," *Proceedings of the Aristotelian Society* 59 (1958-9), pp. 71-82.

[20] Churchill, R. V. *Fourier Series and Boundary Value Problems*. New York: McGraw-Hill, 1941.

[21] Cohen, Paul. *Set Theory and the Continuum Hypothesis*. New York: W. A. Benjamin, Inc., 1966.

[22] Copi, Irving. "The Inconsistency or Redundancy of *Principia Mathematica*," *Philosophy and Phenomenological Research* 11 (1950), pp. 190-199.

[23] Craig, William. Review of *Einführung in die Operative Logik und Mathematik* by Paul Lorenzen, *Bulletin of the American Mathematical Society*, Vol. 63, No. 5 (September, 1957) pp. 316-320.

[24] Davidson, Donald, and Jaakko Hintikka, eds. *Words and Objections: Essays on the Work of W. V. Quine*. Dordrecht, Holland: D. Reidel, 1969.

[25] Duhem, Pierre. *The Aim and Structure of Physical Theory*. New York: Atheneum 1962.

[26] Dummett, Michael. "Frege on Functions: A Reply," Klemke [47] pp. 268-283. Originally published in *Philosophical Review* 64 (1955), p. 96-107.

[27] Feferman, Solomon. "Systems of Predicative Analysis," *Journal of Symbolic Logic* 29 (1964), pp. 1-30.

[28] Feigl, Herbert, and Wilfrid Sellars, eds. *Readings in Philosophical Analysis*. New York: Appleton-Century-Croft, 1949.

[29] Fraenkel, Abraham, and Yehoshua Bar-Hillel. *Foundations of Set Theory*, Amsterdam (North-Holland), 1958.

[30] Frege, Gottlob. "Letter to Russell (1902)," published for the first time in Heijenoort [41], pp. 126-168.

[31] ——. *The Foundations of Arithmetic*. Translated by J. L. Austin. New York: Philosophical Library, 1950.

[32] ——. *Translations from the Philosophical Writings of Gottlob Frege*. Ed. by P. Geach and M. Black. Oxford: Blackwell, 1952.

[33] ——. "On the Foundations of Geometry," Klemke [47] pp. 559-575. Translated by M. Szabo. Reprinted from *Philosophical Review* 69 (1960), pp. 3-17.

[34] ——. *The Basic Laws of Arithmetic*. Translated in part by Montgomery Furth. Berkeley and Los Angeles: University of California Press, 1964.

[35] Geach, P. T. "Frege's Grundlagen," Klemke [47], pp. 467-478. Originally published in *Philosophical Review* 60 (1951), pp. 535-544.

[36] ——. "Class and Concept," Klemke [47], pp. 284-294. Originally published in *Philosophical Review* 64 (1955), pp. 561-570.

[37] ——. and G. E. M. Anscombe. *Three Philosophers*. Ithaca: Cornell University Press, 1961.

[38] Gödel, Kurt. "Russell's Mathemetical Logic," Benacerraf and Putnam [2], pp. 211-32. Originally published in *The Philosophy of Bertrand Russell*, ed. by P. Schilpp. New York: Tudor, 1944, pp. 123-53.

[39] ——. "What Is Cantor's Continuum Hypothesis?" Benacerraf and Putnam [2], pp. 258-273. Reprinted with modification from *American Mathematical Monthly* 54 (1947).

[40] Harman, Gilbert. "Quine on Meaning and Existence, II," *Review of Metaphysics* 21 (1967), pp. 343-367.

[41] Heijenoort, Jean van. *From Frege to Gödel: A Source Book in Mathematical Logic 1879-1931*. Cambridge: Harvard University Press, 1967.

[42] Heyting, Arend. *Intuitionism: An Introduction*. Amsterdam: North-Holland, 1956.

[43] Hilbert, David. "On the Infinite," Benacerraf and Putnam [2], pp. 134-51. Translated by E. Putnam and G. J. Massey from *Mathematische Annalen* (Berlin) no. 95, 1925, pp. 161-190.

[44] ———. "The Foundations of Mathematics," Heijenoort [41], pp. 464-79. Translated by Stefan Bauer-Mengelberg and D. Føllesdal from *Abbandlungen aus dem mathematischen Seminar der Hamburgischen Universität* 6 (1928), pp. 65-85.

[45] Jubien, Michael. "Two Kinds of Reduction" *Journal of Philosophy* 66 (1969), pp. 533-541.

[46] Kleene, S. C. *Introduction to Metamathematics.* New York and Toronto: Van Nostrand, 1952.

[47] Klemke, E. D. *Essays on Frege.* Urbana, Illinois: University of Illinois Press, 1952.

[48] Kreisel, George. "Hilbert's Programme," Benacerraf and Putnam [2], pp. 157-180. Originally published in *Dialectica* 12 (1958), pp. 346-372.

[49] ———. "Mathematical Logic," *Lectures on Modern Mathematics,* Vol. 3. Ed. by T. L. Saaty. New York: Wiley and Sons, 1965, pp. 95-195.

[50] ———. "Mathematical Logic; What Has It Done for the Philosophy of Mathematics?" *Bertrand Russell: Philosopher of the Century.* Ed. by R. Schoenman, London: Allen and Unwin, 1967, pp. 201-272.

[51] Landau, Edmund. *Foundations of Analysis.* Translated by F. Steinhardt. New York: Chelsea, 1960.

[52] Linsky, Leonard. *Referring.* London: Routledge and Kegan Paul, 1967.

[53] Marshall, William. "Frege's Theory of Functions and Objects," Klemke [47], pp. 250-67. Originally published in *Philosophical Review* 62 (1953), pp. 374-390.

[54] Mates, Benson. *Elementary Logic.* New York: Oxford University Press, 1965.

[55] Mooij, J. J. A. *La Philosophie des Mathématiques de Henri Poincaré.* Paris: Gauthier-Villars, 1966.

[56] Moore, G. E. "Wittgenstein's Lectures in 1930-33," G. E. Moore, *Philosophical Papers.* London: Allen and Unwin, 1959. Originally published in *Mind* 63 (1954), pp. 1-15; 289-316; 64 (1955), pp. 1-27.

[57] Mostowski, Andrzej. "Recent Results in Set Theory," *Problems in the Philosophy of Mathematics.* Ed. by I. Lakatos. Amsterdam: North-Holland, 1967, pp. 82-96.

[58] Nagel, Ernst. *The Structure of Science: Problems in the Logic of Scientific Explanation.* New York: Harcourt, Brace and World, 1961.

[59] Parsons, Charles. "Frege's Theory of Numbers," *Philosophy in America*. Ed. by Max Black. London: Allen and Unwin, 1965.

[60] ——. "Ontology and Mathematics," *Philosophical Review* 80 (1971), pp. 151-76.

[61] Pears, David. *Bertrand Russell and the British Tradition in Philosophy*. London and Glasgow: Collins, 1967.

[62] Poincaré, Henri. "Les Mathématiques et la Logique," *Revue de Metaphysique et de Morale* 13 (1905), pp. 815-835; *Revue de Metaphysique et de Morale* 14 (1906), pp. 17-34; *Revue de Metaphysique et de Morale* 14 (1906), pp. 294-317.

[63] ——. *The Value of Science*. Translated by G. B. Halsted. New York: Science Press, 1907.

[64] ——. "Réflexions sur les deux notes précédentes," *Acta Mathematica* 32 (1909), pp. 195-200.

[65] ——. *Science and Method*. Translated by F. Maitland. New York: Dover, n.d.

[66] ——. *Science and Hypothesis*. Translated by "W. J. G.", New York: Dover, 1952.

[67] ——. *Mathematics and Science: Last Essays*. Translated by J. W. Bolduc. New York: Dover, 1963.

[68] Putnam, Hilary. "The Thesis That Mathematics Is Logic," *Bertrand Russell: Philosopher of the Century*. Ed. by R. Schoenman. London: Allen and Unwin, 1967, pp. 273-303.

[69] Quine, W. V. O. "Designations and Existence," in Feigl and Sellars [28]. Originally published in *Journal of Philosophy* 36 (1939), pp. 701-709.

[70] ——. "A Logistical Approach to the Ontological Problem," Quine [86]. Originally printed for distribution in 1939 at the Fifth International Congress for the Unity of Science.

[71] ——. "On What There Is," *Review of Metaphysics* 2 (1948), pp. 21-38. Later reprinted as Chapter 1, [82], pp. 1-19.

[72] ——. "Whitehead and the Rise of Modern Logic," *Selected Logic Papers*. New York: Random House, 1966, pp. 3-36. Originally published in *The Philosophy of Alfred North Whitehead*, ed. by P. A. Schilpp, New York: Tudor, 1951, pp. 125-163.

[73] ——. "Ontology and Ideology," *Philosophical Studies* 2 (1951), pp. 11-15.

[74] ——. "(Rejoinder to Mr. Geach) on What There Is," *Proceedings of the Aristotelian Society*, Suppl. Vol. 25 (1951), pp. 149-160.

[75] ——. "Two Dogmas of Empiricism," *Philosophical Review* 60 (1951), pp. 20-43. Reprinted as Chapter 2, [82], pp. 20-46.

[76] ——. "On Carnap's Views on Ontology," [86], pp. 126-134. Reprinted from *Philosophical Studies* 2 (1951), pp. 65-72.

[77] ——. *Mathematical Logic,* Revised ed., Cambridge, Massachusetts: Harvard University Press, 1951.

[78] ——. "The Scope and Language of Science," Quine [86] pp. 215-232. Originally published in *British Journal for the Philosophy of Science* (1957), pp. 1-77.

[79] ——. "The Philosophical Bearing of Modern Logic," *Philosophy in the Mid-Century: A Survey.* Ed. by R. Klibansky, Florence, 1958.

[80] ——. *Methods of Logic.* 2d ed. New York: Henry Holt, 1960.

[81] ——. *Word and Object.* Cambridge and New York: Technology Press of M.I.T. and Riley & Sons, 1960.

[82] ——. *From a Logical Point of View.* 2d ed. Cambridge, Massachussetts: Harvard University Press, 1961.

[83] ——. "Reply to Professor Marcus," Quine [86] pp. 175-182. Originally published in *Synthèse* 13, (1961), pp. 323-330.

[84] ——. *Set Theory and Its Logic.* Cambridge, Massachussetts: Harvard University Press, 1963.

[85] ——. "Ontological Reduction and the World of Numbers," Quine [86] pp. 199-207. Reprinted with modification from *Journal of Philosophy* 61 (1964), pp. 209-216.

[86] ——. *The Ways of Paradox and Other Essays.* New York: Random House, 1966.

[87] ——. "Russell's Ontological Development," *Bertrand Russell: Philosopher of the Century.* Ed. by R. Schoenman. London: Allen and Unwin, 1967, pp. 304-314.

[88] ——. "Existence and Quantification," Quine [91] pp. 91-113. Originally published in *l'Age de la Science* 1 (1968), pp. 151-164.

[89] ——. "Ontological Relativity," Quine [91] pp. 26-68. Reprinted with some revisions from *Journal of Philosophy* 65 (1968), pp. 185-212.

[90] ——. "Replies," Davidson and Hintikka [24] pp. 292-352. Originally published in *Synthèse* 19 (1968), pp. 264-321.

[91] ——. *Ontological Relativity and Other Essays.* New York: Columbia University Press, 1969.

[92] ——. "Natural Kinds," Quine [91] pp. 114-138.

[93] Ramsey, F. P. *The Foundations of Mathematics.* London: Routledge & Kegan Paul, 1931.

[94] Resnik, Michael. "Frege's Theory of Incomplete Entities," *Philosophy of Science* 32 (1965), pp. 329-41.

[95] Richard, Jules. "The Principle of Mathematics and the Problem of Sets," Heijenoort [41] pp. 142-44. Translated by J. van Heijenoort from *Revue générale des sciences pures et appliqués* 16 (1950), pp. 541-543.

[96] Robbins, Beverly. "Ontology and the Hierarchy of Languages," *Philosophical Review* 67 (1958), pp. 531-537.

[97] Russell, Bertrand. "Letter to Frege (1902)," published for the first time in Heijenoort [41] pp. 124-125.

[98] ——. *The Principles of Mathematics.* Cambridge: Cambridge University Press, 1903; 2nd ed. London: Allen and Unwin, 1937.

[99] ——. "On Denoting," *Logic and Knowledge*, ed. by R. Marsh. London: Allen and Unwin, 1956, pp. 39-56. Originally published in *Mind*, New Series, Vol. 14 (1905), pp. 479-493.

[100] ——. "Les Paradoxes de la Logique," *Revue de Metaphysique et de la Morale* 14 (1906), pp. 627-650.

[101] ——. "On Some Difficulties in the Theory of Transfinite Numbers and Order Types," *Proceedings of the London Mathematical Society* 4 (1907), pp. 29-53.

[102] ——. "Mathematical Logic as Based on the Theory of Types," *Logic and Knowledge* (see Russell [99]), pp. 59-102. Originally published in *American Journal of Mathematics* 30 (1908), pp. 222-262.

[103] ——. *Problems of Philosophy.* New York: Oxford University Press, 1912.

[104] ——. "The Philosophy of Logical Atomism," *Logic and Knowledge* (see Russell [99]), pp. 177-281. Originally published in Monist 28 (1918), pp. 495-527.

[105] ——. *Introduction to Mathematical Philosophy.* London: Allen & Unwin, 1919.

[106] ——. "My Mental Development," *The Philosophy of Bertrand Russell*, ed. by P. Schilpp, New York: Tudor, 1944, pp. 3-20.

[107] ——. *My Philosophical Development.* New York: Simon & Schuster, 1959.

[108] ——. *Autobiography.* London: Allen & Unwin, Vol. I, (1872-1914), 1967; Vol. II (1914-1944), 1968.

[109] ——. and A. N. Whitehead. *Principia Mathematica.* Cambridge; Cambridge University Press, Vol. I. (1910); paperback to *56, Cambridge: Cambridge University Press, 1967.

[110] Skolem, T. A. *Abstract Set Theory.* Notre Dame, Indiana: University of Notre Dame Press, 1962.

[111] Searle, John. *Speech Acts: An Essay in the Philosophy of Language.* Cambridge: Cambridge University Press, 1969.

[112] Schoenfield, J. R. *Mathematical Logic.* Menlo Park: Addison-Wesley, 1967.

[113] Tharp, L. H. "Ontological Reduction," *Journal of Philosophy* 68 (1971), pp. 151-164.

[114] Thomson, J. F. "On Some Paradoxes," *Analytic Philosophy,* ed. by R. J. Butler. Oxford (Blackwell), 1962, pp. 104-119.

[115] Wang, Hao. "The Formalization of Mathematics," Wang [118], pp. 559-584. Originally published in *The Journal of Symbolic Logic,* 19 (1954), pp. 241-266.

[116] ——. "On Denumerable Bases of Formal Systems," *Mathematical Interpretations of Formal Systems.* Ed. by T. Skolem *et al.* Amsterdam: North-Holland, 1955, pp. 57-84.

[117] ——. "Ordinal Numbers and Predicative Set Theory," Wang [118], 624-51. Originally published in *Zeitschrift für Mathematische Logic und Grundlagen der Mathematik* 5 (1959), pp. 216-239.

[118] ——. *A Survey of Mathematical Logic.* Amsterdam: North-Holland, 1962.

[119] ——. "Russell and His Logic," *Ratio* 7 (1965), pp. 1-34.

[120] Wigner, E. P. "The Unreasonable Effectiveness of Mathematics in the Natural Sciences," *The Spirit and the Uses of Mathematical Sciences.* Ed. by T. Saaty and F. J. Weyl. New York: Mc Graw-Hill) 1969.

[121] Wilder, Raymond. *Introduction to the Foundations of Mathematics.* New York: John Wiley & Sons, 1952.

[122] Wittgenstein, Ludwig. *Remarks on the Foundations of Mathematics.* Ed. G. H. von Wright, Rush Rhees, and G. E. M. Anscombe. Translated by G. E. M. Anscombe. Oxford: Blackwell, 1964. Cambridge, Massachussetts: M.I.T. Press, 1967.

[123] ——. *Zettel.* Ed. G. E. M. Anscombe and G. H. von Wright. Translated by G. E. M. Anscombe. Berkeley and Los Angeles: University of California Press, 1967.

[124] Woods, John. "Fictionality and the Logic of Relations," *The Southern Journal of Philosophy* 7 (1969), pp. 51-63.

[125] Zermelo, Ernst. "A New Proof of the Possibility of a Well-ordering," Heijenoort [41], pp. 183-198. Translated by Stefan Bauer-Mengelberg from *Mathematische Annalen* 59 (1904), pp. 514-516.

Index

Index of Special Symbols

(listed by order of first appearance)

Ontology and the
Vicious-Circle Principle

Designed by R. E. Rosenbaum.
Composed by St. Catherine Press, Ltd.,
in 10 point Times New Roman 327, 2 points leaded,
with display lines in Times New Roman.
Printed offset by Valley-Offset, Inc.
on Warren's 1854 text, 60 pound basis,
with the Cornell University Press watermark.
Bound by Vail-Ballou Press
in Columbia book cloth
and stamped in All Purpose foil.

Library of Congress Cataloging in Publication Data

(For library cataloging purposes only)

Chihara, Charles S   date.
  Ontology and the vicious-circle principle.

  Bibliography: p.
  1. Vicious circle principle (Logic)   2. Ontology.   3. Platonists.   4. Russell,
Bertrand Russell, 3d Earl, 1872-1970.   5. Gödel, Kurt.   6. Quine, Willard
Van Orman.   I. Title.
BC199.V5C48 1973   160   72-4569
ISBN 0-8014-0727-3